ETRUSCAN
DRESS

Publication of this volume was assisted by a grant from the Stanwood Cockey Lodge Foundation.

ETRUSCAN DRESS

LARISSA BONFANTE

THE
JOHNS HOPKINS
UNIVERSITY
PRESS
Baltimore
&
London

The Johns Hopkins University Press, Baltimore, Maryland 21218
The Johns Hopkins University Press Ltd., London

Library of Congress Catalog Card Number 75-11344
ISBN 0-8018-1640-8

Library of Congress Cataloging in Publication data will be found on the last printed
page of this book.

To my parents,
Giuliano and Vittoria
Bonfante

CONTENTS

ACKNOWLEDGMENTS

Otto J. Brendel of Columbia University first suggested this book, helped me, and inspired me. I only wish he had lived to see it published. Margarete Bieber, who has long honored me with her friendship and delighted me with her company, patiently read the original manuscript chapter by chapter. Ready, as always, to do more than one should ask, Emeline Richardson gave precious advice and information in the course of two readings of the manuscript. In Rome, at the American Academy, Luisa Banti spent a week reading a final draft, sounded salutary warnings, and made useful suggestions. The appendix on strange costumes was her idea. I also wish to thank Evelyn Harrison and Edith Porada for assistance with comparative material from Greece and from the Near East and Egypt. In excavations at Cerveteri in 1951 Massimo Pallottino introduced me to the Etruscans' presence and their past. In a sense this work began there.

I am grateful for the unfailing courtesy and help of Adolf Placzek and others at the Avery, Fine Arts, and Butler Libraries of Columbia University; of Inez Longobardi and the staff at the American Academy in Rome, whose library makes work a pleasure; and of Hellmut Sichtermann at the German Archaeological Institute in Rome. Jean Owen, William P. Sisler, and the staff of The Johns Hopkins University Press have taught me the difference between manuscript and book. Publication was assisted by the Stanwood Cockey Lodge Fund of Columbia University. For all this distinguished help, I am grateful. Errors are my own.

ETRUSCAN
DRESS

INTRODUCTION

The subject of this book is the dress of the Etruscans as it has come down to us and as it was represented in Etruscan art from the seventh century B.C. to the Roman period. Though there is considerably more information about the way Etruscans dressed than about other aspects of their civilization, the subject has received only incidental attention.[1] Greek dress can be studied from Margarete Bieber's useful volumes;[2] Roman costume, especially the insignia of the emperors, from the works of Andreas Alföldi and Richard Delbrueck. Lillian Wilson has also collected material on Roman dress.[3] In spite of the important recent work and conclusions of scholars like Luisa Banti, Massimo Pallottino, Emeline Richardson, and Otto Brendel, however, a study of Etruscan dress has been missing.

That what is known about the Etruscans is more important than their so-called mystery is an approach finally accepted by the scholarly public and the public at large. Massimo Pallottino, in repudiating the "origin of the Etruscans" as a sterile problem,[4] and Luisa Banti, by her skepticism as well as her insistence on the individual reality of the different Etruscan cities in contrast to some imaginary, composite "Etruscans,"[5] have done much to de-mystify the field. Working tools are now needed to further our understanding of this people, recognized at last as a ranking civilization which played an important role in the history of the world, both in its own time and through its influence on Rome.

Of the two institutions which, according to the ancients, identified a nation—language and dress[6]—the first, the language of the Etruscans, can be studied by way of Ambros J. Pfiffig's newly published grammar and Massimo Pallottino's *TLE*, a concise collection of the most important inscriptions. Here I have organized the material on dress, which has the advantage of being more plentiful and more generally familiar. Focusing on details of dress and development of fashions can be useful in other ways as well. The importance of dress as historical documentation, as a means of dating a monument and identifying the sex, nationality, rank, or name of a figure represented, is evident when one studies another culture through its artistic monuments. The manner of dressing—or, in certain cases, of not dressing—visually demonstrates such distinctions. Certain problems, however, come up repeatedly in the interpretation of this kind of evidence,[7] and they are especially urgent in Etruscan studies, where we are limited to the direct evidence of art and inscriptions for any reconstruction of Etruscan history. When, as happens occasionally, Latin literature gives us a clue about Etruscan matters, for example, revealing the later development of some originally Etruscan type of dress, the problem of interpretation becomes crucial. We are then not only comparing a figured representation with a literary description but also dealing with two different civilizations. All too often Etruscan evidence has been interpreted according to later, Roman standards. Instead, we must derive whatever clues we can from direct observation of the material, notice certain distinctions, and attempt to explain those within their own context.

The following distinctions are fairly regularly made by Etruscan artists, consciously or unconsciously, in their representation of Etruscan dress. Correctly interpreted, they can give us important information about Etruscan history and culture.

1. A real costume, copied from life and familiar to the artist, is distinguished from a costume imitated from another artistic representation. A good example of an Etruscan artist's misunderstanding of an artistic motif imported from Greece, as we shall see, is the Morgan statuette (Fig. 132). There are others.[8]

2. "National" or at least cultural differences are stressed. What made Etruscan figures look different from contemporary Greek or Syrian figures? What still gives them their "Etruscan look"? The long braid for women and the oval, lozenge-shaped Villanovan belt in the seventh century; rounded mantles, pointed hats and pointed shoes in the later sixth century; and short pants, even on the image of Hercules, wearing, as he does, his lion skin modestly draped about his loins.

3. Differences in date are visible and are taken for granted in any study of fashion, which by definition changes in form and meaning. Since fashions change at different rates, the most useful for dating purposes are those styles or accessories fashionable only for a short time, especially when we can fix the dates when they appear or disappear: pointed shoes, or the tassel on women's chitons, or various types of jewelry. It is striking to see how often in the past Etruscan monuments have been dated on the basis of these standards, since stylistic reasons are harder to pin down.

4. Social differences, between men and gods, masters and slaves, men and women—apparently even between live men and dead—can be seen. Goddesses wear archaic dress and pointed shoes long after these are no longer part of normal dress. In the fourth century, priestesses and goddesses are marked by their tassels.

Our study of such details can even teach us to recognize an Etruscan artist's misunderstanding of an artistic motif imported from Greece or the Near East and to distinguish this from a forger's misconception.[9] Not always, however. The Appendix on strange costumes illustrates a number of artistic representations whose costumes seem particularly puzzling, in the hope that isolating the problems in this manner may be a step towards solving them.

In the whole question of dating, which is basic and difficult, certain precise details yield criteria, yet a costume is as securely dated as the monuments on which it appears, and for many Etruscan monuments, dates are controversial and even tenuous. Chiusi, for example, in several cases appears to have taken the lead in representing contemporary Etruscan dress, if one follows the more or less traditional early dating of many of its "primitive" figures. Such a primacy is at first sight hard to explain. The excavations at Murlo, which have opened a new chapter of Etruscan art, will also tell us much about the chronology of this area. It might seem that Chiusi, an inland city, is not as good a candidate as, say, Caere, for originating fashions in either art or dress; the word "provincial" does not explain so much as it points out a difference. Otto Brendel's forthcoming book on Etruscan art will discuss this and other problems of artistic development and differences among the various centers.

Although the chronological aspect of the various Etruscan fashions forms an important aspect of this book, I have organized the material by type of garment rather than by chronology, as a typological arrangement is easier to consult. Each basic garment of fashion is treated in a separate chapter: fabrics, pants, chitons or tunics, mantles, shoes, hats and hair styles.

A chronological division of the text, too, would obscure individual variations in the date of the appearance of some fashions. A number of problematic questions are gathered in the Appendix. The comparative tables that follow attempt to do some justice to the chronological aspects.

The material falls naturally into four broad phases of development:

Phase I	Orientalizing period	650–550 B.C.
Phase II	"Ionian" period	550–475 B.C.
Phase III	"Classical" period	475–300 B.C.
Phase IV	Hellenistic period	300–100 B.C.

The upper limit is set by the first appearance of human figures in Etruscan art wearing recognizable clothes, the lower limit, by the Etruscan adoption of Roman costumes. Disappearance of their characteristic dress as well as their language marks Rome's absorption of Etruria.[10]

Phase I is not really accurately described as Orientalizing, since it includes more local fashions peculiar to Etruria than any other period, not all of which can be directly connected with either Near Eastern or Greek Orientalizing motifs. Breaking at 600–580 B.C., it does not correspond to any phase of Greek art. Included in this period are the Orientalizing or Dedalic fashions of plaid pattern and perizoma or pants (Chapters 1 and 2), as well as the Dedalic chiton (Chapter 3), and of many mantles (Chapter 4), shoes and sandals (Chapter 5), and hats and hair styles (Chapter 6). A break in the middle of this period is especially evident in the development of the mantle.

After 600 B.C. there are different Greek influences, for example, Corinthian; as usual, there are also local developments whose form or chronology does not correspond to Greece. Phase II sees styles suffer fundamental changes: Ionian influence is everywhere evident, in chiton, mantle, and shoe fashions, in hats and hair styles.[11] Even Etruscan fashions which are peculiarly local, such as the tutulus hair style and the pointed calcei repandi, are adaptations of Greek models. Yet a typically "Etruscan look" emerges from this period, one of the most immediately attractive of Etruscan art.

Phase III is marked by the triumph of Attic art and is sometimes difficult to distinguish from the Hellenistic phase which follows it. Its chronological limits are variable. There is a great quantity of material from around the fourth century which is difficult to organize, but when we have a corpus of cistae, mirrors, and sculptured urns from this period, dealing with this material will be a much easier task.

Phase IV corresponds more closely to the Hellenistic period of Greek art and shares many of its characteristics, such as the blend of realistic and theatrical, of "local color" and idealization.

At the end, it is difficult to distinguish between Roman costume and Etruscan usage. For instance, the famous statue of the Arringatore in Florence—recently dated within the first century B.C. (ca. 80 B.C.)—wears a short toga (Fig. 109). Is it a Roman or an Etruscan fashion?

The beginning is as difficult to distinguish sharply as is the end. The study of tomb groups is making the chronology of the seventh century better known, but it is not yet clear.[12] In each case I examine the earliest evidence for a type of garment. Although occasionally an individual search throws some light on the nature of the contacts between the Etruscan cities and the Near East in the very early period, the much-debated question of Etruscan origins lies beyond the reach of this study. By the sixth century, outside influences on Etruscan dress were wholly Greek.

I deal with the subject of foreign influences in a separate chapter, which concludes this study of Etruscan dress in Etruria. In each of the other chapters the subject appears under the following headings:[13]

real fashions: garments and styles which seem to have been actually worn in Etruscan cities;

artistic conventions: the influence of the art of a different culture in the representation of a garment or fashion which might never have been seen in Etruria;

peculiarly Etruscan features: Etruscan art and social customs as reflected in ways of dressing or in the artists' way of representing fashions and garments.

In addition to summarizing these results, I discuss the origins and originality of Etruscan dress and examine connections and parallels with foreign dress.

In a separate article[14] I have described the many details of dress of Etruscan origin which appear to have survived in the derivative art of the Italian north. Much scattered evidence, especially Venetic bronze relief plaques from Vicenza and Este and bronze situlae from Bologna and further north into central Europe, testify to Etruscan influence in northern Italy.

Wherever possible, comparison with the remains of actual garments, such as metal belts or wooden sandals, supplements evidence from monuments. The Greek tradition of *truphe* and the attention paid in Greek literature to the wealth and luxurious habits of "decadent" societies like the Lydians, Ionians, and Etruscans account in part for references in Greek literature to the inappropriately handsome dress of Etruscan slaves, for example, or to Etruscan sandals with gold laces.[15] Descriptions and allusions in Greek and especially Latin literature, the latter referring to Etruscan fashions adopted and long preserved by Romans in their traditions, provide further evidence. They also lead to closer definitions of Latin and Greek terminology for a number of garments. Here Otto Brendel's insistence on greater clarity and precision in descriptions of Etruscan garments depicted in art[16]— an insistence which stimulated the present study of Etruscan dress— has been a constant inspiration.

Another chapter on this subject traces some of the many references in Roman authors, from the Hellenistic period on, to the Etruscan origins of much of the traditional Roman costume.[17] Faced with the threat of Greek culture to their cultural identity in the Hellenistic world, the Romans, in spite of their ambivalence toward Etruria,[18] turned to Etruscan civilization as an ancient culture that they could claim as somehow theirs. Their testimony is, of course, colored by their attitudes. They are loath to credit outsiders with originating some of their most cherished symbols; at the same time, in order to glorify these, according to Roman tradition all Etruscans are kings.[19] The evidence of the monuments, in any case, proves that certain Roman honorary costumes do derive from Etruscan models dating to the late sixth century, traditionally the period of Tarquin's reign in Rome.[20]

This situation suggests further work. There was certainly a good deal of Etruscan art, much of it from the archaic period, available, in Rome and in the Etruscan cities, to the Romans of the late republican and Augustan period. How did they see it? Did they think of it as Etruscan art, and, if so, how did they explain it? Did they not often reinterpret, as evidently happened with the Etruscan bronze statue of the Capitoline Wolf and with statues of Etruscan "*togati*," such monuments as part of their own tradition?[21] We learn something of the Romans' attitude to their own ancient history by comparing Etruscan monuments with references to them in the writings of Roman antiquarians—for example, in Festus—and with descriptions of early Rome in Livy, Propertius, and Ovid. Though a systematic "confrontation" between the literary tradition about early Rome and the archeological evidence is useful, the first task is to understand the Etruscan monuments on their own terms.

CHRONOLOGICAL TABLE OF GREEK AND ETRUSCAN DRESS

ETRUSCAN DRESS AND COSTUME

	men	*women*
PHASE I:		
ORIENTALIZING		
PERIOD		*Worn in Real Life*
750–600 B.C.	plaid fabrics	plaid fabrics
	perizoma	chiton, three-quarter length, or long,
	belts, thick or lozenge-shaped	straight (Dedalic), or "proto-Ionic"
	short chiton(?)[1]	Ionic"
	large mantle (wrapped around)	back mantle
	bobbed hair, beards	back braid, Hathor curls, or front
	pilleus, plumed hats	locks
	sandals	conical hat, wing hat, polos(?)
		sandals
600–550 B.C.	perizoma	long Dedalic chiton
	short chiton	wide Dedalic belt
	long chiton (older men?)	mantle worn over the head, ends in
	large mantle	front
	bobbed hair, some beards	back braid (to ca. 560); single or
		double curls in front

Not Worn in Real Life

700–500 B.C.	nudity	nudity
	"Syrian kilts"	Dedalic capelet
	short pleated chitons	polos
	Egyptianizing loincloths, etc.	flower hat
	Etagenperücke (layer wigs)	

PHASE II: IONIAN		
PERIOD		*Worn in Real Life*
550–525 B.C.	perizoma (cont. in north)	Dedalic chiton (to ca. 540), long
	chiton, short, three-quarter length,	white Ionic chiton; sometimes
	or long white Ionic chiton for	long sleeves
	older men	mantle worn over the head, points in
	himation, diagonally draped	front
	long hair worn loose, beards	long hair worn loose, ringlets, or
	pilleus, petasos, pointed and twisted	tutulus hair style
	hats	rounded "bowler," or pointed hats
	calcei repandi (pointed shoes)	calcei repandi, calceoli (pointed
		shoes)
525–475 B.C.	short chiton; long white Ionic chiton	long white Ionic chiton
	for older men	himation, worn with ends in front
	variety of mantles:	diagonally draped himation
	himation or tebenna diagonally	ringlets, tutulus, mitra
	draped	calcei repandi (pointed shoes)
	rounded, short, worn back to front	
	rounded, long, worn back to front	
	(from 500)	
	ringlets; short hair, sometimes beards	
	calcei repandi (pointed shoes)	

Not Worn in Real Life

550–475 B.C.	nudity	transparent chiton
	animal-skin mantle (Hercules)	Dedalic chiton (divinities)
	Phrygian hat (divinities)	Ionic himation, diagonally draped

**PHASE III:
"CLASSICAL" PERIOD
475–300 B.C.**

Worn in Real Life

men	women
chiton mantle: himation or tebenna, diagonally draped "togati", with or without chiton laced boots (without points, calcei)	long Ionic chiton himation shoes (without points) krobylos hair style, mitra "pearled" diadem, earrings torques, bullae, and bead necklaces

Not Worn in Real Life

475–300 B.C.

men	women
nudity animal-skin helmet (Hades)	pointed shoes (divinities, heroized dead, priestesses?)

**PHASE IV:
HELLENISTIC PERIOD
300–100 B.C.**

Worn in Real Life

men	women
loose chiton or straight tunic himation, tebenna, or chlamys shoes, laced calcei, or sandals thick garlands, short hair banqueters' garlands	loose chiton, belted high heavy himation shoes or sandals lunate diadem or garland variety of necklaces, earrings

Not Worn in Real Life

men	women
nudity theatrical dress: long sleeves, long pants	nudity theatrical dress: long sleeves pointed shoes (divinities)

PRE-GREEK AND GREEK DRESS[2]

**Pre-Greek Period
Minoan,
2000–1500 B.C.**

men	women
perizoma thick belt short chiton(?) long hair high boots	wide tiered skirt, belted stiff short-sleeved bolero, bare-breasted cap; long hair, ringlets

**Mycenean,
1500–1100 B.C.**

men	women
perizoma short or long chiton, long sleeves (Warrior vase) long or short hair, beard (Warrior vase) high, laced, pointed boots	long woolen chiton or full linen chiton (LM III)[3] long hair, back braid

**Geometric Greek,
1100–750 B.C.**

men	women
perizoma heavy mantle: pharos, chlaina laced boots	plaid fabrics long chiton, belted laced boots

**PHASE I: GREEK
ORIENTALIZING
PERIOD
750–600 B.C.**

men	women
perizoma (to 720; later in Crete) short chiton	long woolen chiton (Dedalic peplos); later with overfold

men	*women*
pharos, chlaina, himation long hair, ribbon laced boots, endromides	wide Dedalic belt short capelet[4] polos(?) long hair; back braid (e.g., in Crete, Lemnos)

PHASE II: GREEK
ARCHAIC PERIOD

600–480 B.C.

short chiton (wool or linen); long chiton (older men, musicians, charioteers) mantle: chlaina, himation, chlamys long hair (krobylos, speira, pinned-up braids), short (athletes ca. 550); beards petasos, pilos sandals, laced boots	peplos; sewn linen chiton (ca. 580 B.C. in Ionia; 540 B.C. in Athens) mantle (diagonally draped, ca. 560) with decorated borders long hair, mitra (later) sandals

PHASE III:
CLASSICAL GREEK

480–350 B.C.

short chiton (wool or linen); long chiton (specialized) mantles: chlaina, himation, chlamys short hair; fewer beards sandals, or closed shoes: embades, endromides, etc.	peplos; very thin chiton (ca. 400) long hair (sphendone, etc.) sandals, or closed shoes: laconicae, kothornoi, etc.

PHASE IV:
HELLENISTIC PERIOD

300–100 B.C.

similar to above hair Alexander-style; fewer beards	narrow chiton, belted high, either lightweight, or of heavy wool worn with contrasting light, often transparent, himation

[1](?) indicates a costume which appears in art, but may not have been worn in real life.
[2]Costumes were represented in art, but not necessarily worn, as dress was. The section on pre-Greek and Greek dress has been adapted from Bieber, "Costume." For convenience, the phases have been divided as for Etruscan art.
[3]The long woolen chiton appears in sculpture in Crete by LM III (Banti, "Div. fem. a Creta" 17). The full, linen, "proto-Ionic" chiton may already be represented on Mycenean terracottas: C. Long, *AJA* 58 (1954) 147–148.
[4]The short capelet just might have distant connections with the Minoan bolero; cf. Banti, "Div. fem. a Creta" 1.

1
FABRICS
AND
PATTERNS

Fabrics. Animal skins were used as normal dress in early times, later for special stage costumes or in connection with the games, like the strong man's leopard-skin tights in the circus today. Leather and felt, both durable, sturdy fabrics, were always used for a variety of garments; real leather *perizomas* or pants and fragments of leather backings for metal belts have actually survived. Hats, too, were apparently made of leather or felt. Shoes and sandals were of leather, often reinforced with wooden soles or decorated with metal ornaments. Wool, however, was the textile most used in Etruria, as in the rest of the ancient world.

In Etruria, as elsewhere in Europe, most clothes were made from a thick, heavy, woolen textile, represented on Etruscan monuments, in paintings and sculptures, as falling in straight lines without folds (Figs. 4–6, 8–11, 13–17). Remains of woolen fabric discovered in Scandinavia and elsewhere prove that garments like these were actually worn at a very early period in the European north. Most striking is the oval cloak, woven in a brown and black plaid or twill design, which once covered the body of a man who lived in the Danish Bronze Age, sometime around 1000 B.C. (Figs. 1, 94V).[1] From much closer to home, in the area of Bologna in northern Italy, a region in close contact with the Etruscans, comes a detailed illustration of the various phases of wool working, cleaning, carding, spinning and weaving. The incised decoration of this bronze object (Fig. 2), dating from around 600 B.C., shows us a picture of the most complicated loom known to us from antiquity, two stories high and sturdy enough for a woman to work at it comfortably seated in a throne-like armchair. Aside from its importance for the history of technology, this scene confirms what we know about the later popularity of woolen textiles from northern Italy and Gaul in Rome, and proves that the tradition of wool working was long lived in this area.[2]

Linen, too, was early used in Etruria, as shown by artistic representations and by surviving fragments of linen cloth. It was in linen that, at least occasionally, the Etruscans of the seventh century and earlier dressed the sculptured images of their dead. An early Etruscan funerary urn in roughly human shape, for example, from the vicinity of Chianciano, when found had fragments of purple linen, mixed with bits of gold, adhering to its shoulder.[3] The purple and gold chiton of which this is a remnant was evidently a garment (or shroud) of great luxury. It would seem that Etruscans imported expensive linen cloth from Egypt, just as they imported gold and ivory and fancy patterned textiles for their houses and their tombs. Yet it has been shown that the Etruscans spun their own linen thread and wove it into fabric. The remains of some linen fabric found in a tomb at Veii have been analyzed and indicate that the white linen threads were spun and woven in Etruria. This particular textile, at least, was not imported as a finished product from Egypt.[4] Linen was, in any case, more expensive than wool. Indeed, the fact that it was used even in very early times for fine linen chitons for Etruscan ladies is consistent with what we know—and are told by ancient sources—about Etruscan wealth.[5] Such linen chitons were realistically portrayed on statuettes as early as the seventh century and in painting in the sixth: fine folds distinguished them from the heavy woolen texture of other models (Figs. 7, 62, 63).

In the sixth century, Attic vase painters delighted in representing the contrast between the texture of heavy wool and that of light linen. Etruscan artists picked up this artistic convention, often exaggerating the contrast: for example, in the traditional "stage" costume of the dancing castanet player, a heavy woolen jerkin worn over a fine linen chiton (Fig. 81). This so-called "transparent chiton" on monuments of the late sixth and early fifth century is not a real fashion, but a product of a misunderstanding. A similar convention was used later, in imitation of a Greek style popular at the end of the fifth century B.C., on "classical" figure types on which the nipples show through the thin cloth of the chiton, which contrasts with the texture of the heavy woolen mantle (Figs. 82, 83). Attic art provided the models for all these conventional artistic motifs, for "transparent" garments, and for the heavy folds imitated from works of the Brygos painter.[6]

THE PLAID PATTERN   Heavy woolen garments represented on monuments of the seventh and early sixth centuries are frequently patterned in a plaid or checked design. (The pleated chitons represented on figures of this period are never decorated with the plaid pattern, making it likely that the original was of linen; linen, unlike wool, cannot be easily woven into decorative patterns.)

Plaid or checkered designs have always been the simplest decoration to weave, and the plaid fashion is universal.[7] In Etruria, men and women are shown wearing plaid or checkered chitons and mantles on some of the earliest monuments (Figs. 3-6, 8-11, 13-17). For men, short plaid pants or perizomas were very popular in the seventh and first half of the sixth century (Figs. 11, 35-38). Such garments were actually worn in Etruria. The native Etruscan "back mantle," as well as many other garments decorated with a plaid pattern, appear consistently and in a variety of contexts, ruling out the possibility of special artistic conventions. The plaid or squared panel decoration on the chiton front of some seventh-century female figurines, however, probably did not represent an actual fashion. A standard feature of Dedalic figures like the Auxerre statuette, it seems to have been copied by Etruscan artists from original Greek models, since in Etruria it always appears on the same type of Orientalizing figure.[8]

This checkerboard or plaid pattern was certainly due in part to the archaic artists' preference for an all-over pattern, and certain variations in the representations depend on the material on which the design is shown. The type of design was thus not necessarily realistic, reflecting the original fabric. On clay, the pattern was either painted on, in a more or less complicated design (Fig. 3), or incised into the wet clay, in an easily carved, diagonal, lozenge-shaped pattern (Fig. 35, bucchero, and Tragliatella vase, Fig. 11) or in a simple dotted design (Palermo bucchero oinochoe, Fig. 47). On a series of terracotta statuettes from Chiusi (Figs. 4–6, 8–9) a distinctive waffle-iron pattern was achieved by impressing the wet clay with little squares, so that the surrounding lines stand out in relief, an effect perhaps imitated from mold-made metal-work, as on a silver-plated bronze belt buckle in the Museo Gregoriano.[9] Squared or diagonally incised "lozenges" decorating the garments of bronze or terracotta statuettes (Fig. 10) and ivory figures—such as the situla from the Pania burial at Chiusi (Fig. 13)—have often been misunderstood, the bulging sections formed by the lines cut into the soft ivory being explained by modern scholars as representing quilted material.[10]

These simplified, stylized representations of the monuments probably reflect only a small part of the variety of such plaid patterns existing in real life. Some representations do, however, show alternations of different colors, like the modern Scottish plaid. There were also textured, three-dimensional weaves like our tweeds or twill, if the waffle-iron patterned dress of some early figurines from Chiusi is at all realistic (Figs. 4–6, 8–9). We have seen that the cloak from Gerömsberg, Sweden (Fig. 1), was patterned with both color and texture, in a black and brown plaid or twill pattern. Another anthropomorphic vase in the Museo Gregoriano (Fig. 3), providing us with one of the earliest clear examples of the plaid fashion in Etruria, has the design of the garment painstakingly painted on the surface of the clay. Evidently copied from an original textile is the complicated pattern of inscribed squares and little crosses, a realistic rendering of a textile design popular throughout the seventh century which appears frequently on figures of this period.

After the beginning of the sixth century this plaid design all but disappears. Only on provincial, retarded figures repeating a seventh-century motif is the pattern still to be seen. Some ivory plaques in Bologna, of unknown provenance (Fig. 17), generally dated in the first half of the sixth century,[11] illustrate a somewhat more refined late example of plaid decoration, a kind of patchwork quilt of patterns, originally brightly painted in yellow, blue, red, brown, and gold, in zones and bands, on chiton and mantle. It is tempting to connect this representation with a description of sixth-century Ionic dress by a certain Democritus of Ephesus: "the garments of the Ionians are violet-red, and crimson, and yellow, woven in a lozenge pattern; the top borders are marked at equal intervals with figured patterns";[12] we seem to recognize here the zoned decoration, the "rhomboidal" pattern, and the colors of the dress of the Bologna figures. Any originally figured decoration on the borders would, of course, have been stylized beyond recognition, or simply omitted on such small figures.

The models for this seventh-century Etruscan fashion—in art and to some extent no doubt in real life also—were in some cases Greek Orientalizing monuments (cf. Figs. 19, 21), in others apparently the same kind of Near Eastern models which inspired the Greeks. The enormous popularity of the artistic convention in Etruria, where it took over more insistently, though for a shorter time than it did in Greece, can be explained in several ways. The Etruscan artist's love of detail might be one explanation. It also seems to have been closely connected with real fashion, encouraged by imports from the Near East. See, for example, the plaid patterns illustrated on ivories from Nimrud, of a type which inspired Etruscan artists (Fig. 20). The central figure represented on an engraved tridacna shell imported from the East, with its long-sleeved plaid chiton (Fig. 22), could almost have served as a "fashion plate" for Etruscan tailors and dressmakers of the seventh century. At least one of these tridacna shells was found in Vulci, in Etruria; they were certainly a regular item of commerce in Near Eastern-Etruscan trade. So were real fabrics, which, though they played such a large part in the commercial and artistic relations of this period, perished completely, leaving their traces only on such figured monuments as these.

The bright colors of all these fabrics, local or imported, though originally reproduced on the monuments—Homeric descriptions of purple-dyed ivory might refer to such designs—have rarely survived. Only a few artistic representations, such as the plaques in Bologna (Fig. 17), which, we have seen, still retain traces of their variegated colors, or the terracotta statuettes from Cerveteri, with their deep red mantles and chitons bordered in a deeper color, give us some idea of their original appearance (Figs. 14–16).[13]

APPLIED DECORATIONS   Aside from woven decorations, in the early period gold plaques in a variety of designs were sewn or otherwise attached to the material to form decorative designs. It is difficult, however, to know what these looked like: usually the thin gold plaques found in tombs survived long after the woven material on which they were sewn had perished.

Both embroidery and appliqué decoration were far more common in the Near East and Asia Minor than among Greeks or Etruscans in the West. Complex Oriental patterns were executed by means of appliqué metal or ivory plates in the form of squares or rosettes;[14] these luxurious fabrics were then copied both locally and abroad, in cheaper models, with cheaper means, such as weaving.

Borders were a typical and constant feature of Etruscan dress. Their special historical interest has to do with a later chapter of the history of costume, since the use of borders was taken over by the Romans, along with other aspects of Etruscan dress, and used symbolically as a sign of honor and social position. Technically, there was a very good reason for the existence of these borders. In Etruria, in Greece, and in the ancient world in general, there was no question of weaving a large bolt of cloth, as we do today, and then cutting pieces out of it to make different garments. Each garment was woven to order, all in one piece, to fit the person for whom it was intended.[15] Each piece of cloth, therefore, constituted a garment, the edges of which were not sewn or hemmed, but were finished off right on the loom. The loose threads at the edges, which were simply cut off from the loom, formed a fringed border, which was sometimes worked back into the cloth, forming a smoothly bound border. Sometimes, instead, especially on Near Eastern garments, this fringe was used as decoration.

The borders of the garment were often emphasized by being woven in a contrasting color. Ancient paintings contain many examples of such brightly decorated borders on the edges and on seams. The figures on the sarcophagus of Haghia Triada, Syrian tributaries on Egyptian paintings (Fig. 54),[16] and Etruscan figures of all periods have chitons, mantles, and pants decorated with patterned or colored borders.

Apart from the realistic depiction of the actual cloth, moreover, we deal once more with an artistic representation. In Etruria artists generally prefer the detail to the mass, the individual decorative motif to the main composition. A linear outline style emphasizes the borders of shapes. Such basically realistic details as seams and stitching, edges, and border decorations are often emphasized because of their ornamental quality (Figs. 31, 81, 130). On some of the bronze relief panels of the Loeb Tripods (Figs. 79, 80), the artist makes use of elaborate borders on the garments to obtain a finely chiseled decorative effect. A similar ornamental use of borders in the composition can be seen on painted terracotta plaques from Caere (Figs. 71, 73-75). Border decorations set off the forms of the dress in bold relief. When the rounded mantle or *tebenna* first appears, sometime after the middle of the sixth century,[17] the curve is emphasized by the border, which follows only the outer edge, as on the bronze statuette of a boy in the Bibliothèque Nationale (Figs. 102-103), or outlines the shape of the mantle all around, as on the Apollo from Veii (Figs. 104-105).

Tebennae with dark red woven borders eventually develop into the later Roman *togae praetextae*; the dark-bordered mantle of one of the mourners in the Tomba degli Auguri at Tarquinia already looks very much like the Roman *praetexta pulla*, the proper formal dress for state funerals.[18] There is no evidence, however, that any specialized, symbolic meaning for this fashion existed for the Etruscans, who regularly wore bordered garments of all kinds.

The custom of decorating the borders of mantles and tebennae continues in Classical and Hellenistic times, as the paintings of the period show. Pliny (34.98) says that the Romans used to paint the borders of the *togae praetextae* of honorary bronze statues with purple pigments. The Etruscans may have treated some of their bronzes the same way. Generally, the border is decorated with an incised design (Figs. 119–120) and, on the well-known statue of the Arringatore, with a binding all around (Fig. 109).

OTHER PATTERNS   Chitons and mantles were dyed bright colors, as we see on the Tarquinian tomb paintings, sometimes brightened further with all-over patterns of dots or small rosettes. A popular decoration in the late sixth and the fifth century is a border pattern of dots or of zig-zags and circles (Figs. 81, 107, 119).[19] In the fourth century, the dog-tooth pattern and modified meander are to be seen, especially on square *himatia* (Fig. 87).[20] The Hellenistic period brings more luxurious designs, such as the elaborate representation of figures dancing a war dance on the triumphal mantle of Vel Sathies, a himation, not a toga, but surely related to the Roman triumphal *toga picta* (Fig. 135).[21]

CONCLUSION   The earliest evidence shows Etruscans wearing garments woven all in one piece, of either wool or linen. Woolen clothes, in the seventh century and the beginning of the sixth, were often decorated with a textured or colored all-over plaid pattern and a solid-color border. The use of linen cloth is also attested as early as the seventh century by actual remnants, as well as by the representation, on some garments, of fine folds apparently showing the fine texture of the material in contrast to the heavier, stiffer texture of wool. The fact that these garments with folds are never decorated with the plaid pattern confirms this indentification, since linen, in contrast to wool, dyes poorly: the original material would thus have been left in its natural color, dyed or bleached. Aside from their use of linen chitons at this exceptionally early date, Etruscan textile fashions of the Geometric and Orientalizing periods were not very different from those of contemporary mainland Greeks. Both Etruscans and Greeks differed from the peoples of Asia Minor and the Near East in their preference for woven over embroidered or applied decoration.

The popularity of the plaid design in the seventh century in Etruria was due in great part to a "realistic" rendering of such a pattern on homespun or imported textiles. The taste of Greek Geometric and Orientalizing art for squared, lozenge-shaped, and plaid designs further reinforced the artistic fashion, and the Near Eastern trade brought both actual textiles and art objects—ivories, tridacna shells, etc.—on which such squared textile patterns were represented. The colder climate of Etruria may also account in part for the long-lasting Etruscan fondness for warm woolen plaids, a taste that continued in northern Italy and Europe long after it had been forgotten by the Greeks and still exists in Scotland. In short, the plaid-patterned decoration seems to reflect real clothes actually worn in Etruscan cities more closely than do contemporary illustrations of similar designs in Greece. This characteristic of Etruscan art, more realistically inclined than Greek art, helps to explain the surprising, relatively isolated instance of "folds" on seventh-century representations of linen chitons. The taste for representing decorative details in the Mediterranean world, an important, somewhat "primitive" element of an international Orientalizing style, remains a basic feature of Etruscan art.

Other artistic conventions copied from Greek and Near Eastern models also account for the way cloth was represented in Etruscan art. The convention of showing the fineness of the cloth by allowing the forms of the body to show through has sometimes been misunderstood by scholars. Two female busts of the seventh and early sixth century B.C. were probably not meant to appear bare-breasted, although the nipples are clearly defined: necklace, belt, and, in one case, bracelets seem to define the top of a chiton (Figs. 57, 58; cf. 60). In fact, however, since Etruscan artists were not fond of representing nude female figures, except when directly copying Oriental models, the artist was perhaps influenced by such a foreign model when he emphasized the breasts, even in his depiction of a dressed female figure.

In the construction of the actual garments, a peculiarly Etruscan taste for "shaped" and sewn garments seems apparent. The garments were woven to size and fitted, often with complicated shapes, in contrast to Greek clothes, which had basically simple shapes but complicated folds and drapery, at times even pressed into shape.[22]

PERIZOMA AND BELTS

2

In the early period, down to the middle of the sixth century, Etruscan men were normally represented wearing short pants or trousers, varying in length from very brief to knee-length (Fig. 23). We shall use the Greek name for this garment, *perizoma*. It was probably not its Etruscan name, but it was a word which a literate, Greek-speaking Etruscan would have recognized.

In Greek, aside from περίζωμα, which I have adopted as a general term,[1] pants were referred to as a διάζωστρα[2] or διάζωμα,[3] and the verb forms περιζώννυμι or διαζώννυμι were also used, meaning "to put on the perizoma."[4] The Latin equivalent is the *subligaculum, cingulum, licium,* or *campestre*.[5] Modern words used to translate these terms, such as "girdle," "belt," "apron," "kilt," "skirt," or "*schurtz*," give an old-fashioned or effeminate connotation to a perfectly ordinary article of men's clothing. They also usually give a wrong impression of a garment which, like modern pants, is primarily designed to cover the sexual parts. "Loincloth" is better in this respect, since it implies that part of the garment goes between the legs. Since, however, "loincloth" sounds more like the dress of a primitive tribe than of a civilized people, I shall only use the word to describe a special shape of draped garment, which differs from the fitted and sewn perizomas or "bathing drawers" of so many Etruscan and Cypriot figures.[6]

The history of garments like the perizoma goes back to earliest times, and it is in this wider context that the Etruscan perizoma must be studied. According to the Bible, the perizoma was the oldest garment of all. Adam and Eve invented it to cover their nakedness, after eating of the fruit of the tree of knowledge in the Garden of Eden (Gen. 3:7):

καὶ διηνοίχθησαν οἱ ὀφθαλμοὶ τῶν δύο, καὶ ἔγνωσαν ὅτι γυμνοὶ ἦσαν, καὶ ἔρραψαν φύλλα συκῆς καὶ ἐποίησαν ἑαυτοῖς περιζώματα.

The purpose of the perizoma was to avoid being γυμνοί, or naked. Being γυμνός, however, is relative; under most circumstances women were γυμναί even when wearing pants. So Eve's was an emergency measure, and women soon developed other clothes. Men long continued to wear the perizoma, or pants, as normal dress. The Egyptian phallus sheath, *schenti*, the Minoan loincloth, and the short pants of Etruscan kouroi are all varieties of the same basic garment, used throughout the whole of the Mediterranean.

The traditional type of Greek perizoma, however, can be traced back to Crete, where from Minoan times various forms of loincloths were regularly worn by men,[7] and by women, who, as in later times (Fig. 52), wore short pants when performing as acrobats.[8] On the

THE PERIZOMA IN THE MEDITERRANEAN

Knossos fresco, for example, the female bull-jumpers wear a typically Cretan form of perizoma, cinched tightly at the waist and cut high on the sides.[9]

Some kind of perizoma was worn in the Aegean throughout Mycenean and later times.[10] As often happens, fashions in clothes bridge the gaps where art does not: there is more continuity in dress than in architecture or even in the minor arts. In Crete the perizoma continued to be worn without interruption, and was still the normal sports costume in the Orientalizing period. On a bronze plaque from Rethymna, each athletic youth seems to be dressed in a short-sleeved shirt and bordered plaid perizoma[11] with a triangular front section, evidently derived from the earlier Mycenean fitted garment with separate codpiece, as in the Knossos fresco. Such a perizoma always remained at home in Crete, as seen on a bronze figurine of a *kriophoros* in Berlin dating from ca. 600 B.C., whose Cretan provenance renders the costume, a typically Orientalizing variant of the ancient loincloth, especially interesting.[12]

The perizoma, universal throughout the eighth and seventh centuries, appears in its typically Orientalizing form during this period in Greece, Etruria, Asia Minor, and Cyprus (Figs. 34, 40) on proto-Corinthian vases,[13] ivories, terracottas, and many other monuments of this period, worn not only by the favorite Dedalic male figure type of the "Master of Animals" but also by realistic figures such as the warriors on the proto-Corinthian Chigi vase. Such a garment was therefore really used.[14] Its representation was not merely an artistic convention but agrees with explicit statements in Greek literature that Greek men at this time normally wore the perizoma in order not to expose their genitals. In the *Iliad*, indeed (2.261–264), Thersites is still threatened by Odysseus with the public humiliation of being run naked through the camp.

A change occurred with the introduction in Greece of the idea of "heroic nudity," that is, of appearing publicly at the games without any perizoma. This change was so important that the date was recorded by tradition: it took place, we are told, after the fifteenth Olympiad, in 720–716 B.C., when a contestant won the footrace by allowing his perizoma to fall off along the way. He was identified by some later authors as Orsippus of Megara. Thucydides, on the other hand (1.6.5), believed it was the Lacedaemonians who set the example of contending naked, and started a custom which had recently—or not very much earlier—become universal in Greece.[15] Though the change certainly did not occur overnight, the date in the late eighth century given by the literary tradition agrees with the beginning of the series of statues of naked Greek kouroi.[16]

This important change introduced a custom which the Greeks shared among themselves and set them apart from others. Thucydides, conscious of this cultural difference and of its significance, stated

(1.6.5) that wearing the perizoma was one of the customs which the barbarians of his day shared with the ancient Hellenes. Clearly the Etruscans must be numbered among these barbarians. For the Etruscans, the perizoma was a normal male garment long after the Greeks had abandoned it,[17] as it was in Cyprus, Samos, Ionia, and other areas that remained as provincial outposts of the earlier widespread cultural area of the Orientalizing and early archaic period.

After 550, Greek influence caused the perizoma's disappearance from Etruscan art. Etruscan artists by this time were more interested in representing Athenian fashions than local styles. In real life, however, it continued in daily use, and never ceased to be worn in Italy, as we know from Dionysius of Halicarnassus, who tells us (7.72.73) that the Romans "preserve this ancient Greek custom to this day."

Even after men in Greece had abandoned the use of the perizoma and were exercising in the nude, however, women performers and athletes continued to wear it, both in real life and in art. In southern Italy especially the motif of the woman acrobat achieved lasting popularity. A great number of Italiote vases show a woman doing the handstand or performing the sword dance (Fig. 52), and as late as the fourth century A.D., on a mosaic from Piazza Armerina in Sicily, the women athletes wearing brassieres and shorts, an abbreviated sports costume or "bikini bathing suit," still follow this tradition. The Greeks nevertheless considered this semi-nudity—not to mention the public exposure—indecent for women. There was little difference, in their eyes, between such a costume and total nudity, and in real life dancing girls dressed this way were likely to be confused with courtesans. Athenaeus, in an anecdote, describes the reactions of a party of Arcadians in Athens, out-of-towners who saw, for the first time, dancing girls dressed in such topless suits: "When the drinking was going on and there entered . . . those Thessalian girls who danced, as their custom is, naked wearing only the *diazostra*, the men could no longer restrain themselves, but started up from their couches and shouted aloud at the wonderful sight they were seeing . . . and they proceeded to commit many other vulgarities" (Deipn. 14.607C).

Etruscan banquet scenes represented in art are considerably less rowdy. The women are all respectably dressed: they are wives, not courtesans. Neither here nor elsewhere are they represented naked; and by the same token, men are often shown wearing a perizoma rather than nude in the Greek style. Etruscan youths are shown wearing at least shoes, or jewelry, to keep them from being as naked as the Greek kouroi.

About each fashion we must ask: "Was such a garment really worn?" This really means asking whether it could be worn, and how. For the perizoma, this means asking how it was fastened. A perizoma which was actually worn had to be fastened in some way so that it could be

THE ETRUSCAN PERIZOMA

easily put on and removed, yet stay in place during strenuous movement, for the perizoma was first and foremost worn by active men (women and older men wore the more sedate chiton).

Ancient sources are vague about its form. We must turn to the monuments to see what this garment looked like. Fortunately, Etruscan artists were fond of using realistic details in a decorative manner, telling us a great deal about the practical construction of Etruscan clothes from their representation on the monuments.

The perizoma was pinned, buttoned, belted, or tied in place. Fibulae or safety pins never appear in representations of the perizoma. We know from literary evidence, however, that the Romans used them to pin their *cingulum* in place,[18] so it is logical to assume that the Etruscans also fastened their perizomas this way. Of the many fibulae found in Etruscan tombs, some may have been used for this purpose. Some of the small metal objects found in the tombs were probably originally sewn on the garments as buttons or fasteners, and buttons were also made of wood and other perishable materials.[19] A perizoma might be held together by a narrow self-belt made from the same fabric as the garment. Several artistic representations (Figs. 24, 39) and an actual model of a Roman leather perizoma found in London clearly illustrate its construction (Fig. 23).

Belts are much better known: in fact, the large number of bronze belt plates and buckles found throughout the Mediterranean, the Aegean, and much of Europe from the ninth century throughout all of the seventh provides us with some of our most secure evidence for the chronology and interrelations of this early period. They also afford us a unique opportunity to compare actual objects with their representation in art. Like the jewelry, these belts were precious and prestigious. They were carefully represented on human figures and were buried with the dead in their graves. They called forth the best of the metalworkers' craft, and reflected both typical local style and currently fashionable exotic specialties. They were brought home by travelers abroad. Best of all, and most convenient for us, they survived, while the cloth and leather and wood of those times have almost completely disappeared. Of course, the bronze plates we find today were once attached to cloth or leather backings which were glued or sewn on, as the holes on the borders of the bronze show; and the bronze buckles fastened leather belts much like those in use today.

We can identify with some certainty at least one of the two types which were worn with the perizoma of the men. The first type, a wide belt, cinching the waist tightly, which suggests the rigid metal surface of the original bronze belts, is easily recognizable by its peculiar willow-leaf or lozenge shape, broadest in front and tapering at the sides. On the figurines wearing it this shape is repeated in back, as though the belt were made up of two such oval or lozenge-shaped sections (Figs. 35–38); and indeed bronze plates for such a belt, hinged at the sides and designed to be fastened in back, were found in the Barberini tomb at Praeneste. This local Etruscan type appears with the plaid perizoma (Figs. 35–38, 41), another typically Etruscan garment of the seventh century B.C. The painted scene on a recently discovered vase from Cerveteri, for example, shows the exaggerated points of such a lozenge-shaped belt clearly drawn above the short, checkerboard perizoma (Fig. 41). The belt also appears on a contemporary ivory group from Praeneste (Fig. 43), together with an exotic type of perizoma which we shall examine later; there too, it gives a note of purely local color.

It has been suggested that such belts were originally intended as protection, like the wide belts worn by motorcyclists, and indeed most of the figurines wearing them do represent riders, soldiers, or acrobats involved in violent exercise. Yet the majority of actual bronze belts, or rather plaques of this shape, come from women's graves; and occasionally, for example on later monuments from the conservative north, at Este, where this fashion lasted much longer than in the Etruscan cities, such a belt is worn by women, so we cannot be sure whether these belts had any connotation for the Etruscans of the seventh century B.C. other than that of decorative luxury items. Such belts are typical of Villanovan II (eighth- and seventh-century) graves in Tarquinia, Populonia, Veii, and elsewhere. They have a wide distribution in Italy and were even exported, in the eighth century, as far abroad as mainland Greece, in Euboea. The decoration is related to that of the Urnfield and the Hallstatt Iron Age, but like the shape it is a purely Italic type. Like the metal fibulae, these bronze belts disappear from art and grave groups after around 600 B.C., just about the time of the change from the Orientalizing Etruscan fashions.[20]

Monuments of the seventh century also represent wide belts of uniform width, which appear with both the men's perizoma and the women's chiton. These representations are not all alike, and are not as easy to identify as the lozenge-shaped belt. The most peculiar type looks as though it consisted of some material which stood out from the body, forming a roll about the waist. The roll might be a folded cloth belt, fastened with a fibula or a buckle, or it might represent an exaggerated rendering of the cloth or leather backing of a flat metal belt: compare the realistically rendered ridges around the borders of a lozenge-shaped belt (Fig. 43).[21]

In contrast, a simple flat belt could represent one of several types of which traces have actually been found. The most typically Etruscan must have been the leather belts originally fastened with metal buckles, found at early Etruscan sites: the most distinctive type has double horse-head hooks or prongs which fasten into round holes on the other side of the buckle.[22] The gilded belt buckle of the statuette from the Isis tomb (Fig. 99) may show such an original fastener. It may, instead, represent another type, the flat Orientalizing bronze belt which was one of the most characteristic features of Dedalic art, like the wide patterned belt clearly shown on several Etruscan female figures of this style (Figs. 57, 58, 60).

Different local types of Orientalizing belts which have actually come down to us are being identified, and various influences can, as a result, be traced: a single-clasped Ionian bronze belt studied by Boardman, for example, had Phrygia as its source of inspiration. Examples of another widely used type have been found in Italy as well as in Greece; and an Etruscan bronze plaque has been attributed to Etruscans inspired directly by Phoenician work, as an example of "Orientalization" at work.[23]

The greatest variety of forms of the perizoma occurs in the early period, as is to be expected, since throughout the Orientalizing period it was the typical male garment in both Greece and Etruria. Real fashion and artistic convention were at this time close, if not identical; that is to say, real garments were usually represented.

Early types of perizoma represented on monuments in Etruria include an "apron" type, covering only the front, and a similar type, like a skirt, covering both front and back; a very abbreviated type, something like a codpiece, covering and lifting up the sex; several versions of a fitted type, with separate pieces cut and sewn; and longer, knee-length "Bermuda" shorts.

Some forms, obviously never worn in Etruria, testify to artistic borrowing rather than to realistic renderings of real perizomas. We shall take these up later. In either case, the variety of forms illustrated tell us a good deal about Etruscan commercial and artistic relations in the Orientalizing and early archaic period. Down through the first half of the sixth century—though there are by then fewer examples and less variety—most representations can still be recognized as continuations of these types.

The words "apron" or "skirt" describe some of the earliest examples of the perizoma, apparently native forms. A seventh-century figurine on a belt buckle from Sovana gives a good example of this apron form, represented with a particular detail which permits us to recognize it here: "apron strings," or ends tied in back, hold the front panel in place.[24]

A second type of perizoma is little more than a "phallus sheath," or separate codpiece, enclosing and lifting up the sexual organs. This type of scanty slip with thick belt is represented on a series of bronze statuettes, the earliest of which belong to the seventh century, and on the oinochoe from Tragliatella (Fig. 11). It seems to be a local development, centering in North Etruria.[25]

The fitted type of perizoma was the most common. We can often reconstruct the original models and even the patterns from which the separate pieces were cut, according to the peculiarly Etruscan preference for fitted, sewn garments.[26]

Some of the earliest examples of this form are three of the fragmentary sandstone statues from Vetulonia (Fig. 28).[27] The statues were almost life size, and except for the fact that they were dressed, would fit into the series of Greek kouroi because of their pose, with arms at the sides and left leg slightly advanced. The perizoma fits very snugly and seems to be made of a soft material.

Another series of bronze statuettes, the earliest of which date from the seventh century, wear a similar fitted perizoma.[28] The best-known figure of this type is a small bronze in the Louvre (Fig. 29), long erroneously labeled "Cretan" because of this very perizoma.[29] All are similar in pose and dress. They stand with parted legs, arms bent, and hands out in front[30] and wear their hair in a long bob. Their tight-fitting short pants stand stiffly away from the body on many examples: the originals were evidently made from some rigid material, coarse wool, fur, or leather. Often a border or hem is represented. They might have been acrobats, their costume representing an early model of the leopard-skin tights of modern-day "strong men" and circus performers. It is hard to tell what they originally held in their hands: swords, lances, and musical instruments have all been suggested.

The group is remarkably homogeneous. Again, the type is localized in northern Etruria.[31] The many surviving examples seem to illustrate a change in style, from the Dedalic type of the turn of the sixth century to softer, less angular types of later times.[32] Yet the greater popularity of the perizoma fashion in the northern Etruscan centers is probably due to their "provincial" taste, which leads them to continue to make statuettes wearing the perizoma after male nudity has been accepted in the South. Many of these figures are therefore likely to be dated earlier than they should be because of the roughness of their style. They should be considered "retarded" rather than genuinely archaic.[33]

Various individual figures of kouroi wear a similar perizoma, like that of the beautifully detailed bearded kouros from Castello, near Florence (Figs. 31–32),[34] on which waistline, front seam, and lower borders of the perizoma, decorated with a finely incised braid design, reproduce the woven or stitched decoration of the actual cloth garment. The front seam, which shows exactly how the pieces of the garment were sewn together, is one of the clearest representations of stitching in Etruscan art, though it is by no means unique.[35] Judging by the more complicated forms of their garments, the Etruscans were handier with the needle than either the Greeks or the Romans.[36]

The artists' fondness for detail also led them to represent these complicated forms and stitched patterns on the monuments, as on the stele of Larth Ninie (Fig. 33). This stele, showing an armed warrior[37] wearing a perizoma very much like that of the youth from Castello, comes from Fiesole and is approximately contemporary to that statuette. We seem to have evidence of a specific fashion in Etruria in the latter half of the sixth century.

Where did it come from? A number of striking parallels in the fashion of Cyprus and Etruria in the second half of the sixth century, including the stitched center seam on the perizoma of a contemporary statuette from Cyprus (Fig. 34),[38] apparently testify to direct cultural and commercial contact between the two areas.

The relationship between Cypriot and Etruscan perizoma fashion has been noticed before. Hus, in discussing the perizoma of the Vetulonia statue fragments, argues for a Cypriot provenance for the fashion as a whole,[39] but there is no basis for considering the general type of the Cypriot perizoma to be earlier than the Etruscan, as he does. The two are contemporary: in fact, the earliest surviving Etruscan examples precede the Cypriot. The perizoma fashion existed in Greece, Etruria, and Cyprus in the same period. In the sixth century the fashion was abandoned in Greece but was maintained in Cyprus and Etruria. Similar forms of perizoma were used in Etruria, Cyprus, and Asia Minor.

The pattern for all these forms of perizoma was essentially that used for modern pants or trousers. This is true of both the short pants and the longer versions of them; for the longer version, see the rider on a bucchero vase (Fig. 35) or on some bronze figurines of soldiers and acrobats (Figs. 36–38).[40]

A slightly different form, reproduced in detail on the elegant statuettes of the warriors from Brolio (Fig. 39), consisted of a more or less triangular front piece pulled up through the legs in front and over the pieces at the sides. This fitted model seems to be a development of the Orientalizing draped model like the perizoma of the archaic Greek *kriophoros* from Crete in Berlin. A number of later versions of the originally draped form, from outside Etruria, include the Greek wrap-around model worn by a woman athlete (Fig. 24) and by Atalanta as a female wrestler (Fig. 51), with the ends tied in front, and two contemporary Cypriot examples, one with the ends tied in front and one with the triangle reduced in size and cut and fitted into place over the crotch, like modern underwear (Fig. 40).

The perizoma is often decorated with a plaid design: see the brief shorts of the Tragliatella vase (Fig. 11) and the longer, fitted pants of the bucchero rider from Cerveteri (Fig. 35) and of some bronze figurines in Siena (Figs. 36–38). These plaid pants are often worn with the typical lozenge-shaped belt of the period, as we have seen, for example, on the seventh-century vase from Cerveteri (Fig. 41),[41] which probably translates into local dress a mythological scene taken from a Greek model.

By the later sixth century, of course, the perizoma was no longer represented in Greece, though Etruscan, Cypriot, and Ionian figures still appear in this costume (Figs. 34, 40). An important difference between the Etruscan examples and the others is that in Etruria a short-sleeved chiton like a shirt was rarely represented together with the perizoma.[42] Two small bucchero statuettes do represent a perizoma worn over a short plaid chiton so realistically that we seem to see the shirttails hanging down on either side,[43] but this is unusual. Cypriot statuettes, on the other hand, normally wear chiton and perizoma, as do the figures on the Rethymna plaque and others (Figs. 34, 40).

Aside from these illustrations of actual garments there are artistic representations of two types of perizoma which were never actually worn in Etruria: the Syrian or Cretan kilt and the Egyptian draped loincloth. The kilt is represented on a large statue from Marciano, for example (Fig. 42), and on numerous figures of the "Master of Animals (Fig. 56), all evidently imitated from foreign models.

A particularly puzzling example of such a kilt is that of an ivory figure, one of several from the seventh-century Bernardini and Barberini tombs at Praeneste (Fig. 43). The original group consisted of three human figures and a lion;[44] today only the figures of the lion and the youth lying on the lion's back remain. The youth is stretched out full length, legs bent, arms thrown back, hair streaming out behind him. His pose is the traditional one of an acrobat (cf. Fig. 38).[45] The streaming hair and outstretched arms could signify that he is leaping over the animal: Minoan bull-jumpers are frequently represented in this pose,[46] and the artist who carved the ivory figures might have had just such a composition in mind. Of course, he knew as little about real bull-jumpers as he did about real lions and was merely copying and combining various compositions he had seen. An example of the kind of model he could have used is an ivory in Syrian style from Nimrud, showing two lions attacking a bull. A man is lying between their legs, on the bull's flank (Fig. 44).[47] This ivory group has proved as difficult to interpret as the one from Etruria. Perhaps the original influence, as well as the confusion of motifs between animal-jumper and animal victim, is the same on both ivories. The costume is certainly similar, especially the pleated drapery of the Syrian figure's knee-length short skirt, which is close to that of the Etruscan lion-jumper.

The ivory group from Praeneste seems to be of Etruscan workmanship but is closely connected with Near Eastern ivories,[48] through which, apparently, came the garbled motif of the lion-jumper. The costume, like the style, is part native Etruscan and part exotic. The craftsman added two contemporary, realistic Etruscan touches of local color to the figure: the hair style and the lozenge-shaped belt, typically Etruscan in contrast to the rectangular Oriental belts.[49] Another realistic touch on this particular belt is the ridge all around the edge where the leather backing protruded from behind the bronze plate. The rest of the costume, however, is unreal. The pleated kilt-like costume below the belt,[50] worn with a chiton top, is not the normal Etruscan perizoma. It is impossible, in fact, to tell whether the artist actually meant to represent short pants, or a very short wrap-around skirt with the right section overlapping and the end hanging down lower in front. He was evidently copying a costume he himself did not understand, having seen only artistic representations of it on the Near Eastern models he used for his work.[51]

Other interesting artistic changes occur in the sixth century. Then the fashion of heroic nudity in art differed in Etruria and in Greece, and some peculiar modifications of Greek traditional mythology occurred, in accordance with local custom. The Etruscan equivalent of a Greek kouros wears a perizoma, and mythological figures such as centaurs are shown wearing short pants.[52] Even Hercules, traditionally a nude hero, in Etruria often wears his lion skin draped modestly about his loins (Figs. 45, 86; cf. Fig. 160).[53]

In the latter part of the century a type of perizoma was imitated from abroad, perhaps from Egypt (Figs. 23J, 50). This garment, which does not appear in sculpture, seems to have consisted of a piece of cloth draped and tied about the waist and thighs.[54] It appears on a few paintings or reliefs, where, except for the mysterious figure of Phersu (Fig. 49)[55] and figures of dancers, it is worn by mythological figures or foreigners: see Achilles in the Tomba dei Tori (Fig. 46) and Theseus and the Minotaur on the bucchero oinochoe from Chiusi (Fig. 47).[56] On the Caeretan hydria with Heracles and Busiris (Fig. 48),[57] the artist's desire for authenticity may have dictated the representation of this costume on Nubian slaves, which resembles a garment shown on workmen and slaves in Egyptian painting (Fig. 50).[58] The draped loincloth perizoma of Phersu (Fig. 49), worn with a mottled animal-skin shirt or chiton, on the other hand, seems to represent some kind of stage costume. Such representations were evidently reinforced by the existence of a plain "wrap-around" perizoma often worn by servants, a scarf or piece of cloth simply draped about the waist like a sarong.

CONCLUSION The perizoma fashion in art belongs in the context of the Dedalic style in Etruria. Its latest representations on "normal" figure types like the kouros from Brolio or Achilles in the Tomba dei Tori coincide with the end of the Dedalic fashions and the beginning of Ionian influence in dress in the middle of the sixth century. It will be useful, once again, to distinguish real fashions from the artistic conventions by which they are represented.

The perizoma was surely worn, in Etruria as in the rest of the Mediterranean world, during all of the Orientalizing period. That the type of garment represented on the earliest Etruscan male figures corresponds to a real fashion is proved by the variety of styles of these short pants. Their patterns can be reconstructed, since we can understand how the garment was fitted, worn, and fastened. They can also be compared with styles worn elsewhere and reflect actual contacts at various periods. The basic fashion of these short pants was originally adapted from Crete by Mycenean Greeks, who by the Orientalizing period had influenced Ionian Greeks, Cypriots, and Etruscans alike. Most striking of all is the parallel between Etruscan and Cypriot fashion around 550–525 B.C. The principal difference was the fact that the Cypriots wore these trunks with a shirt—the *chitoniskos*—unlike the Etruscans. The Cypriots followed the non-Greek, Oriental custom of covering the body. The Etruscans, as always, were more open to purely Greek influence.[59]

Certain representations of the perizoma reflect foreign artistic conventions: the *schenti*-like skirt and shirt of the Barberini lion-jumper, for example, or the Egyptianizing loincloths on the Busiris vase. Artistic conventions, however, had above all a negative effect in the representation of the perizoma in Etruscan art. The very idea of the nude kouros represents the victory of Greek artistic fashion. Because of the overwhelming prestige of Greek art, the nude male figure type was accepted in Etruscan art; and though Etruscan men, like other non-Greeks, continued to wear the perizoma, they no longer represented it on their monuments. Women athletes, on the other hand, continue to be shown wearing two-piece or one-piece "bathing suits."

The perizoma fashion therefore illustrates the artistic receptivity of Etruria, which adopted such a variety of specific perizoma styles, both in art and in fashion, and then abandoned their representation altogether when Greek fashion so dictated. Greek art triumphed despite the fact that such garments were worn in real life, despite such barbarian traits as the "realistic" tendencies of Etruscan art, and despite the consistent Etruscan reluctance to represent totally nude figures.[60]

In the construction of the actual garments, the peculiarly Etruscan taste for "shaped" and sewn garments accounts for some of the details—the set-in crotch, self-belt, seams, and decorated borders—so carefully depicted by Etruscan artists. The Cypriots shared this taste, judging by the close similarity of some of their models to Etruscan examples.

Another feature worth noting is the tendency for normal garments to become special costumes, like the lion-skin perizoma of Hercules, which owes its origin to the natural Etruscan aversion to nudity and often takes the place of the lion-skin mantle as the regular attribute of the god in Italy,[61] even after the representation of the perizoma is no longer common.

3

CHITON AND TUNIC

The robe or shirt worn from earliest times in Etruria by men and women alike is the *chiton* (Fig. 53). This Greek name can serve as a general term for a garment long used not only by Greeks and Etruscans, but by people nearly all over the Mediterranean region. The word by which Homer refers to this basic garment, the χιτών,[1] is itself of Near Eastern origin and has the same root as the Latin *tunica* and our own word "cotton."[2]

If *tunica*, the Romans' name for this garment, really came into Latin by way of Etruscan,[3] which is possible, we might be coming close to the Etruscan name for it if we called it "tunic" rather than "chiton." Aside from the fact that the Etruscan derivation is far from certain, however, I prefer to use the word "chiton," not only because the word "tunic" is by now too closely identified with the later Roman form of the garment; but because its use might imply that there was a real difference between the basic form of the Greek chiton and the contemporary Etruscan chiton, while in fact no such difference existed.[4]

The history of the chiton style in Etruria can be divided into four phases.

THE CHITON IN ETRURIA

1. In the first period, which included the seventh and the first half of the sixth century B.C., chitons are of the type common in the Dedalic period throughout the Greek world, though at the same time various details point to direct contact with the Near East.

2. The second phase begins with the introduction of the Ionic, linen chiton. This new style, which marked an important change in both artistic style and real fashion in Athens as well as in the cities of Etruria, occurred slightly earlier in Etruria, and with somewhat different results. This Ionic fashion persisted in the art of Etruria as staunchly as had the Dedalic, well into the fifth century B.C.

3. At the close of this period came a third phase, when a peculiarly Etruscan variation of the chiton can be observed. The lady's dress with the fringe at the shoulder indicates some kind of social status which has significance only within the context of Etruscan society.

4. The Hellenistic urns of the third and second centuries B.C., and other monuments of this period, show certain forms and ways of wearing the chiton which are different from the usual Greek representations.

As usual, in all these periods, we have to remember that we are dealing with local variants of Greek fashion and to try to distinguish between actual fashions and artistic conventions.

In the early period we find certain differences between the Greek and the Etruscan chiton fashion, the latter exhibiting a greater variety of forms. Aside from the usual long Dedalic chiton of the women and the short *chitoniskos* of the men, the monuments of this period in Etruria also record two more unusual garments: a three-quarter-length chiton and a long chiton whose folds indicate a loose, wide garment, a "proto-Ionic" chiton made of a lighter fabric than the Dedalic model. The last two, all but unknown in contemporary mainland Greece, were apparently adopted in Etruria directly from Near Eastern models.

The Long Dedalic Chiton

This form, reaching down to the feet or a little above, and frequently plaid-patterned (Figs. 4–6, 11, 14–16), was worn by both men and women. While the normal dress for active men was the perizoma, older men, represented in more solemn contexts, wore a long chiton. A figure from Cortona, a figure on the funerary urns from Chiusi,[5] and three seated terracotta statuettes from Cerveteri all wear this long chiton under a mantle (Figs. 14–16).

Men usually wore it unbelted. Women always wore it belted, either with a wide ornamented belt like that of Dedalic figures (Figs. 57, 60) or with a thick rolled belt similar to those worn with the men's perizoma (Figs. 55, 62; the rolled look may derive either from the leather or cloth lining of the metal belt or from folds of cloth). Often the chitons of Orientalizing female figures show a plaid-patterned zone down the front of the skirt which looks more like an artistic convention than a real fashion.

This narrow, straight, columnar Dedalic chiton was the normal dress for women in the seventh century B.C. and is one of the earliest costumes we recognize on an Etruscan monument (Figs. 41, 65). It was narrow and tight enough to be fairly form-fitting. This accounts for a conventional motif often represented, as on the female figures of the gold earring from the Regolini-Galassi tomb (Fig. 56), for example: the skirt has a characteristic V-shaped fold at the joining of torso and legs (Figs. 60, 62, 63, 155).[6] On many female busts this chiton appears as a short-sleeved garment. We have already mentioned the terracotta vase in the form of a bust in the Museo Gregoriano (Fig. 3), dressed in what is to be reconstructed as the top of a long Dedalic chiton. The design painted on the neck indicates a choker necklace, a piece of jewelry often worn with the Dedalic chiton and which is closer to the Near Eastern than the Greek fashion.[7] Female busts of the seventh century B.C. and later also show the top part of the chiton: on the fragmentary stone torso from the Pietrera tomb in Vetulonia, for example, the borders of the short sleeves and neckline are clearly marked on the surface of the stone (Fig. 57; cf. Fig. 58). The neckline was usually adorned with a necklace or what looks like a fringe decoration, and bracelets often hide the edge of the short sleeve.[8]

This fashion continued to be depicted until the middle of the sixth century B.C. and even after. The female statuette from Brolio and her male companions wearing the perizoma (Figs. 60, 39) were made some time around the middle of the sixth century B.C., yet their costume is pure seventh-century fashion. A wide Dedalic belt clasps the female figure's long, tight chiton, on whose skirt is worked the V-shaped fold, in the manner of figurines of the preceding century. The taste for decoration— leading the artist to represent with great care the choker necklace and incised basket-weave design on borders, side seams, and belt—, already noted in the representation of the perizoma is also typical of seventh-century representations of the Dedalic chiton.

These long Dedalic chitons are not very different from the fashion in Greece during the Orientalizing period. The occasional presence of long sleeves is, however, peculiar.[9] Long sleeves appear on two figures on the Monteleone chariot (Fig. 61), more or less contemporary with the statuettes from Brolio, shortly after the middle of the sixth century B.C. and likewise retaining Dedalic features.[10] The long chitons of the standing female figure and of the smaller female figure lying under the biga, as well as the short *chitoniskos* of the men, are richly decorated with incised designs along all borders and seams. Other elements, too, are still in the Dedalic tradition: the straight skirt of the long chitons, slightly flared at the bottom, with a curved hemline revealing the feet in front, and the belt, hidden by the curve of the arm but clearly indicated by the fit of the garment. The jewelry and fringe ornament on the lower border of the chiton of the female figure often identified as Thetis, on the other hand, is connected with Near Eastern models. If the garment of this standing figure represents normal dress, without the connotations of barbarian costume which long sleeves acquire in classical Greek art, the long sleeves may be a feature of local costume adopted in the period when the chariot was being made, around 550–540 B.C.

A contemporary representation of a long-sleeved chiton in Greek art, that of an early Attic *kore* in Lyons,[11] also represents a costume of the period of transition, at the beginning of the popularity of the Ionian chiton. Both the Etruscan and the Attic costume are eventually to be traced to the Mycenean and Near Eastern chiton style, in which long sleeves were a feature of the earliest chitons (Fig. 54) and always remained in use. In form, the Etruscan sleeves are most similar to the narrow Mycenean sleeves of the figures on the Warrior vase. Their appearance on this monument might illustrate the transition from the Dedalic to the Ionian style, as does another element of the costume of the figures, the pointed shoes of the naked kouroi, which marks one of the earliest appearances of the *calcei repandi*, adopted along with the Ionic chiton at this period. These two elements—long sleeves and pointed shoes—seem to reflect a real fashion, coming from Ionia, adopted during the years ca. 550 B.C.

An unpatterned chiton with folds appears on certain small female figures of terracotta, ivory, or bucchero (Figs. 7, 62, 63). On the Chiusi "ziro" burial urns this is the dress of the smaller female figures,

The Long "Proto-Ionic" Chiton

contrasting with the plaid mantles of the smaller male figures and the more elaborate dress—plaid chiton and back mantle—of the larger female figures crowning the lids (Figs. 4–5). This distinction of costume may indicate the relative importance of the wearer, but we cannot be sure. What is certain is that, in Etruscan art of the seventh century B.C., we find represented two different kinds of chiton worn by women. The difference between them probably reflects an artistic dependence on two different traditions: the "Dedalic" tubular chiton, often patterned on the surface and tightly cinched with a wide belt, and a fuller, Near Eastern chiton with folds. The "realistic" tendency of monuments on which these garments appear (Figs. 4–9) shows that two such styles of dress, a heavy woolen chiton with a woven pattern and one made out of a thinner fabric, either linen or fine wool, were probably really worn by Etruscan women. If such a loose, wide chiton with folds was then a familiar garment in Etruria in the middle of the seventh century, it preceded the adoption in mainland Greece of the famous "Ionic fashion" by about a century. Examples of a loose "Ionic" chiton with many folds represented on Greek monuments (but not in Athens) in the early sixth century are probably to be attributed to Eastern influence. They are isolated instances, however, which may not reflect a "real" costume, as they do in Etruria.[12]

The Three-Quarter-Length Chiton

A belted chemise reaching only to mid-calf, with elbow-length sleeves, appears very early in Etruscan art, on the two bronze figurines from the Tomba del Duce in Vetulonia (Fig. 65). The length of the sleeves is unusual and is not found again in Etruria. The shorter hemline, however, is a regular feature of early Etruscan dress[13] (Figs. 73–75, 104–105, 107). Yet it is somewhat surprising to find such a very short chiton at this date on a female figure. In the seventh century this form of chiton was a man's costume, both in the Near East and on the rare Greek illustrations of this originally Oriental garment (Figs. 19, 21, 66, 67).[14] The three-quarter length of the chiton on the Tomba del Duce statuettes, which obviously represent female figures, seems to be a local peculiarity. The shortness of the chiton might have been exaggerated by the artist, for the long chiton was always a bit shorter in Etruria, and there are many examples of female figures of the seventh and sixth century where the ankles, and even part of the legs, show below the hem of a shorter long chiton (Figs. 11, 62, 70).

The actual three-quarter-length chiton seems to have been a male garment in Etruria. In Etruscan art it does not clearly appear on men except on monuments dating from the middle of the sixth century, such as a terracotta painted plaque in the British Museum or a stone relief stele from Volterra with the figure of an armed warrior (Figs. 73, 69). Normally worn unbelted, it is the dress of younger men who wear neither the longer "formal" chiton nor the perizoma of active heroes, warriors, or athletes.[15]

At some point the connotations of this type of garment changed. Still a male dress, it also indicated the lower status of the wearer. On a recently discovered series of terracotta friezes from Poggio Civitate, in North Etruria, dating, according to the excavator, from the middle of the sixth century, the servants attending their masters are distinguished by the kind of chiton they wear (Fig. 72). In the scene with seated figures the two smaller male servants standing behind their seated masters wear three-quarter-length unbelted shirts. The female servant carries feminine instruments, a handled pot and a fan, and wears a longer, belted chiton. In the procession frieze, too, the two figures leading the horses wear the beltless three-quarter chiton; the smaller female figures following the carriage carry fans, vases, and household furniture and wear, as appropriate, the long, belted chiton.[16]

The Short Chiton

The practical short chiton of the men, the chitoniskos, was much rarer in Etruscan art of the seventh century than it was in Greece. Its place was taken by the perizoma, as on the four fragmentary male statues from the Tumulo della Pietrera in Vetulonia, which show in some detail the costume of the seventh century in Etruria (Fig. 28).[17] Many examples of the short chiton in Etruscan art of this period are indeed to be considered imitations of Near Eastern artistic models rather than representations of garments actually worn in Italy. On an ivory pyxis from the Regolini Galassi tomb at Cerveteri[18] a youth engaged in taming lions is dressed in a short tunic with close-set pleats, a costume as exotic as the scene itself (cf., on Fig. 56, the young men fighting lions on the earring from the same tomb).

In the sixth century the picture changes. Under the influence of Greek art, the short chiton becomes more frequent and begins to take the place of the perizoma as the aristocratic costume of the hero. This change takes place around the middle of the century. In Greek art, Theseus, for example, who often wears a perizoma in the seventh century, usually wears a chiton in the sixth.[19] In Etruria, the figure of Achilles in the Tomba dei Tori (Fig. 46) wears a perizoma; in the more or less contemporary scene on the Monteleone chariot, where he receives the arms from his mother, he wears a short-sleeved, elaborately decorated short chiton (Fig. 61). All the active figures on the Loeb tripods, of the last third of the sixth century, wear the short chiton (Figs. 76–80).

But the short chiton worn alone does not last long as an aristocratic costume. Already the man with a scepter on one of the terracotta plaques from Cerveteri is wearing an elaborate short mantle over his short chiton (Fig. 71),[20] and so does the figure of Paris on the slightly earlier Boccanera plaques (Figs. 73–75). By the end of the sixth century, again following the influence of Greek art, the simple short chiton worn alone had become the mark of slaves and attendants like the young boy in the Tomba degli Auguri.

In any case, with or without mantle, the chiton was always more common in Etruria than in Greece. Whereas in Greece the aristocratic dress of younger gods and citizens consisted of heroic nudity or, for older gods or philosophers, the himation worn alone, in Etruria the chiton appears more often, and in different contexts. Etruscan gods, for example, are represented with both chiton and mantle, unlike Greek gods after the archaic period: see the Apollo of Veii (Figs. 104–105) or the figure of Zeus on the Pyrgi pediment. In fact, Etruscan figures, both divine and human, as noted in the case of Hercules, tend to be dressed more fully than the Greek prototypes.[21]

PHASE II: THE IONIC CHITON

The change to the Ionic fashion took place in Etruria, as in Greece, within the space of about twenty years after the middle of the sixth century. The change applies especially to the long chiton. The chitoniskos of the men retained its original length, which became that of the Roman tunic, but was often represented with folds showing its finer texture and greater width.[22]

The difference between the long Dedalic chiton and the later, modernized Ionic style can be seen by comparing the statuette from Brolio (Fig. 60) with another bronze statuette, fifty years or so later in date (Fig. 130). This later figurine is dressed in a loose garment forming numerous folds below a thin belt (here, as often, not actually shown). The skirt was very full, as can be seen from the width of its lower border: though a fold of it is pulled up and held in the figure's left hand, it is still not pulled tight. This gesture of holding up the skirt,[23] necessary with the full, trailing Ionic chiton, would be impossible with the narrow Dedalic chiton; furthermore, the linen fabric of the Ionic chiton forms folds quite different from those of the heavy wool of the straight Dedalic chiton.

The sleeves of the Ionic chiton, too, are different. At first sight they look rather like the elbow-length sleeves of the figurine from the Tomba del Duce (Fig. 65). But these "sleeves" are not woven to shape at all; as the fine folds on the upper arm show, they are simply formed by pinning together the edges of the fabric on the shoulders (Fig. 53).

The difference between the two types of chitons can perhaps best be understood by comparing the reconstructed patterns of the original garments. A Dedalic chiton with sewn sleeves, like that of the Brolio statuette, was made according to pattern No. 1 (Fig. 53).[24] The Ionic chiton of the other bronze figure was at least twice as wide as the early archaic type, so that the thin fabric fell in soft folds all around the body.[25] The construction of the "sleeves" is clearly illustrated: because of the great width of the garment, the openings for the arms are left in the upper seam along the neckline, not at the sides, as in the early, narrow sheath chiton of patterns No. 1 and No. 2, and the extra material on the top edge, which comes down below the shoulders, forms full "sleeves" over the upper arms. As so often, Etruscan artists develop this realistic detail of the construction of the sleeves as a decorative element. The characteristic points at the elbow, which appear on Etruscan monuments from ca. 520 B.C. (Figs. 130, 132–133), actually represent the upper points of the rectangle, which now come below the arms (Fig. 53).[26]

The change in fashion, which occurred gradually, is illustrated by many monuments of the period 550–520.[27] Unlike mainland Greece, where the Attic *peplos* with overfold constituted the normal fashion preceding the introduction of the Ionic chiton, the Dedalic fashion in Etruria continued throughout much of the sixth century, replaced only by the Ionic style.[28] In Etruria, the peplos with overfold, familiar only from artistic models (it appears, for example, on the François vase, from Chiusi, representing a compendium of current Greek fashion ca. 570 B.C.), was shown on such an Attic figure as Athena, but it was not really worn and is therefore never shown as a normal dress.[29]

The transition from Dedalic to Ionic, we have seen, can be followed in monuments like the Monteleone chariot (Fig. 61), where both the long sleeves of the female figures and the pointed shoes of the nude kouroi show the artist's acceptance of Ionian influence in dress.

The two series of painted terracotta plaques from Cerveteri also show the gradual adoption of this style of dress. On the earliest of the group, the so-called Boccanera slabs in the British Museum, the two chiton types appear simultaneously. The straight Dedalic chiton, of heavy red wool with brightly decorated seams and borders, is worn by an imposing female figure leading two mourners, and also by Athena in the scene of the Judgment of Paris. Hera and Aphrodite, the two more feminine goddesses, and other female figures on the plaques all wear the new, soft style of the Ionic chiton (Figs. 73–75).[30] This chiton is not yet worn alone, however, but appears either under a heavy mantle pulled over the head or, on the figure of Hera, below a heavier red chiton, pulled up to show the new style below.

On the somewhat later plaques in the Louvre, the "archaizing" image of a divinity standing on a pedestal is still conservatively dressed, with only the edge of the Ionic chiton showing below the edge of the heavier woolen tunic (Fig. 71),[31] on another plaque, two old men seated on folding stools already wear, under their purple mantles, the current soft Ionic chiton with sleeves forming points at the elbows. On their feet are the calcei repandi which regularly accompany the new chiton fashion (cf. the Monteleone chariot, Fig. 61, and the Boccanera plaques, Figs. 73–75).

Another set of monuments, the Loeb tripods (Figs. 76–80), dating from the third quarter of the century, illustrate variations in the artistic representation of the Ionic chiton which might reflect changes in the actual fashion. The artist of tripod B, for example, shows a pouch formed at the waistline, as well as the characteristic points at the elbow. The chitons of the figures on tripod C, instead, have elaborate border decorations which resemble those of some earlier Dedalic chitons (Figs. 60, 61). The changes in style might be useful as chronological criteria to date the various tripods. If the representation of the Ionic chiton on these tripods reflects the contemporary fashion in art and costume, rather than simply the age or training of the artist, then tripod A seems to be somewhat later—perhaps ten years or so—than tripods B and C.

Our usual questions must now be asked: what was a real fashion, what was due to artistic convention, and what was the origin of each?

There is no doubt that this loose linen chiton was a real fashion adopted sometime after 550 B.C. In Ionia, the fashion is attested as early as 580–570 B.C.[32] In Athens, the shift to the Ionic chiton took place within the course of a complete change in fashion which occurred between 540 and 530 B.C., at the time of the change from black- to red-figure paintings. The change is documented on the series of marble korai from the Acropolis and in contemporary vase painting.[33] In Etruria, the change took place about this same time—a few years earlier, if we can trust the dating of representations of this chiton style on a number of monuments now generally dated soon after 550 B.C. (e.g., the Boccanera plaques, Figs. 73–75).

There is, in any case, evidence for an independent adoption of this style in Etruria. It would seem that an originally Oriental chiton fashion first came into Etruria directly from some Ionian intermediary, and not by way of Athens, since the context was different in Athens and Etruria. In Etruria the new chiton fashion was accompanied from the first by other fashions, such as pointed shoes and, especially, types of hats unknown in Athens. Then too, the Etruscans might have remembered the older "proto-Ionic" chiton fashion of the second half of the seventh century, represented in Etruria half a century or so before the earliest examples of the Ionian chiton in Ionia. (As far as we can tell, it had disappeared from art sometime before the beginning of the sixth century.) This would have facilitated the adoption of the new fashion, which came, this time, no longer directly from Near Eastern models but by way of the later "arbiters of fashion," the Ionians.

Artistic conventions soon followed Attic Greek models, however. By the end of the sixth century many details of wearing the Ionic chiton, not necessarily connected with actual Etruscan custom, were being imitated in Etruscan art from Attic vase painting and sculpture. The gesture of holding out the chiton at the side makes little sense when the figure wears the shorter Etruscan version of the chiton. Nor does the representation of apparently "transparent" chitons, which appear on figures of dancers on monuments of the early fifth century, have much to do with reality.[34] The fine texture of this very full, flowing chiton skirt of extremely sheer fabric, worn under the *ependytes*, a short-sleeved colored jacket of heavy contrasting texture (cf. Fig. 81), is imitated from a stylization very common in Greek red-figured vase painting of the end of the sixth and beginning of the fifth century, which shows the outline of the leg and thigh below the fabric of the chiton as though it were made of transparent fabric.[35] The woolen jacket represents a real garment, a special dancer's costume regularly worn by figures of castanet players in both Greece and Etruria, made of wool and often plaid-patterned (Fig. 81).[36] Other differences between the Etruscan and the Attic fashion in this period concern the mantle worn over the chiton and will be treated in the next chapter.

The Ionic chiton was still worn by Etruscan ladies throughout the late fifth and fourth centuries. Except for the length, which was slightly shorter in Etruria, the Etruscan fashion follows the Greek. Around 400 B.C., as in Athens, artists once again exaggerate the contrast between the heavy texture of the mantle and the soft folds of the linen chiton, which cling so tightly to the body that breasts and nipples show through the material (Fig. 82).

There also appears, some time before this, a peculiarly Etruscan fashion which has no counterpart at all in Greece. Two tassels hanging from the chiton on each shoulder, front and back, are very clearly represented on all types of monuments—mirrors, reliefs, statues, and vase paintings—and surely correspond to a real fashion. The tassel appears to have consisted of a long strand of braided wool, like a fillet, attached on the shoulders at the seam and hanging free at both ends. It was worn by figures of divinities, priestesses, and ladies of some rank (Figs. 83, 85, 86, 87, 159). On the sarcophagus from Vulci (Fig. 85) the lady on the front panel, probably the owner of the sarcophagus, wears it, while her attendants do not: it obviously had some special significance, and was the sign of some social status, like the pointed shoes with which it was often, though not always, worn.[37] The tassel is clearly visible on two monuments of the classical period from Chianciano, the sarcophagus with a deceased man (Fig. 159), where it is worn by the winged female figure seated at the foot of the bed, and the enthroned female figure with child, the so-called Mater Matuta—human mother, divine mother, or "angel"? The latter, recently cleaned and restored, seems to be dated by an Attic vase of 470–460 B.C., found inside the statue, to sometime around the middle of the fifth century.[38] This date gives us an early starting point for the style and helps to close a chronological gap which would otherwise be puzzling. For the tassel appears, somewhat surprisingly, around 500 B.C., on the chiton of a bronze figure, the so-called Vertumnus (Figs. 107, 108), who also wears a diagonally draped rounded mantle and pointed calcei repandi. This, its earliest appearance and the only instance I know of it on a male figure, underlines its symbolic meaning as a sign of rank: it is clearly a god who wears this feature of costume which, like the pointed shoes, was later reserved as a symbol for figures of goddesses and important women. This tassel remains in use throughout the fourth century, until it is displaced by the Hellenistic chiton style of the early third century.

Men in this period have no such special Etruscan fashion. They are often represented without a chiton, wearing tebenna or himation directly over the body.[39]

From the early third century on, fashionable women are shown wearing a narrow, sleeveless chiton tied in a high-waisted "Empire" style, with a narrow belt which comes just below the breasts in front. Still made of

PHASE III: THE CHITON OF THE CLASSICAL PERIOD

PHASE IV: THE HELLENISTIC CHITON

fine linen, but not as full as the classical and archaic Ionic chiton, it had a long overfall and was simply pinned once at each shoulder, giving a sleeveless effect contrasting with the earlier form (Figs. 89, 92). The fashion seems to derive from Alexandria, where the native linen was used. The earliest Greek figures wearing such dresses date from after 275 B.C. or so, and the Etruscan fashion seems to start around this same time.[40] Portrait figures reclining on the covers of Hellenistic urns give us the best picture of such chitons, as they do in general of fashions of the third through the first centuries B.C. The men are shown bare-breasted or with tunics, with their himatia wrapped about their legs; the ladies appear with sleeveless chitons, sometimes with richly decorated "body jewelry," a long chain crossing the breasts in front, fastened with a rosette brooch (Figs. 89, 92), always with a variety of bracelets, necklaces, torques, earrings, and diadems.[41]

Other monuments of the Hellenistic period show a rather curious mixture of conventional artistic motifs and realistic details. The heroic nudity or partial draping of many figures (Figs. 90, 91) is represented, along with real fashions, especially jewelry or shoes, which add a touch of local color.[42] Terracotta urns and incised mirrors also show some very strange garments, to be interpreted as stage costume rather than real fashions, which is not surprising because they reflect scenes from tragedies, shown as though on a stage (Fig. 91).[43] So we see on a number of terracotta urns representing the death of Myrtilus, Pelops' charioteer, figures dressed in the long, plaid-patterned pants reserved for archers or charioteers. The long sleeves appearing in these mythological scenes from dramas may also be explained as "barbarian" dress, appropriate to Asiatic figures. Some representations of sleeves which appear rather extraordinary to us—shown, for example, *without* an attached chiton on one funerary urn with the story of the death of Oenomaus (Fig. 90), look as though they show the real construction of stage costume.[44] Even theater dress was shown realistically by Etruscan artists.

The representations on these reliefs, then, must be used very cautiously in attempting to reconstruct the "real" dress of the Hellenistic period. It is hard to say, for example, whether long-sleeved chitons were actually worn in Etruria or not: our evidence comes mostly from mythological scenes on reliefs or mirrors (Fig. 91).

The dress of the female demons who so often flank these scenes on the urns is a costume suitable for violent action, similar to that of Artemis the huntress. It consists of a short skirt, baring the knees and the whole upper torso and breasts; high boots or *embades* with soft leather tops; and straps crossing the breasts, often fastened by a brooch in the center, which often look more like the Hellenistic "body jewelry" of the ladies reclining in finery on the lid of the urn than the baldric they originally were meant to represent. These Etruscan Furies, whom we may call Vanth, are similar in costume and pose to those of earlier south

Italian vases, which served also as models for the winged figure of Lyssa on the frieze of the Villa of the Mysteries.[45]

Another problem confronting us in the fourth century and Hellenistic period is the relationship between Rome and the Etruscans.[46] A better understanding of the political relation between the two in this period would make the interpretation of certain Etruscan costumes easier, for the historical situation was undoubtedly reflected in the significance attached to the dress of magistrates and various other important personages. We do not understand when or in what context the Roman symbolism of a costume was accepted or shared by the Etruscans. The famous triumphal painting of Vel Sathies in the François tomb shows him wearing a figured mantle (Fig. 135). It is not a Roman toga picta, for it is a himation rather than a rounded *tebenna* (see Chapter 4), but it clearly has the same significance as the Roman triumphal garment.[47] When did the toga come to signify to the Etruscans what it did to the Romans? A monument which must be interpreted according to this chronological and social context is the famous statue of Aule Metelius (Fig. 109), an example of Etruscan portraiture identified by an inscription in Etruscan which gives his titles in the Roman style. The date of this statue, long under discussion, has recently been put as late as 80 B.C., largely on the basis of his dress.[48] The chiton he wears, with vertical stripe down the side, has been called the *angusticlavus*. Such a white tunic with red vertical stripe was already common in Etruscan wall paintings of the fifth century, where it represented normal dress. With the Romans, however, it developed into the symbol of a certain social standing. It is apparently with its Roman significance that Aule Metelius wears this garment.[49] In the first century B.C. Roman influence would dictate the use of the symbolic dress of a Roman magistrate for a man who held an official position in an Etruscan city: *toga praetexta*, *calcei*, gold ring, and tunica with *clavus*. The Arringatore properly enough wears all of these.

The shorter length of the toga, on the other hand, so often cited as evidence for an early date, could be a matter of fashion rather than symbolism. Since these garments were originally Etruscan, Aule Metelius could still follow Etruscan rather than Roman fashion in details of dress not specifically dictated by protocol, even around 80 B.C., when he was legally not only a *togatus* but also a full-fledged Roman citizen.[50]

CONCLUSION

The chronological development of chiton styles in Etruscan art allows us to follow changing forms and to reconstruct the real fashions behind them. In the first phase, the seventh and the first half of the sixth century, two basic types of chiton were worn: the "Dedalic," or "Achaean" chiton, a heavy woolen robe, often decorated with the ubiquitous plaid pattern of this period, and a long, loose linen garment I call the "proto-

Ionic" chiton. There were also certain variations unknown in contemporary Greek fashion: a shorter version of the long "Dedalic" chiton, which might be classified separately as the "three-quarter-length" chiton, and longer sleeves, as on the "Dedalic" dress of figures on the Monteleone chariot or on the figurines from Tomba del Duce in Vetulonia. Furthermore, the chiton in Etruria was always shorter than in Greece.

Does this greater variety of what seem to be "real" fashions imply a variety of cultural influences in Etruria, or is it that because of the "realistic" tendencies of the artists different styles are represented more faithfully in Etruria than in Greece? Both answers are true. There were, certainly, different influences at work. The basic Dedalic chiton fashion is Greek, or rather Orientalizing, and therefore widespread, while a number of details, such as the longer sleeves, the three-quarter-length chiton, and the "proto-Ionic" chiton, seem to point to direct contact with real Near Eastern fashions.

The introduction (or reintroduction?) of the Ionic linen chiton style shortly after the middle of the sixth century brings us to the second phase, ending sometime after the second half of the fifth century. From now on, both women and old men wear the long linen chiton, while active, younger men wear the short chiton or chitoniskos, which is a substitute for the perizoma. Even the long chiton is still never as long, however, as the original Ionian chiton: no "trailing-robed Ionians" here. The mid-calf-length chiton of the Apollo of Veii almost seems to continue the tradition of the three-quarter-length chiton for men, while women's chitons were never so long that they really had to lift their skirts out of the way with that typical gesture of the Greek kore. Direct connections with actual Ionian fashions, independent of mainland Greek intervention, are implied by the date and context of the adoption of the Ionic chiton in Etruria.

The third period, extending throughout the later fifth and most of the fourth centuries—the Classical period in Greece—is characterized by a special Etruscan fashion, a chiton with tassels on the shoulders, formerly worn by the figure of a god and now signifying the rank or priestly status of higher-class women. Men are rarely shown wearing chitons in this period, though this may or may not correspond to real-life custom.

In the Hellenistic period women wear sleeveless narrow linen chitons pinned at the shoulders, belted high at the waist with an overfold, and often decorated with a necklace or "body jewelry" crossing the breasts. Men's chitons are rarely represented on funerary portraits, and differ from those of the women only in being unbelted, undecorated, and somewhat narrower. In each period certain artistic conventions modified the manner in which "real" chitons were represented. The folds I interpret as signifying the texture of linen chitons on the "proto-Ionic" chiton of seventh-century figurines are a local artistic convention apparently worked out by "realistically" inclined Etruscan artists to illustrate a real dress. For the Dedalic chiton, there existed a number of widely accepted conventions, which may not always have corresponded to the actual local fashion: the geometric design on the front panel of the skirt, the V-shaped lines on the skirt, the curved edge of the skirt above the feet, and even the representations of decorative elements such as the broad Dedalic belt, fringed necklines, sleeves, or jewelry.

Later, in the sixth century, conventional ways of depicting the Ionic chiton included the front "pouch" over the belt in front, the gesture of holding up the long Ionic chiton—quite unnecessary with the shorter Etruscan model—and the "transparent" chiton shirt of dancers.

This mannerism of showing the forms of the body through the thin cloth occurs again in the women's chitons of the Classical period, on which the nipples seem to show through the fine material. In the fourth century, too, the representation of men reclining without chitons under their mantles may represent Greek artistic convention rather than actual Etruscan custom.

Imitation of artistic models also accounts for representation of the short chitoniskos for men in the seventh century and the peplos for women in the sixth or fifth; neither of these chiton types was ever really worn at that time in Etruria. In the Hellenistic period, furthermore, there appear on the relief scenes of ash urns from Volterra and other monuments a whole series of representations of figures wearing what looks like theatrical costume rather than normal dress, including chitons with long sleeves, thick belts, and overfolds. Female figures, no doubt mythological, even appear bare-breasted, contrary to all Etruscan ideas of propriety.

Peculiarly Etruscan chiton fashions include the proto-Ionic chiton in the seventh century and the women's fringed chiton in the fourth. Etruscan receptivity to outside influences accounts both for the variety of actual chiton types and details adopted from the Near East, the Ionian cities, and Athens, in that order; and the artistic conventions adopted almost exclusively from Attic art of the last quarter of the sixth century.

The colder climate might have something to do with the preference Etruscan men and women always had for wearing both chiton and mantle. We do not know whether long sleeves were a real fashion or not, or, if so, for how long, but if they ever were, the reason might have been warmth; it might also be related to the custom of wearing more clothes than the Greeks. Etruscan taste for ornamentation in art and fashion is illustrated by the brightly colored or incised borders and seams of so many chiton representations,[51] while set-in, apparently sewn sleeves show the taste for sewn, fitted clothes in contrast with the plainer Greek models.

Finally, the similarity between the long Dedalic chitons of men and women in the seventh century and the three-quarter-length chiton may indicate an important feature of Etruscan dress, the frequent identity of fashions for men and women in the seventh and sixth centuries (though men's and women's chitons were actually pretty much alike anywhere).

4

MANTLES

The most obvious difference between Greek and Etruscan fashions is the variety of shapes of Etruscan mantles, in contrast with the consistently rectangular shape of all Greek mantles, from the ample himation to the smaller chlamys.

Many of these Etruscan inventions, having found favor with the Romans, enjoyed a long history. The most characteristic Etruscan mantle, the rounded tebenna of the later sixth century, survived into Roman times as the toga, and still later, draped in a different way, was modified into the priest's cope, worn in the Roman Catholic Church today.

Even though cloaks and mantles changed more rapidly than other fashions, their development can still be conveniently separated into four successive phases. Of these, the earlier part of the first period, the seventh century, presents a stable picture. One type of mantle served for men, while women wore first the back mantle, a peculiarly Etruscan fashion, and then a kind of cape, something like a raincoat. About 600 B.C. the picture changes, and some new and unexpected representations of mantles and ways of wearing them appear. In the second half of the sixth century the most striking change is the introduction of the rounded mantle, the Etruscan tebenna, and the development of a number of peculiarly Etruscan fashions based on this special shape. Finally, in the Classical and Hellenistic periods, the alternation of tebenna (or toga) and himation as a costume for men presents the problem of the possible symbolic significance of these garments within the context of Etruscan culture. Certain stylizations in the way mantles were represented in each period are connected with artistic rather than with actual fashions and are related to artistic influences at work in Etruria at various times.

PHASE I: SEVENTH CENTURY

Throughout the seventh century, people undoubtedly wore the kind of heavy woolen cloak, often plaid-patterned, which appears on the monuments. The men wore their wide mantles wrapped about the body and fastened over the right shoulder with a brooch to allow the right arm freedom of movement;[1] these are best illustrated by some of the small figures from the ziro burial vases from Chiusi (Figs. 8, 9). One can still see, in some cases, the holes where miniature metal fibulae or brooches with pendant ornaments were once attached.[2] This wide, enveloping type of mantle, the simplest kind of warm covering for men, was worn throughout the Mediterranean world. The Homeric χλαῖνα and φᾶρος were also used as such combination mantles and blankets[3] (Fig. 94; cf. Figs. 6, 84, 145).

The "back mantle" represented on so many seventh-century figures of women (Figs. 4–5, 62, 65, 94) is instead typically Etruscan and has no parallel elsewhere. It consisted of a long, rectangular piece of heavy wool, fastened at the shoulders so that it hung straight along the length of the back down to the hem of the chiton. It was probably sewn or pinned at the shoulder seams of the chiton, there being no other visible fastening: the mantle had to be securely fastened to keep the heavy woolen fabric from dragging it down. This back mantle, worn over the straight Dedalic chiton with a long braid hanging over it in back, appears on some of the earliest figures of the period, like the statuettes from the Tomba del Duce in Vetulonia (Fig. 65), the largest female figures on the burial urns from Chiusi (Figs. 4–5), and some of the pyxis supports from Cerveteri (Fig. 62).[4]

A second type of mantle for women appearing in the latter part of the century is a kind of cape "raincoat" with holes for the arms in front. This is worn pulled up over the head on a bronze statuette in the British Museum (Fig. 95) and, later, on archaizing statuettes of the mid-sixth century (Fig. 96).

PHASE I: EARLY SIXTH CENTURY In this period many earlier styles continue, though new artistic influences change the way in which they are represented. Men are rarely shown wearing the heavy mantle in the manner of the seventh century, though a square or rectangular mantle continues to be worn throughout, nor is the narrow back mantle for women any longer to be seen; its place is taken by a wider cloak worn over the head, illustrated, for example, on one of the ivory situlae from Chiusi (Fig. 13). The cloak, a large square or rectangle frequently made of a heavy plaid fabric, as in the seventh century, here covers the hair entirely. Later in the sixth century some of the hair appears at the sides, following the Greek fashion. Often this cloak or the raincoat is worn over the long braid of the seventh century, which shows up in profile as a hump under the mantle (Fig. 96).[5] Several statuettes illustrate this overlapping of two fashions: the back braid of the seventh century, which survived longer than the back mantle, and the later style of mantle worn over the head.

The dating of many figures dressed in this manner has been controversial, both because of this overlapping of an actual fashion and because the retarded, conservative style of many of these statuettes is confusing. Since this fashion actually spans the whole of the sixth century, we must find some other detail of dress as a dating criterion: this, as we see in the following chapter, is provided by the pointed shoes. The consciously archaizing statuette in Florence (Fig. 96), wearing an eclectic costume consisting of a "raincoat" mantle over the back braid of the seventh century, must actually be dated after 550, in spite of its primitive appearance, because of the calcei repandi, which were not generally adopted before the middle of the century. It could easily date even later, around 540 or 530 B.C.[6]

The same date holds for the much-discussed Greek figurine from the Vix crater (Fig. 97), whose costume is so similar to that of the statuette in Florence. This monument has also, at times, been dated earlier than 550 B.C.; recently a date as early as 575 B.C. has been proposed,[7] mostly on the basis of comparisons with Corinthian monuments.[8] Yet here, too, the Ionic shoes give us a *terminus ante quem non* of ca. 550 B.C.

The principal innovation in this period is in the field of art, not fashion. Rather than any radical changes in real dress, representations of mantles between 600 and 570 B.C. reflect the experiments and adaptations of artistic influences from Greek art by Etruscan artists. These include, first, the representation of mantles which never existed in Etruria at all but were merely copied from Greek monuments; and second, the representation of mantles which were probably really used in Etruria but which the artists presented in accordance with certain Greek artistic conventions.

Of the first type of influence we have a clear instance in the Dedalic capelet, shown on figures of dancing women on a relief from Chiusi dating from the middle of the sixth century (Fig. 98). This little cape was the normal costume for Orientalizing female figures like the statuette from Auxerre and was a characteristic garment of the seventh century in Crete. It had never been worn in Etruria and was unknown to the Etruscan artist. He evidently copied from a seventh-century monument, perhaps one of those bronze plates from Crete on which it occasionally appears; or he might have come in contact with a South Italian or Sicilian monument. On a contemporary relief from Sicily, the artist seems to be using this Cretan costume consciously to characterize Europa on her way to Crete.[9] This imitation is proof of the complex artistic influences at work in Etruria in the sixth century and is also an instance of the continuing appreciation for Dedalic style, which continues well into the middle of the century.

Two other representations of mantles in this period, when the artistic style was changing, are also puzzling. The types of mantle shown were probably actually worn; but the artists stylized their appearance in a way that makes it hard to decide what the original garments looked like. The first of these is the plaid mantle worn by three terracotta statuettes from Cerveteri, dating from sometime around 600 B.C. and marking the end of a period as well as the beginning of the next (Figs. 14–16); the mantle's rounded edges are stylized rather than realistic (see infra Appendix I). Another mantle difficult to interpret is that of the alabaster statue from the Polledrara tomb at Vulci (Fig. 99).[10] Here the artistic conventions obscure the rendering of the actual garment. It seems to have been a rectangle, with two long ends hanging over the shoulders in front. Though at first sight the closest comparison seems to be with the mantle of the central female figure on the Monteleone chariot (Fig. 61), the mantle of the Polledrara statue may represent a real-life fashion in which the front panels have actually been added separately. Long front panels are also worn by a group of women on a relief from Chiusi strongly influenced by Corinthian art (Fig. 101). Similarly, Greek representations of mantles with long panels in front might have been the models for the Vulci artist, and perhaps the statue foreshadows the importance of Corinthian influence.

From the second quarter of the century Corinthian influence can be recognized in a number of stylizations. The manner of representing the mantle on the head with some hair showing on the forehead follows the Corinthian style (cf. the Vix statuette, Fig. 97), in contrast to the mantle of the seventh century, when, following the Near Eastern style, it covered the head completely (Fig. 13). Another stylized feature is the "Corinthian point," the lower edge of the mantle formed by a diagonal line, as though it dipped down in back to the heels (Fig. 18). This characteristic of the Corinthian style of vase painting appears on various Etruscan monuments, especially ivories and small reliefs, like one of the Pania situlae (Fig. 13), the ivories from Bologna (Fig. 17), or a relief from Castellina in Chianti.[11] The gesture of holding the mantle out before the body with both hands, creating a dowager-like silhouette christened the "Penguin woman" by Beazley,[12] was especially popular in Greece in the first half of the sixth century (Fig. 18). In Etruria it appears on the ivory plaques from Bologna (Fig. 17). The gesture of holding the cloak out with only one hand, as Hera does on the Pontic amphora by the Paris painter in Munich (Fig. 146), is common in archaic Greek art representing a bride or wife.[13]

PHASE II:
SECOND HALF OF
SIXTH AND EARLY
FIFTH CENTURY

A radical change took place in Etruscan fashion soon after the middle of the sixth century and affected the most striking and long-lived characteristic of Etruscan dress, the rounded form of the mantle. We are now confronted with an exhilarating variety of forms and fashions and changes as rapid as those of fashion styles today.

Tebenna

The rounded shape of the cloak of a number of figures of the second half of the sixth century (Figs. 71, 102–105, 107) ushers in a new fashion, a garment the Etruscan name of which was preserved in Greek as "*tebenna*," destined to become the basic form of the mantle in Etruria. The representations on the monuments reflect an original model woven with curved edges, in a roughly semicircular or elliptical form, foreshadowing the shape of the later Roman toga.

The rounded tebenna was originally used by Etruscans as the rectangular himation had been, as a general covering. Women wore it as well as men, says Varro, and it was the all-purpose cover, a dress by day and a blanket by night.[14] The monuments in part confirm this Roman literary tradition. On a monument of ca. 400 B.C., a rounded mantle is clearly shown draped as a blanket over the figures of a deceased couple embracing (Fig. 84).[15] A number of bronze figurines of women (Fig. 106)[16]—dating from the late sixth and early fifth centuries and therefore contemporary with male figures wearing the rounded tebenna—wear a diagonally draped mantle which at first sight also looks like a tebenna. Like the Ionian figures which inspired them, however, they actually wear rectangular himatia, as we can see from the square corners appearing below the edge of the mantle. Nevertheless, it may be that women were represented wearing the rounded mantle. The description of a statue of Cloelia on horseback as *togata* (Pliny *HN* 34.28), seems to agree with the appearance of a series of Etruscan figures on horseback wearing a short tebenna, like a rider in Detroit (Fig. 134) or figures on Etruscan urns. There may actually have been statues of women wearing rounded mantles which have not come down to us, and an Etruscan statue of the archaic period in Rome may have been interpreted in later times as representing a heroine of early Roman times.[17]

This rounded mantle was worn in three different ways, each of which was eventually used in Rome as a regular costume with its own connotations. It was worn like the Greek chlamys, around the shoulders and fastened by a brooch, as on the Cerveteri terracottas (like the later Roman *paludamentum*); it was draped like a himation, or the later Roman toga, over the left shoulder and under the right arm; it was worn "back to front," with the curved edge hanging down in front and the two ends thrown back over the shoulder, like the much longer, later Roman *laena*.

The diagonal draping of the tebenna adapted from the Greek style of draping the himation represented the more formal manner of wearing this mantle. The original form, borrowed from Near Eastern fashions,[18] is Ionian: the male Branchidae, seventh-century terracotta statuettes from Rhodes, and Samian statuettes all wear this diagonally draped mantle. In Athens the style came in together with the Ionic, crinkly chiton, and evolved into the well-known stylized type of the small diagonally draped mantle, characteristic costume of archaic korai, whose intricate folds and points were favored by Attic artists and widely imitated.

The gesture of draping this tebenna is illustrated by a bronze figure of a youth putting on a short, semicircular mantle (Figs. 102–103) whose curved edges are emphasized by a border decoration all around. What this mantle looked like when draped can be seen from the statue of the Apollo from Veii (Figs. 104–105). Here the artist has clearly shown not only the long end hanging in a point in back but also—in spite of the stylization of the drapery—the realistically zig-zag folds of the rounded outer edge, the latter further emphasized by the red, *praetexta* border decoration. It would be impossible for a rectangular Greek himation to form such folds. This fashion characterizes a type of figure which may be conveniently, if anachronistically, called a togatus.[19] The so-called Vertumnus in Florence, dating around 500 B.C., wearing laced boots and carrying a staff, is one of the best examples (Fig. 107). A series of such standing bronze statuettes comes from northern Etruria: see the bronze statuette from the island of Elba, in the Naples museum, recently attributed to Populonia.[20] Many of these statuettes wear only the toga without a tunic underneath, thus resembling the type of statue described by Pliny as dressed in the archaic fashion, in *toga sine tunica*.[21] Figures wearing a chiton under the tebenna seem to represent divinities.

From about 530 to 500 B.C. there also occur, in paintings and reliefs, groups of seated figures wearing rounded tebennae draped diagonally, equipped with *lituus* or staff and pointed boots (Fig. 110). The earliest appearance of this type may be on the Campana slabs from Cerveteri (but the original painting is hard to see, and the two old men at least seem to be wearing himatia rather than tebennae).[22] Two reliefs from Chiusi and Velletri showing similar figures, dated by scholars respectively ca. 500 and 475 B.C., interpreted as councils of local magistrates in session on the basis of the (Roman) symbolism of the costume, probably represent judges at the games, like the togatus with *lituus* at the Tomba degli Auguri, or—in the case of groups including female figures—assemblies of divinities, like the council of the gods of the Siphnian Treasury or the Parthenon reliefs:[23] Zeus appears with *lituus*, pointed boots, and stool on one of the Loeb tripods (Fig. 78). The tebenna, the folding stool, and the calcei repandi have not yet been reserved for the use of the magistrates, and the *lituus*, as we see from the Tomba degli Auguri, was used by judges of the games as well as by gods and priests.[24]

A variation of this diagonal drape was the rounded toga worn low on the body, like a heroic himation drape, leaving the torso bare. A series of sacrificing youths wear it actually only draped about the loins (e.g., the Monteguragazza bronze, Fig. 123).[25] Similar to the himation drape is the short rounded tebenna worn by a man on horseback (Fig. 134), surprisingly like the *trabea* of the knights on the *decursio* on the base of the column of Antoninus Pius in the Vatican Museum. The statue of Cloelia on horseback described by Pliny as togata (*HN* 34.26) must have looked something like this.

Another manner of wearing the tebenna, a more informal draping worn by active young men and dancers, became popular in Etruria. The ends were thrown over the shoulders in back, while the rounded section hung down the front in a horseshoe-shaped pattern (Fig. 118).[26] This rounded mantle, worn short, without a chiton underneath, is illustrated by a dancer in the Tomba dei Leopardi, ca. 470 B.C. (Fig. 113), and on a number of vase paintings and statuettes.[27] Women, especially dancers, also wore it occasionally, but always with a chiton.

This fashion of wearing and representing a short mantle seems to have been adopted from Greece, where Attic vases of ca. 530–500 B.C. occasionally show a small rectangular scarf or *chlaina* worn draped like this in back or in front (Fig. 115).[28] The name "chlaina" might even have been adopted along with the fashion, since the Latin word *laena*, used for a later development of this type of mantle and manner of wearing it, derives from the Greek word chlaina, χλαῖνα, by way of Etruscan.[29]

Certain contemporary examples from Cyprus (Fig. 116)[30] are even closer to the Etruscan models, both because of their detailed similarity and because they appear to indicate an established fashion and not merely an accidental, whimsical draping, as is the case in Greek art. Here we have yet another example of the similarity between archaic Etruscan and Cypriot dress fashion in the sixth century. The chief difference is that the Cypriot mantle is rectangular and worn over a chiton, whereas in Etruria male statuettes wearing it are usually nude. In this custom, as in the habit of dressing a statue of a kouros in a short chiton or shirt along with the perizoma—the Etruscan kouros wears the perizoma alone—the Cypriot fashion is more fully clothed and therefore closer to Oriental models. The Etruscan fashion is closer to the Greek ideal of nudity, modified—the mantle worn in this manner very often covers the sexual organs in front—but never quite forgotten.

The rounded chlaina becomes progressively longer, until in the early years of the fifth century on some figures it hangs down as far as the knees (Figs. 117-120).[31] This longer mantle is never worn by women. A triangular version also appears on some monuments dating around the turn of the fifth century (cf. Fig. 119).[32]

The long rounded mantle is frequently illustrated on the series of relief cippi from Chiusi, most of which date well into the fifth century. Here, along with the tebenna, it is the most common dress for men, usually worn over a long chiton by figures taking part in funerary rituals and other solemnities[33] (a horseback rider, for whom the long chiton would be impractical, wears the chlaina alone, as do most statuettes).[34] Perhaps these scenes reflect the beginning of the use of this garment as a ritual fashion, like the Roman laena which was its descendant.

The representation of these garments on the cippi reliefs does not seem to be consistent. Although in many cases we can recognize the shape of the semicircular tebenna, with its two pointed ends shown hanging in back, sometimes the artist instead shows rounded edges in back echoing those in front. The mantle appears to be round, worn like a poncho, with a hole in the middle for the head.[35] (The curved edges in back could, however, simply represent the continuation of the curved outer outline of the mantle. We could perhaps imagine the actual garment as an elliptical rounded mantle, which could be worn like a poncho or else folded in half, doubled over to form a semicircle, and draped front to back).[36]

The rectangular himation continued to be worn after the tebenna became fashionable (Figs. 94, 113), nor does there seem to have been any reason except personal taste to account for the use of the one rather

Himation

than the other. During the course of the late sixth and fifth centuries the representation of the himation was affected by the influence of Greek art: relatively narrow at first (Fig. 94), by the second quarter of the fifth century it was shown billowing out in ample folds (Fig. 113) in imitation of the style of the Brygos painter.

Active figures often tied their mantles around their waists to get them out of the way; this manner of draping became popular for figures of dancers, musicians, and fighters. The attractive pattern of large knot and flying ends thus formed was long appreciated by Greek and Etruscan artists (Fig. 115).[37]

Styles for women also changed. The toga-like draped himation worn with chiton and pointed shoes, which appears briefly around the end of the sixth century on a type of bronze statuette similar to the male togatus (Fig. 106), is no longer seen after this early period.[38] Short mantles, rounded or rectangular, were worn by dancers back to front or tied about the waist; himatia or rounded mantles were draped over the shoulders with the ends in front (Figs. 124, 127).[39] Usually women preferred the rectangular himation. Its shape can best be seen on Loeb tripod C (Fig. 80), on which a female figure flees at full speed, while the mantle, which she had been wearing pulled up over her head, spreads out behind her. It is richly decorated with a border all around.[40]

The ends or the points of the rectangle were often pulled down in front over the breasts, as the men's himation sometimes was in Greece. Eventually the basic rectangle was modified, and the long strips which hung down the front seem to have been woven or sewn on separately.[41] On a relief cippus from Chiusi (Fig. 127), a woman holds out for inspection a mantle on which the two upper ends were apparently shaped and perhaps even provided with a kind of fold or lapel on the sides of the collar.[42] Of course it is often difficult to distinguish, as on the statue of the Polledrara (Fig. 99), whether these panels represent conventional folds exaggerated by the artists or whether they represent separate panels sewn onto the garments. The panels on the wide mantle of the dancer in the Tomba delle Leonesse seem to be made of separate material because the artists show the blue strips contrasting with the deep red of the mantle; but this distinction by color did not always correspond to reality. The blue horse on another wall painting from Tarquinia makes us wary of trusting this type of evidence.

Another type of proof is more trustworthy. The bronze statuette from Rapino (Fig. 128)[43] and another in the Florence Museum (Fig. 130)[44] clearly show the stitching used to sew separate parts of the mantle together. Stitches are visible at the shoulders on the statuette from Rapino. On the back of the Florence statuette, too, which seems to be constructed of two separate strips, I take the dots to represent the stitching.

Once more we see Etruscan and Greek—or Attic—fashions going their separate ways. The shaped mantle is absolutely foreign to Greece, where the basic rectangular form of the himation never varied. On the other hand, the most popular way of wearing the himation in Athens and much of Greece and southern Italy in the late archaic period, the diagonal draping of the archaic Acropolis korai,[45] was never adopted in Etruria as a real fashion. The few representations of it in art, most of which seem to come from southern Etruria, are more or less faithful imitations of Greek artistic models (Fig. 132).[46] Some statuettes reproduce the effect of the mantle in front but break down entirely where the back is concerned (Fig. 133). Evidently the model the artist was using, a two-dimensional drawing or vase painting, did not give him an example to follow for the back of the figure.

PHASE III:
CLASSICAL PERIOD

The fashions just reviewed continued to be represented and worn down to 475 or 450 B.C. There is, after this, a notable lack of any new, distinctive fashions until about 400 B.C. Men continue to wear the tebenna or the himation, bare-breasted or over a chiton. Women wear a heavy himation draped about the lower part of the body, over a light chiton (Figs. 82–88), the contrast in textures emphasized by the artist according to a Greek artistic fashion current at the end of the fifth century (Figs. 81, 83).

What sets the Etruscan fashion apart from the Greek in this period is the presence of details with a special significance—Etruscan symbols which we cannot always understand, such as the special tassel on the chitons of goddesses or women of high rank, the pointed shoes, no longer a common fashion at this time, and perhaps, for the men, an alternation of himation with tebenna which might no longer be altogether casual.[47]

Since much of the evidence we have comes from funerary monuments, it is possible that the special dress of many figures dating from this period has to do with Etruscan symbols concerning the afterlife and the dead. Why, for example, does the figure in the front panel relief of a sarcophagus from Vulci (Fig. 85) wear a himation, where we would expect to see him in a tebenna? The contrast is made more obvious by the fact that his attendants are dressed in the round-edged tebenna.[48] Just as his wife wears a dress with tassels as a sign of rank, whereas her attendants do not, the dress of the deceased probably sets him off from the others. Does he, perhaps, wear the himation as the dress proper for the heroized dead?[49] Sometime later Vel Sathies, in the François tomb, also wears, over a tunic with stripes, a himation (Fig. 135). Since this decorated garment seems to qualify as a *vestis picta*, he is shown as *triumphator*—but does not wear the Roman *toga picta*, which would have rounded edges and would be worn a different way.[50]

Another example of a peculiarly Etruscan symbolism is the dress of the so-called *haruspices*, represented on a fourth-century mirror and a statuette (Fig. 137; cf. 138).[51] On this rough, fringed shawl pinned in front, the fibula is clearly emphasized, evidentaly as part of the ritual dress of this priest or *haruspex*, along with his special twisted hat. One is reminded of the dress of the Roman *flamines* who, according to Varro, were *infibulati*, their mantles held up by means of bronze fibulae.[52] The mantle of these Etruscan figures resembles that of Greek bronze statuettes of Arcadian shepherds of the sixth century, the best known of which is the one dedicated by a certain Phaulos to the god Pan (Fig. 136).[53] Here, too, the heavy, fringed mantle is prominently fastened in front with a large pin. The costume is designed for cold winter weather; Hesiod recommends just such a leather mantle and warm *pilos* for the peasant of Boeotia, to keep away the bitter cold.[54] Whereas the Arcadian costume looks like sensible, everyday dress, however—the pilos is still an ordinary hat in the sixth century—the Etruscan outfit looks anything but normal. It has evidently been adapted as religious dress. On the statuette the mantle, modified into the typically Etruscan rounded shape, is worn, Etruscan style, over a chiton reaching almost to the ankles, and is therefore impractical for anything but solemn ritual wear. Furthermore, hats for men were in general no longer usual in Etruria by this date, especially not this peculiar style. The figure has a special function, for which his way of dressing marks him out. The Etruscans, having apparently adapted a foreign costume for their own religious use sometime during the fifth century, retained it well into the Hellenistic period.

PHASE IV: HELLENISTIC PERIOD There is not much difference between the mantles of the Classical period and those of the later Hellenistic period. Both tebennae and himatia were still worn (Figs. 91, 92, 109). The significance of the clothes is now more clearly similar to that of those of the Romans. The mantle worn over the head, so that the wearer is virtually *capite velato*, a way of wearing the mantle which first appears on statuettes from Carsóli in the third century B.C., becomes common on portraits of the deceased reclining on Hellenistic Etruscan relief urns from Volterra.[55]

Yet much of the clothing represented in this period is conventional Greek "stage costume" rather than realistic dress, as is to be expected in a period in which dramatic scenes are more popular than scenes of local color. Scenes on engraved mirrors and cistas of this period show Greek heroic dress: nude figures of men or women carelessly draped, with heavy mantles slipping down about their legs, or youthful male figures with a Greek chlamys flying behind their shoulders (Fig. 91). Figures on relief friezes of Hellenistic urns also tend to wear the theatrical Greek chlamys and himation proper for mythological figures rather than more practical or realistic dress.[56]

CONCLUSION Because forms and fashions of mantles changed more often than those of chitons, it is easier to trace influences and native tendencies there, both in the case of real garments and in the case of artistic conventions.

Real fashions can all be included in the following three categories:

1. Native, original mantles developed in Etruria, for which no exact Greek or other foreign equivalent can be found: the back mantle of the seventh century; the rounded tebenna, worn diagonally or forming a rounded shape in front; the fitted women's mantles of the sixth century and later; and the pinned cloak of the haruspex in the fifth.

2. The Greek type of mantle adopted in Etruria as real dress—basically, the rectangular cloak we first see represented as the wide men's mantle of the seventh century—which remained continuously in use from the earliest times down to the Roman period. This rectangular mantle, universally used, appears both in Etruria and in Greece in the guise of the wide himation and as a finer, lighter scarf called a chlaina. In Rome it was called a *pallium*.

3. Ways of wearing the actual mantles borrowed from Greek fashions, rather than the garments themselves. Most fashions of draping the himation illustrated on Greek vases eventually find their way into Etruscan art; some, which become especially popular, represent styles taken over in real life. The diagonal draping of the Greek himation for men was adapted for the tebenna. The back-to-front draping of a mantle, which in Etruria was almost always rounded, was represented on Greek vases of the late archaic period: what was an occasional style of draping in Greece was developed into a real fashion in Etruria. (Both these ways of wearing the tebenna, diagonally over one shoulder, or with both points thrown over the shoulders in back, were eventually taken over by the Romans.) The diagonal draping of the archaic Greek korai, on the other hand, was never adopted in Etruria as real dress. Aside from a few exceptions, in the Classical and Hellenistic periods the Greek style of drapery prevails.

The tebenna and the longer chlaina were worn only by men after the end of the sixth century. It was as men's costumes that the Romans received these types of mantles, though apparently there was still a memory of a time in their own distant past—the period of Etruscan influence in Rome, in the late sixth century—when both men and women wore the toga as a conventional garment.

The change in artistic conventions allows us to trace influences of Greek art in Etruria. This is difficult in the seventh century and the early years of the sixth. Though the strange rendering of the mantles on the terracotta statuettes from Cerveteri may mark the influx of new artistic ideas,[57] it is not easy to track these down.

From 580 to 570 B.C., in the second quarter of the sixth century, however, we can begin to identify the successive waves of Greek influence. They are listed chronologically in the following summary, showing to some extent the changing direction of Etruscan interests:

1. The long-lasting influence of Orientalizing art (as evidenced, for example, by the appearance of the Dedalic capelet on a relief from Chiusi [Fig. 98]).

2. The influence of the black-figure Corinthian style of the first half of the century, which leads artists to depict a "Corinthian point" in back of the mantle, and to adopt the pose of the "Penguin women," the curls shown under the mantle pulled over the head.

3. Around the middle of the century, some contact with Laconian art, either directly or by way of Magna Grecia—e.g., Tarentum—which accounts for the similarities between the bronze statuette from Vix (Fig. 97) and Etruscan figures wearing a mantle over the head and pointed shoes (Fig. 96). Some artistic stylizations are similar: a Laconian statuette from Olympia offers a close parallel to the Etruscan fashion for women of wearing two ends of the square mantle hanging down over the shoulders in two long panels (Figs. 99, 101). On the back of the Spartan figure, though, the mantle is not spread out wide, but rolled up like a scarf. The motif, widespread in Greece, of the wife or bride holding out the mantle before her may have come from Laconian art directly or by way of southern Italy.[58]

4. The influence of Attic art in Etruria, very slight before ca. 530 B.C., which bursts into full flower at this time. Etruscan artists start to copy archaic fashions on black- and red-figure vases and in sculpture. The diagonally draped himation of the late archaic korai, for example, was never actually worn but was imitated from works of art; the attractive pattern resulting from the draping of the short mantle back to front had its models in Attic vase painting; the representation of the himation was affected by its appearance on Attic red-figure vases by the Brygos painter.

5. The strikingly close Cypriot parallels, as in the draping of the short mantle back to front on a terracotta statuette (Fig. 116).[59]

A study of forms and fashions in mantles confirms certain conclusions about peculiarly Etruscan features of their dress.

1. The Etruscan preference for fitted and sewn garments over models simply draped in the Greek style is shown not only by the popularity of rounded or curved shapes but by the complicated construction of some of the mantles for women.

2. The tendency for women to wear the same fashions as men in the late sixth century is illustrated by the diagonal and rounded back-to-front draping of tebenna and chlaina on both men and women. Etruscan women also apparently adopted a male Greek fashion of the sixth century, the draping of the square himation with ends pulled down in front.[60]

3. A tendency to wear mantles more frequently and more sensibly than in Greece, especially in the early period, may, of course, be more apparent on monuments than in real life, since the Greek ideal of heroic nudity in art certainly did not condemn Greek men in life to

suffer from the cold by walking around naked at all times. On the other hand, this may have been a real tendency in Etruria, for two reasons. First, the colder climate of northern Italy may have necessitated warmer covering, which would explain the wide mantles of the seventh century, the women's choice of heavy mantles worn in back, rather than draped coquettishly about the body; the double—or at least longer—chlaina; and the warm mantle of the haruspex. Compare also the long-lived and extended use of the plaid fabric, and the greater use of the chiton. Second, the Oriental, barbarian habit was to express greater respect for a figure by dressing it more fully. The Etruscans of the seventh and sixth centuries were certainly not Oriental, but they were, as we already noted, "barbarians" in comparison with the Greeks of that period.

SHOES⁵

S hoes figure prominently in Etruscan dress and costume. Proof of their importance, as well as evidence for their actual form, comes from the monuments, from references in Greek and Roman literature, and from actual remains of Etruscan footwear.

In the earliest period, heavy shoes and sandals were undoubtedly worn but are hard to recognize on human figures represented in art. On a primitive statuette, a bare foot can look as big as a shoe. Details of shoes or sandals, originally painted on, are often lost. Only occasionally did a few representations survive, such as a votive model shoe from Vetulonia, for example, which gives us an idea of the appearance of those early sturdy shoes.[1]

Among the earliest representations of sandals to have come down to us is an ivory foot from the Barberini tomb, on which the arrangement of the straps is clearly visible. They are represented in relief; three side thongs and a strip coming through the first and second toe. A fragment of an actual leather sandal with such a strap coming up between the toes was found in the same tomb. The type of sandal worn throughout the Greek and Etruscan world is also shown by a Rhodian leg-shaped vase found in Etruria,[2] probably dating from the mid-sixth century, on which a side strap above the toes holds the sole firmly. Such a strap appears on the contemporary Polledrara statue from Vulci (Fig. 99), though here the sandals, visible in front under the curved hemline of the Dedalic chiton, have a thick sole which follows the contour of the foot.

This thick sole might be connected with a type of sandal mentioned in Greek literature, the so-called Etruscan sandal, described as having wooden soles about three inches thick and golden laces.[3] The Athenians of the fifth century considered such sandals to be objects of great luxury,[4] and imported them from Etruria[5] or at least imitated Etruscan models.[6] It is not easy to be certain as to what feature originally distinguished the "Etruscan" form from ordinary Greek sandals. The gilded laces were incidental. Thick soles were extremely common throughout the Greek world. They were usually made of a flexible material like cork or leather, sometimes even of wood. There was something special, however, about the footwear the Etruscans themselves used in life and placed beside the deceased in their tombs after death: they had soles made of movable parts. Could these "Etruscan sandals" be so called by the Greeks because of their construction?

Real sandals found in tombs of the seventh century at Bisenzio, Cerveteri, and elsewhere give plentiful evidence of this special type of construction. The best-preserved examples (Fig. 140)[7] clearly show the bronze frame, originally nailed to a wooden sole several inches thick and contoured to fit the shape of the foot. On some the prints of the

PHASE I:
SEVENTH CENTURY
Sandals

wearer's toes are still visible. The sandal was fastened to the foot by means of leather thongs, now gone; the thin straps represented on the feet of the statue from Polledrara (Fig. 99) give us an idea of what they looked like.

The most remarkable feature of these sandals, the hinged sole, consists of two separate wooden pieces framed by a bronze or iron frame and articulated at the instep by means of leather straps. These movable parts followed the movement of the foot and made it easier to walk on the thick wooden soles.

Such sandals remained in use from earliest times to a late date: not only are a large number of actual sandals of this type found in early tombs, but there are frequent representations of similar footwear on later monuments. The sandals of the statue of Polledrara (Fig. 99) date from close to the middle of the sixth century. A pair of sandals with thick soles and thin straps for the foot appears in the third-century Tomba dei Rilievi at Cerveteri, at the bedside of the deceased woman. They were even exported or at least imitated in the very fashion capital of the ancient world, Athens, in the fifth century. When elegant Athenian ladies in Aristophanes' time flocked to their shoe merchants or shoemakers to buy a pair of Etruscan sandals, they were perhaps buying these sandals with high hinged soles, rendered even more exotic by their golden laces.

The sandals of the men, which seem to have been much simpler in style, were standard footgear, worn at all times. We see a pair placed on the low table by the funerary couch together with the high women's shoes of the late sixth century.[8]

PHASE II:
IONIAN INFLUENCE,
550–475
Calcei Repandi

In contrast to the sandals, the laced, pointed shoe with upturned toe represents a purely local style. It is never mentioned outside of Italy, yet for us, as for the Romans before us, it is the most characteristic Etruscan style.

We generally call these Etruscan shoes *calcei repandi*, assuming that this was the Latin name for them and that we are using the contemporary technical term. It may well be so, but the name appears only once in ancient literature, in the first century B.C., and even then in the diminutive form. In a famous passage Cicero describes the attributes of the Italic goddess Juno Sospita of Lanuvium, "whom not even in your dreams do you ever see without her goatskin, her lance, her shield, her *calceoli repandi*." By the latter term, "little pointed shoes," he seems to refer to pointed slippers of some kind.[9]

Several archaic monuments show a female figure who can be identified as Juno Sospita[10] on the basis of Cicero's description. A bronze relief from Perugia now in Munich (Fig. 142), once part of a tripod base, represents the goddess, clearly recognizable by her attributes: fully armed—not, indeed, with a lance, but holding a large shield—she wears the goatskin, which serves as her cuirass, like a mantle over her head and pointed shoes on her feet. A number of tripod bases from Vulci of approximately the same date show Hercules accompanied by a female figure, probably also Juno, wearing a mantle on her head and pointed shoes.[11] Clearly the image later identified with the goddess was crystallized at the end of the sixth century, when pointed shoes formed a part of the normal archaic costume.

After the first decades of the fifth century they were no longer universally worn but appear only on female figures and denote a certain status. Goddesses, in particular, were still represented wearing laced pointed shoes: Juno, in the famous mirror from Volterra with the symbolic adoption of Hercules (Fig. 143), is conspicuously dressed in these native shoes. So these laced pointed shoes, which seem to have become more and more a specialized costume, were eventually identified with a specific type of iconographic figure of Juno which remained unchanged from archaic times. No wonder that Cicero saw the image of Juno Sospita wearing this characteristic costume of archaic times; by Roman times it was preserved for her alone.

We shall call this early Etruscan form of the pointed laced shoe the *calceus repandus*. For the Romans, the *calceus* was also the type of Etruscan shoe from which they believed their own patrician *calceus* was derived. Cicero, therefore, used the diminutive form of the word, *calceoli*, in referring to a woman's shoes or slippers, to distinguish them from the high Roman calcei which were in his time a purely masculine insignia of rank.[12]

The standard form of the calcei repandi as they appear in Etruria just after the middle of the sixth century can be seen in relief plaques from Loeb tripods B and C (Figs. 77–80). They are high boots, reaching at least to mid-calf, red or black in color, as we know from their representation in painting on the plaques from Cerveteri, for example. A thin sole of a different color follows the foot all the way to the pointed, upturned curve of the toes. The intricate system of lacing includes three sets of laces: a cross-lacing down the front (this is shown three-dimensionally on the woman's shoes on the terracotta sarcophagus from Cerveteri [Fig. 145], where another set of horizontal straps or *corrigiae* binds the ankle), three, four, or five, according to the monument,[13] and above these another strap, passing through a circular ivory buckle later called the *luna*[14] and fastened at the junction of the high rounded tongues or *lingulae*.

The fashion of pointed shoes in general, and calcei repandi in particular, lasted in Etruria for about three-quarters of a century, from at least ca. 550 to ca. 475 B.C. They are illustrated on a sizable group of monuments dating from ca. 550.[15] Their adoption coincided with the introduction of the Ionic chiton. On the Boccanera plaques in the British Museum (Figs. 73–75) boots appear side by side with both types of chiton, the older Dedalic form and the newer, thin Ionic.[16] The Monteleone chariot shows long-sleeved chitons in the Ionic manner

(Fig. 61), and on the side a nude kouros sporting the new shoe fashion. We are therefore in the period of transition between these two fashions, ca. 550 B.C.

Another indication of relative date is given by the Tomba dei Tori (Fig. 46), representing, as we have seen in the case of the perizoma, a moment of transition between two styles of costume. Troilus appears unarmed, completely naked except for the blue pointed shoes on his feet. Achilles, on the contrary, is armed and is dressed in the perizoma of the archaic Etruscan warrior. After the middle of the sixth century, the perizoma was no longer represented as heroic dress.[17] This is the only Etruscan monument I know on which perizoma and pointed shoes appear side by side.[18] Near Chiusi, in Poggio Civitate (Murlo), pointed shoes appear on a type of seated terracotta figure dated to the second quarter of the sixth century (Fig. 121).[19] Perhaps pointed shoes came into Etruria sometime before the middle of the century, and settled down as a fashion around 550 or 540 B.C. Something like this, as we have seen, seems to have been the case with the "proto-Ionic" and Ionic chiton.

The calcei repandi were, from the first, worn by men and women alike. They were frequently shown on the so-called togati (e.g., Fig. 107). For fashionable Etruscan ladies in the second half of the sixth century, calcei repandi or pointed shoes, an essential part of any ensemble, were worn with a number of fashionable outfits: with the Ionic chiton, with the mantle pulled up over the head, or, slightly later, with tutulus or pointed hat, as on the figure of Aphrodite herself on the Pontic amphora by the Paris painter (Fig. 146). In a banquet scene by the Paris painter a number of stylishly dressed and cloaked female figures have removed these shoes, as was the custom, and hung them up above the couch on which they recline (Fig. 147).[20]

Other Pointed Shoes

When the fashion for pointed shoes was first introduced in Etruria, it was adopted with enthusiasm and applied indiscriminately to all types of closed shoes. One type of pointed shoe, the laced boot we call the calceus repandus, was certainly the most conspicuous. At the same time there also appears on the monuments a different type, a soft shoe like the Greek *soccus*, with a high back, but open in front in a deep V shape, without any lacing. The shoes worn by Troilus in the Tomba dei Tori are of this type (Fig. 46).

At first these simpler shoes seem to have been used interchangeably with the calcei repandi. Togati wear them with the tebenna, as in the Tomba del Barone. So do fashionable Etruscan ladies: these are the shoes represented on both Pontic amphoras we have just examined (Figs. 146, 147). Strictly speaking, the term calcei repandi should perhaps be reserved for high boots with pointed toes on which the lacing is clearly visible. It is worth noting that the shoes worn by Juno are always represented as laced. In using the term loosely, however, we allow ourselves the same latitude exercised by the Etruscans of the archaic period in their use of the shoes, since laced boots or soft, unlaced shoes were shown without apparent distinction. So scholars normally refer to any kind of pointed shoes represented in Etruscan art as calcei repandi.[21] After 520 B.C. or so, the soft, pointed soccus was more and more reserved for figures of dancers or nude figures of youths.[22]

PHASE III: CLASSICAL PERIOD

Throughout the fifth and fourth centuries sandals remained practically unchanged. Shoes, however—after ca. 475 no longer pointed—were usually low, without the high boot-like tops of the calceus or the back flap of the soccus. A common type, illustrated on numerous mirrors of this period, had a cross-strap at the instep. Fourth-century paintings also illustrate sandals and shoes of this period, generally of a standard, simple type not very different from contemporary Greek models (Figs. 81, 83).[23]

After 480–475 B.C., however, shoes very similar to the laced calcei repandi also continued in use, unchanged in form except for the loss of the point. Many representations of such laced boots appear on bronze mirrors. The boots worn by the figure of Perseus on a mirror from Chiusi (Fig. 148) are closer in form to the calcei repandi, with their front cross-lacing and the four or five horizontal *corrigiae* above the ankle, than to contemporary Greek representations of laced boots.[24] The shoes hung by the bedside of Helen, on the charming mid-fifth-century mirror in the Museum of Villa Giulia (Fig. 149), at first recall the shoes hung up in a somewhat similar scene on the Pontic amphora in New York (Fig. 147); but the fashion for the pointed toe has gone out in the interval between the two representations, and Helen's shoes are shown with blunt toes according to the contemporary style.

A problem is the significance of the pointed shoes still represented on a number of Etruscan monuments after they ceased to be a normal style. Until around 480, pointed shoes, both laced calcei repandi and socci, were worn by everyone indiscriminately. By the first century B.C., as we have seen, pointed calcei repandi were the exclusive attribute of a divinity, Juno Sospita.[25] Sometimes between these two dates the significance of the calcei repandi changed. How this change took place is not easy to see. Some phases we can follow; others are more difficult to pin down. To begin with, after 480 B.C. pointed shoes are always the laced calcei, not the soft dancer's soccus; and they are never represented on men. Female figures now wearing this fashion include many divinities, especially Juno, almost regularly shown with laced calcei repandi, as in the mirror from Volterra with the adoption of Hercules (Fig. 143), or other mythological figures, like Leda in a later mirror. A series of bronze statuettes wearing the tasseled chiton and heavy mantle of the Classical period often—though not always—also wear laced, pointed shoes (Fig. 82). We have seen that there is some controversy as to the identity of these figures: do they represent divinities or humans offering their devotion to the goddess?[26] Do pointed shoes already have a special significance at this time? The figure of the deceased lady painted on the walls of the Tomba degli Scudi at Tarquinia wearing the fourth-century tasseled chiton, mantle, and pointed shoes is undoubtedly human, and so is her maid. Perhaps, though, pointed shoes, by now a special, archaic fashion, are appropriate to them in the kingdom of the dead.[27] By the Hellenistic and Roman period, pointed shoes appear only on figures of female priestesses and divinities.[28] Presumably their symbolic connotation had by then crystallized, and they were well on their way to becoming specialized as the attribute of the chief Etruscan—and Roman—goddess Juno in her character as Juno Sospita.

PHASE IV: HELLENISTIC PERIOD

On monuments of the Hellenistic period, from the third to first century, there is a variety of representations of shoes and sandals. Sandals appear in their standard form, which remained in fashion for a long time, with heavy sole and laces. A good example from Cosa has thongs and a sole painted dark red.[29] On mirrors young men also appear, gods or heroes, wearing sandals with long laces which criss-cross at the ankle and above, tying halfway up the calf. Of course these are mythological figures, naked or wearing only a chlamys; but given the continuing Etruscan passion for footwear and the presence of actual fashions in jewelry in the same pictures, it seems likely that this too was a real fashion.

The tradition of showing nude youths wearing shoes or sandals goes back to the figure of Troilus in the Tomba dei Tori (Fig. 46). Low shoes continue to be worn, but not as frequently as in the fourth century; now shown, on mirrors and funerary urns, are the high boots with flaps the Greeks called *embades* (Figs. 89–91).

"Italic" Shoes

It is difficult, as in the Hellenistic period, during the last years of Etruscan independence, to distinguish between Etruscan and Roman connotations of originally Etruscan dress. In the case of shoes or calcei there is some literary evidence to guide us in our interpretation of figured representations.

A number of figures of togati illustrate the transition between Etruscan laced boot and official Roman calceus; a bronze statuette in the Louvre dating from the third century still wears the standard form of the shoe, with cross-lacing and four corrigiae above the ankle.[30] This form of shoe may have been known as the "Italic" shoe, mentioned in a literary reference of the second century B.C. Prusias, king of Bithynia, wishing to show his submission to the Romans, "went to meet the Roman generals wearing a Roman garment of the kind called tebennus and Italic shoes, with his head shaved and wearing on it a *pilleus*, as slaves sometimes do who have been freed in their masters' wills."[31] The rounded tebenna or toga, together with the Italic calcei, identified him as a Romanized togatus and showed his loyalty; the pilleus showed that he was their client.

The distinction between real fashions and artistic imitation may be less relevant in the case of footwear than other fashions. Most of the shoes illustrated seem to have been really worn. If any representations of shoes were imitated from art rather than everyday life, it would be certain forms of sandals, which, unlike the closed shoes we have been discussing, were purely Greek. The types of sandals pictured on Etruscan monuments all have counterparts in Greece, beginning with the earliest example, the statuette from the Polledrara tomb (Fig. 99).[32] Yet, as we have seen, a special type of sandal for which Etruria was famous in the ancient world can perhaps be identified with the peculiar hinged models from Etruscan tombs (Fig. 140), which were certainly actually worn.

The fashion of the calcei repandi, the most typical item of Etruscan dress from ca. 550 to 475 B.C., developed from a special form of the Greek *endromides*. These were usually red, high-topped, decorated laced boots which, in the second quarter of the sixth century, appear on Spartan and Ionian figures. They may have come to Etruria by way of the Greek colonies of Sicily and south Italy (Fig. 141). Very closely related were the shoes called *laconicae* in Athens. Another type of pointed shoe, the Greek soccus with pointed toes, was also worn by both men and women in archaic Etruria; on Spartan monuments such as the Chrysapha stele, it appears as a woman's shoe. The most characteristic "Etruscan look" for female figures in the late sixth and early fifth century is a combination of various fashions, the Ionic chiton, pointed hat or head dress, and pointed boots or soft shoes.

After about 475, when pointed calcei repandi were no longer fashionable for daily use, the style survived in various forms on special figure types. The male togatus wore the blunt-toed calceus which the Romans eventually took over as a special costume; so did various divinities and mythological figures. The pointed laced shoe remained as the attribute of Juno Sospita.

In the Hellenistic period, shoes represented on monuments reflect more closely the styles found in Greek art. Most styles represented were actually worn in Etruria too. Etruscan artists, always fond of adding local color to traditional representations from mythology, were especially shoe-conscious. Very popular in the fourth century was a soft, low woman's shoe with a strap. In the Hellenistic period a special type of high laced sandal appears, along with heavy Greek boots.

The Etruscan fondness for showing shoes where Greek artists would show sandals or bare feet may be related to a tendency, already noted, to dress more heavily than was the Greek custom. The corresponding reluctance to show completely naked figures accounts for the fact that, even where a Greek nude kouros type was copied, the Etruscan artist often added shoes or jewelry to avoid the effect of total nudity.

Interest in shoes from the economic point of view may also have encouraged the representation of an important local product, as with images of bronze products found on Praenestine bronze mirrors and cistae by artists who were, so to speak, advertising their wares.[33] The special Etruscan sandals so sought after in Athens in the fifth century and the popular calcei repandi of the sixth certainly testify to the special skill of Etruscan craftsmen in this field.[34]

6
HATS, HAIR STYLES, AND BEARDS

There is a wealth of material on hats, allowing us to draw certain conclusions about their symbolic, social, or chronological significance. Less tied to utilitarian considerations than other garments, fashions in hats are more apt to be given special meanings (see, for example, the crown or mitre) and can teach us more than other garments about Etruscan life, myths, and religion. Hats, like shoes, were generally more popular in Etruria than in mainland Greece and flourished in a variety of forms.[1]

As usual, in distinguishing chronological periods within which to separate "real" from "artistic" or conventional styles, we can divide the period into the following four phases:

1. the seventh and first half of the sixth century, when we find both "real," local Etruscan styles and Orientalizing conventions;

2. the second half of the sixth and the first quarter of the fifth century, in which local styles coexist in art with a variety of Ionian-influenced fashions and some "special" types of pointed hats, as well as diadems and crowns;

3. the "Classical" period, from ca. 480–475 through the fourth century, when Attic Greek styles are adapted in real life and in art; and

4. the Hellenistic period, when the clean-shaven look brought in by Alexander the Great is taken over by men, and women adopt more informal hair styles.

PHASE I:
ORIENTALIZING
AND EARLY
ARCHAIC PERIODS
Real Styles for Men

Hair. Men wore short bobbed hair, cut bluntly just below the levels of the ears and combed straight back, as shown on a large number of examples from this period (Figs. 35–38, 41). The fashion is so common that it even whimsically appears on the figure of an "Etruscanized" lion carved by an artist of the seventh century. Sometimes it is shown blown back by the violent action on such figures as the "lion-jumper" from Cerveteri (Fig. 43).[2] At the same time a longer hair style was worn tied back behind the ears by a ribbon.[3]

Beards. Beards are shown with a certain ingenuous charm on several seventh-century monuments; for example, they are scratched on the long chins of figures from ziro burial urns from Chiusi (Fig. 6).[4] There are also numerous clean-shaven male figures, especially of the Orientalizing hero. The Etruscan male terracotta statuette from Cerveteri is as smooth-chinned as his female companions (Fig. 16). Nevertheless, it seems that beards were actually worn throughout most of the archaic period in Etruria (Fig. 121). In Greece, bearded warriors were represented as early as the twelfth-century Warrior vase; the beginning of the black-figure style brought a profusion of beards even for gods and heroes, including such novelties as a bearded Apollo and Heracles' luxuriant mustache on the Proto-Attic Nessos vase.[5] In the sixth century the fashion for beards flourished in Etruria too, and was reflected in art on Achilles of the Tomba dei Tori (Fig. 46), as well as on warriors and other figures of the period around 540–530 B.C. (Fig. 31).[6]

Hats. The hats men used for everyday wear were the wide-brimmed *petasos* and the brimless, pointed *pilleus*. It is not always easy to tell the two apart; there seems to have been a certain amount of overlapping.

The pilleus, a plain cap with a more or less conical crown, appearing on a number of figurines of the eighth and seventh centuries,[7] probably represents a real hat of felt or leather, an early form of the Greek πῖλος.[8] This type of hat has deep roots in the Near East: the Etruscan pilleus bears a striking resemblance to a form of hat depicted on Syrian statuettes of nude male figures as early as the third millennium B.C.,[9] which continued to be worn in Syria and the Near East without interruption.[10]

The pilleus and πῖλος became thoroughly naturalized, however. The same shape was often used, in the early period, for helmets as well as for soft hats, and in early Etruscan and Italic art it was often represented as a local costume on primitively realistic figures.[11] In its traditional brimless, conical, or rounded form, it appears throughout the fifth century and later on figures engaged in outdoors work or sports, like the charioteers in the tomb of the Olympic Games at Tarquinia and the Tomba del Colle in Chiusi.[12] Its use as a practical hat for workers of all kinds in Italy eventually led to its becoming, in the Roman period, symbolic of the "lower middle class" of citizens.[13]

The broad-brimmed petasos of Greek costume,[14] in its early, narrow-brimmed form which closely resembles the pilleus, was also popular in Etruria, though usually appearing in more specialized contexts. The plain petasos remained in use at all periods in Etruria, as shown by the well-known Hellenistic bronze statuette from Arezzo of a ploughman.[15]

The original use of the petasos as a traveling hat made it an appropriate attribute for Hermes, as in its earliest recognizable appearance, on one of the painted "Boccanera" plaques from Cerveteri (Fig. 73).[16] A somewhat similar later figure, the statuette from Isola di Fano (Fig. 107), also holds a staff and wears a petasos, originally with a spike on the crown. It probably represents a divinity, which we cannot identify with certainty.[17] A petasos, without spike, probably identifies the figure of Hermes sitting in a council of the gods on a terracotta plaque from Velletri (Fig. 110). Elsewhere, too, this type of hat was the attribute of Hermes (Fig. 117, 119).[18] This hat has sometimes been identified as a priestly costume because of its similarity to Roman priestly hats, but the variety of shapes of Etruscan pilleus and petasos, which contrasts with the constant form of certain special Etruscan hats as well as of Roman priestly headgear, suggests that they reflected passing fashions rather than ritual form. Yet the wearing of a hat may itself have some special significance. Emeline Richardson suggests that gods wore hats.[19] Excavations at Poggio Civitate (Murlo, near Siena) have brought to light a terrocotta akroterion in the form of a seated male statue wearing an extraordinary wide-brimmed "cowboy hat" or petasos (Fig. 121). Though the identity of the figure is still uncertain, the remarkable hat certainly marks it as someone special.[20]

On a "Boccanera" plaque from Cerveteri the figure of Paris, standing opposite Hermes in the Judgment of Paris scene, wears a relatively soft hat made of leather, felt, or cloth, twisted into a point at the crown (Fig. 73). This type of hat, appearing here for the first time, represents a special form of pilleus, perhaps appropriate for a Paris in peasant or shepherd costume (cf. Fig. 136). Later, it seems to have developed into a peculiar form regularly worn by figures identified as haruspices or priests (Figs. 137, 138).[21] Much later, similar twisted hats worn by dancing mimes appear on a Roman bronze oinochoe in the Louvre.[22]

One of the most striking seventh-century fashions is the luxuriant crown worn by several male figures, especially bronzes (Fig. 10). On a bronze figure from the Bernardini tomb in Praeneste (Fig. 150), the crown is made up of eight gradually thickening, club-like projections radiating out from the center. Other seventh-century male figures wear a similar hat.[23] Sometimes this "crown" appears simply as an ornament. What these frond-like projections represented cannot be known for certain, since nothing exactly like this headdress has been found outside Etruria. Was this something actually worn in Etruria, or was it a misunderstanding of some (unidentified) artistic motif? If an original existed, and such a hat was actually worn, was it really made of feathers or plumes, grasses or plants?

The very strangeness of these decorations suggests that they reflected a real fashion in Etruria. Could they not have been made of great ostrich plumes, of the type imported in this period for ivory-handled fans?[24] Such a special hat of feathers resembles those of much earlier Near Eastern figures,[25] traditionally connected with soldiers, music, and the dance, as well as animal-taming. A comparison with the figure of a foreign (probably Persian) musician and lion-tamer on a relief from the palace of Ashurbanipal at Nineveh is instructive.[26] Several Etruscan figures wearing the feather hat are also represented with lions.[27] The Bernardini figures seem to represent warriors taking part in a ritual war dance connected with animals, as do other groups in this same period.[28] Confirming this interpretation of the feather crown as a special hat connected with war dances is the later appearance of female dancers wearing a feather crown on Lucanian vases around 400 B.C.[29] There are also references in later Roman literature and art to gladiators, especially animal-fighters, wearing plumes in their hair as their characteristic costume.[30] It therefore seems at least possible that this was a special costume actually worn in Etruria on certain occasions.[31] If our examples are indeed copied from real life, this would account for their strange appearance, which cannot easily be explained by reference to any artistic models, though the appearance of the feather crown on a number of monuments of Oriental and Orientalizing art—in particular, Bes figurines (Fig. 150)—shows that the feather crown was a favored artistic motif in this period in the eastern Mediterranean.[32]

Real Styles for Women

Hair. As in other civilizations and other times, women's hats and hair styles constitute the most characteristic feature of local costume. The seventh century was characterized by the back braid, the late sixth by the famous tutulus hair style.

The long back braid[33] can be seen most clearly on terracotta statuettes and bucchero figurines dating from the middle of the seventh century or shortly after (Figs. 5, 62, 63). The hair, combed smoothly back behind the ears and braided in a single thick plait hanging down the back, reaches below the hemline of the back mantle and fans out in a fringe at the end, below the round clasps or fasteners which bind its lower edge.[34]

This was the favorite hair style of the seventh century: it appears regularly on female figures of this period.[35] It went out of fashion soon after the beginning of the sixth century. Still represented—in profile—on one of the sixth-century ivory situlae from the Pania burial at Chiusi (Fig. 70), perhaps its latest appearance occurs around 570–560 B.C., on the alabaster statue from the Polledrara tomb in Vulci (Fig. 99).[36] Here, the normal seventh-century braid has been modified into a shorter more elaborate model formed by nine smaller braids joined together at the bottom.[37]

Other hair styles represented on monuments of the seventh century were also probably worn in real life. Sometime later than the back braid, but still of the seventh century, is the fashion of wearing a lock of hair hanging down over each shoulder in front. Around the middle of the seventh century, this style was usually in the form of so-called Syrian curls or Hathor locks—long ringlets ending in a flat spiral, as on the bucchero figurines from Cerveteri (Fig. 62; cf. Fig. 63);[38] on most examples these appear together with the local fashion of the back braid. The name "Syrian curl" has been given to this fashion by scholars who connect it with Near Eastern models, and especially with Syrian ivories of the eighth and seventh centuries, like some ivory heads from Nimrud. It has also been called the Hathor curl, after the traditional figure of the goddess on which it frequently appears (Fig. 153).[39]

Later than the Hathor curl were two other fashions connected with Greek styles of wearing locks of hair in front. Thick braids hanging down over each shoulder as far as the waist are illustrated on a series of stone busts from Chiusi ranging in date from the end of the seventh century to some time in the sixth.[40] Long spiral or corkscrew curls appear, for example, on one of the crowning figures of a ziro burial urn from Chiusi, the so-called Cinerario Gualandi. On this monument the combination of front curls and back braid is an indication of its relatively late date; other female figures on the ziro burial vases wear only a back braid (Figs. 4–5). This statuette is probably to be dated in the third quarter of the seventh century at the earliest. Similar long front curls appear around the turn of the century on the bronze bust from Vulci in the British Museum (Fig. 58).

Spiral hair holders of gold or bronze, found in great numbers in the seventh and early sixth centuries and probably used to hold such locks of hair, testify to the popularity of the fashion among Etruscan women at this time.[41] Under the impact of Greek influence, it develops further and becomes the most popular style of the first half of the sixth century; it is beautifully pictured on one of the figures from Brolio in Florence (Fig. 60). By the middle of the century, however, the contemporary Greek fashion of two or three curls on each side (Fig. 152) was becoming more popular, as on the statuette from the Polledrara tomb (Fig. 99).[42]

A puzzling motif, peculiar to Etruria, is that of figures grasping these locks of hair in front.[43] The gesture appears on some very early figurines (Fig. 63), on which exceptionally long Hathor locks are held tightly with both hands at waist level. It is a favorite motif of Italic art from ca. 650 to 550 B.C., perhaps the latest example being one of the mid-sixth-century bronze statuettes from Brolio (Fig. 60), which still features several elements of seventh-century costume. The gesture is shown on figures holding Hathor locks, long spiral curls, or braids (Figs. 151, 152).[44] The origin would appear to be an Etruscan adaptation of a Near Eastern motif, probably Syrian:[45] the Oriental motif of the naked mother-goddess holding her breasts (Fig. 153; cf. Fig. 161). The gesture is necessarily modified: the figure is no longer represented naked but dressed according to Etruscan taste, and the breasts are no longer visible.[46] The hands are then represented either holding locks of hair or simply folded over the breasts. An amusing variation occurs on bucchero figurines holding the ends of wings rather than locks of hair (Fig. 55).[47]

Women apparently did not usually wear hats during the seventh and early sixth centuries. Examples from this period are rare and can in most cases be traced back to Oriental prototypes. One style adopted in this period, however, a conical brimless hat inspired by Oriental models (Fig. 153),[48] continues to be shown on sixth-century figures (Fig. 154)[49] and seems to reflect a real fashion, as a precursor of the popular rounded or pointed hats of the later sixth century.

This brings us to representations of a number of special fashions and stylizations, hats and hair styles reflecting artistic borrowings rather than "real" fashions. During this early period these consisted mostly of Orientalizing motifs adopted throughout the Greek world.

Fashions Not Really Worn

The *etagenperücke* or "layer-wig" of early Greek art was a stylized version of a fashion perhaps really worn in Greece: the name suggests the artificial appearance of its rigidly geometrical, horizontal,

Fashions for Men

wig-like ridges. It is found sporadically on Etruscan monuments: on a bronze centaur in Hanover and on the figure of Avile Tite on a stone relief stele in Volterra (Fig. 68). Both of these examples date later than the height of the *etagenperücke* fashion in Greece in the seventh century—the centaur early in the sixth century and Avile Tite probably in the later part of the century.[50]

Fashions for Women   Two types of women's hats, the polos and the "flower-hat," clearly represent artistic motifs rather than real fashions. These, as well as the rounded or pointed hat represented in this period, can be traced to Oriental models. The polos (cf. Fig. 151) was a motif common in Greek Orientalizing art.[51] The "flower-hat," on the other hand, seems to be an interesting local development. It appears on a number of bucchero figurines of the seventh century (Fig. 62),[52] on which the stylized, two-petaled flower has been transformed into a wide-brimmed hat. A remarkably close Oriental parallel, an ivory from the Southeast Palace of Nimrud in the British Museum,[53] carved in the form of a flower, might almost have served as a model for the Etruscan artist. Etruscans were particularly fond of the flower motif.[54] Whereas the Oriental artist used such a decoration on human figures only to provide a support for a caryatid,[55] the Etruscans adapted it, in a more "realistic" context, as a hat for women and for fabulous animals. The centaur of the Bernardini bronze, for example, wears this jaunty hat as a companion piece to the great plumed hats of the hunters (Fig. 150).[56] The motif undoubtedly came to Etruria directly, not through mainland Greece, where it was never as widely or as imaginatively used as in Etruria. Greek examples of bronze female figures with flowers on their heads from the Acropolis in Athens all belong to the late archaic period,[57] and are therefore considerably later than the Etruscan models. The Attic flowers, as well as the bust-length statuettes themselves, are typically more decorative and less realistic than the Orientalizing Etruscan models.

It is difficult to say whether such a hat represents a real fashion in Etruria or an artistic motif. On the one hand, it does appear on female figures wearing realistic, local Etruscan seventh-century fashions, such as the long back braid and back mantle (Fig. 62). On the other hand, the use of these caryatid figures as supports and the fact that the hat was considered to be an appropriate costume for the fantastic figure of a centaur are consistent with a basically decorative use of this flower motif, interpreted realistically according to Etruscan artistic taste.

Wings   A good example of this "realistic" tendency of the Etruscan artist is the representation of wings, which appear on a number of figures of the seventh and sixth centuries as a decorative motif without any connotation of divinity.[58] Etruscan art has a number of interesting local variations on the theme of wings, originally adopted from the Orient as part of the Orientalizing repertoire. The wings spring not from the back but from the waist, an Etruscan peculiarity adopted from Oriental animal figures. Wings rarely appear this way in the Orient on human figures, but monsters, like the Assyrian human-headed lions or bulls, have bird-breasts, so that the wings seem to start in front.[59] In provincial Tell Halaf as well, artists misunderstood the original organic Assyrian wing disposition and created strange combinations[60] similar to those four-winged figures long the favorites of Etruscan artists.[61] In Etruria the tendency to render details "naturalistically" led to whimsical variations on the wing motif. Figures are shown with wings instead of arms;[62] sirens have wings as well as arms[63] or hold locks of hair at their breasts (Fig. 152).[64] We have already seen how this last motif leads to the peculiarly Etruscan gesture of holding wings at the breast as though they were locks of hair (Fig. 55),[65] a "realistic" way of showing details: if wings were real this is how they would grow and how one would hold them.

The late archaic period saw many sudden changes, most of them due to Ionian influence in art and fashion.

Hair. By and large, the trend during the sixth century was toward long hair. The change can be observed on the series of kouroi with perizoma, the earliest of which wear their hair in the straight bob of the seventh century (Fig. 29), while a later example, the bearded youth from Castello, has long hair hanging over the shoulders in back in a flat, compact mass (Fig. 31).[66]

Long hair continues to be in vogue until the end of the century. It is shown as a solid mass on both men and women on Loeb tripod C, for example (Fig. 79–80), and on reliefs and paintings in the Ionian fashion dating from the second half of the century. On the Caeretan hydriae the men wear shoulder-length, windblown hair; so does the fourth figure on the Pontic amphora in the Metropolitan Museum, which might well represent a male (Fig. 147).[67] A contemporary fashion for men was to wear long hair in long ringlets or corkscrew curls. On a terracotta relief from Velletri (Fig. 110) most of the male figures wear their hair loose; but one of the seated figures, perhaps Hermes, wearing a pointed petasos, has his hair combed in long, separate ringlets or curls, two of which come down over his chest in front. This new fashion of "corkscrew curls," popular for men during the last quarter of the century, is illustrated on the terracotta sarcophagus of the "bride and groom" from Cerveteri (Fig. 144). On another terracotta figure from southern Etruria, the Apollo from Veii, a ribbon holds the hair in place (Figs. 104–105).[68]

This fashion for long hair coexists with the new style of short hair, which appears in Etruria as a normal style on male figures in the Tomba degli Auguri around 520 B.C. From then until the beginning of the fifth century, monuments show men wearing either short or long hair, though generally both styles are not shown together on the same monument. After the early years of the fifth century male figures usually have close-cropped hair. Finally, in the Tomba dei Leopardi, dated around 475, both men and women wear short curls framing the face (Figs. 113, 114).

As usual, early archaic fashions persist longer in Etruria than in Greece. Two special Greek styles of the late archaic period, the *speira* and the *krobylos*, appear on Etruscan monuments, though not always at the same time or in the same context as in Greece. The speira, formed by rolling the hair around a metal *torulus* or ribbon, appears on a small bronze figure of about 470, which is dressed in a typically Etruscan rounded mantle (Fig. 118; cf. Fig. 129).[69]

In the krobylos style a twisted mass of long hair is fastened with a headband in back of the head at the nape of the neck. This style was fashionable for men and was also worn by women in Greece around 480 B.C. Thucydides records the end of the fashion in the generation before his own.[70] In Etruria it was often worn by figures of kouroi. It was also one of the most typical fashions for women in the Classical period, from its appearance on a relief from Chiusi around the middle of the fifth century down into the fourth century; it is the style regularly worn with the fringed chiton and heavy mantle of Classical women's dress (Fig. 160).[71]

Beards. We have seen that beards were worn in Etruria, as in Greece, during the seventh and most of the sixth centuries. In mainland Greece the change from black- to red-figure painting coincided with a change in the taste for beards, brought about by the influence of Ionian fashion and art. From around 520 on, it was normal for younger gods and heroes, such as Achilles, Apollo, Hermes, Peleus, and Perseus, to be depicted as smooth-shaven.[72] This change in fashion extended to real life as well, as it would seem that younger men were normally clean-shaven. Beards are shown only on older divinities such as Zeus and Poseidon and on subhuman creatures such as centaurs and sirens, as well as old men and philosophers. The strong man Hercules is also usually represented with a beard, for example, on the crater by the Niobid painter, perhaps because, like Samson, his hairyness is a sign of his strength.[73]

In Etruria, apparently, this change was gradual in life and fitful in art. Most interesting in this respect are two bronzes from Castello, found together: one a nude, beardless kouros, the other bearded, dressed in a perizoma (Fig. 31). Around 520 B.C. a citizen of Cerveteri, in the prime of life, is shown reclining beside his wife on a couch: he wears a beard (Fig. 144), perhaps as a mark of respect. On the Loeb tripods, dating from the last quarter of the sixth century (Figs. 76–80), all the male figures are beardless, following the new fashion;[74] their cheeks look smooth, rounded, and Ionian. In fact, the coincidence of Ionic chiton and smooth male cheeks, fashions from the same Ionian source, suggest that Etruria might have adopted both independently of Athens and a little earlier, rather than a little later.[75] Even Hercules, traditionally a bearded hero in archaic Greek art, is regularly represented in

Etruria without a trace of a beard (Fig. 45). The change from a bearded to a beardless Hercules has been taken as a sign that the figure type was adopted from outside mainland Greece, perhaps from Cyprus.[76] From about 500 B.C. on, the beardless look is normal for most male figures, in Etruscan as well as in Greek art, although older men always wear beards and mature men still wear them in the full Classical period.[77] Alexander's young, smooth-cheeked good looks had finally caused beards to go completely out of style, even for older men, by the end of the fourth century.

Livy makes good use of the dramatic significance of costume, in his description of the old senators who remained in Rome to be killed by the Gauls during the Gallic invasion in 390 B.C. The splendor of their triumphal robes at first awed the barbarian invaders, and stopped them cold. It was only when a Gaul pulled one senator's beard, to see whether he was a statue or a real man—"for at that time," Livy explains, "men wore their beards long"—that the senator hit him on the head with his ivory staff. Then at last the illusion was shattered, and the slaughter began.[78]

Hats. Pilleus and petasos continue to be worn in the late archaic and the Classical period. The twisted hat which made its appearance in the sixth century (see above) now develops into the special costume of the haruspex (Figs. 137, 138), found as late as the Hellenistic period.

A peculiar hat with a point appears on several monuments of the late sixth century. Quite clearly a special Etruscan costume worn in real life by figures connected with games and theatrical performances, it is represented on the figure of "Phersu" in the Tomba degli Auguri (Fig. 49), as well as in other similar scenes in tombs in Tarquinia and in bronzes of this period. The theatrical costume consisted of this tall, pointed stiff hat, to which a bearded mask was attached, and either the draped perizoma (Fig. 49) or a short decorated chiton, brightly patterned with loud checks or mottled like an animal skin.[79]

Hair. In the later sixth century the monuments reflect the contemporary coiffures of women, who wore their long hair either loose or pulled up on top of the head in the characteristic tutulus. On Loeb tripod C, both men and women wear their hair in a long compact mass (Figs. 79, 80). On the terracotta sarcophagus from Cerveteri (Fig. 144) both husband and wife wear long ringlets or "corkscrew" curls; the man has single curls on each side, the women two curls, as a trace of the earlier fashion.

By far the most characteristic hair style for women during the late sixth and early fifth centuries, however, was the tutulus. The name "tutulus," used in Roman times for the ritual hair style of the Flaminica, which preserved a very ancient fashion,[80] seems appropriate for the original Etruscan fashion from which the Roman religious style developed. If not actually an Etruscan word,[81] it is at least a very ancient name corresponding, for the Romans, to an ancient ritual hair style.

Real Styles for Women

Often erroneously used today to refer to the rounded hats so popular in Etruria in this period, in fact it represented a manner of dressing the hair.

Varro's description of this traditional tutulus hair style, formed by separate twisted locks of hair brought up to the crown of the head and bound in place with ribbons,[82] is recognizable on a number of archaic Etruscan figures. A bronze statuette in Florence (Figs. 130-131), on which details of the costume are rendered realistically, shows the separate strands of hair pulled up to the top of the head, in the characteristic swelling shape or bulge of the tutulus,[83] what we would call a high bun or chignon. In this case, a kind of coronet is worn with it. On another bronze statuette, broad spiral bands with incised decoration probably represent the ribbons or *vittae* binding the hair in place.[84]

The conical shape of the tutulus is visible even under a veil or mantle. In an exuberant period of Etruscan fashion, this profile formed part of one of the most characteristic Etruscan looks, as, for example, on the female figure on the wall painting of the Tomba del Barone or on the Pontic amphorae by the Paris painter (Figs. 146, 147).[85]

By 480-470 B.C. the fashion died out completely, leaving few traces in Etruscan art of the later fifth century. The fashions of the tutulus and calcei repandi end at the same time. On a mirror in the Villa Giulia Museum in Rome (Fig. 149), Helen wears her hair neatly bound with interlaced bands which resemble the vittae of the tutulus more than they do the Greek kerchief or *mitra*; but both tutulus and calcei repandi have lost the characteristic point of the archaic period.

Hats. The popularity of hats for women in the second half of the sixth century shows some peculiar developments. In the first place, it contrasts sharply not only with the earlier Etruscan custom of going bareheaded—or with a mantle pulled up over the head—but with the contemporary fashion in mainland Greece. There, hats, never popular in any case, were even less so for women, who led a sheltered life and wore at most a soft bonnet indoors. The variety of pointed or rounded hats which suddenly appears in Etruria at this time shows that this new fashion was adopted in real life as well as in art and evidently came from the Ionian cities as a result of direct contact.[86]

In the second place, this oval or pointed hat is an originally male fashion adopted for women. In the Near East, though pointed or oval or "sugar-loaf" hats do appear on both male and female figures, they represent a predominantly male fashion. In Cyprus, too, it is male figures who are shown wearing hat shapes resembling the contemporary Etruscan fashion. The local situation in Etruria is well reflected on the sarcophagus from Cerveteri in the Villa Giulia, on which the woman wears a handsome brimmed hat, while the man is bareheaded (Fig. 144).[87]

Fashions Not Really Worn   The "Phrygian" hat, frequently represented in Greek art as the attribute of archers or hunters, as well as mythological figures of Oriental origin,[88] appears in Etruria in special contexts. The most interesting is a group of statuettes of about the last quarter of the sixth century, whose costume does not fit any recognizable Greek iconography. A bronze statuette in the Louvre (Fig. 157), with a quiver strapped in place under the arm, wears a Phrygian hat and an animal skin wrapped about the body, its head covering the genitals in front. To the three known bronzes of this type[89] is to be added a terracotta figure from Veii, which has not, as far as I know, been connected with the bronzes but which has similar attributes (Fig. 158).[90] The figures have at various times been identified as Amazons or, more frequently (especially in the case of the bronze from Este, which is bearded), as Hercules. There is no indication that any of them is female, however, and Giglioli already questioned their identification as Hercules. The animal skin is not that of a lion, and Hercules does not normally wear the animal skin in quite this fashion.[91] The figure may be simply a hunter; but Emeline Richardson identifies the garment as a fawn skin, and suggests that the figure may represent Silvanus. This is apparently an instance of an Etruscan hero or deity for whom a special iconography was invented in the latter part of the sixth century, but it is difficult to be certain of his identity, in the absence of such literary evidence as we have for the figure of Juno Sospita.[92]

PHASE III:
CLASSICAL PERIOD
Real Styles

From about 500 b.c. on, men wear short hair (Figs. 113–114), and even mature men appear, perhaps more often than in Greece, without beards.[93] In the fourth century there develops a consistent, recognizable style of dress. At this time, for example, the taste for jewelry affects men almost as much as women. They appear wearing bullae on their arms and wreaths or diadems on their heads. Much of this jewelry is known to us from representations on the monuments, as well as from actual examples found in tombs. A garland, something like that represented on the deceased in the fourth-century Tomba degli Scudi, but executed in real gold leaf, was found buried in a tomb.[94] Many bullae, too, have been found, of gold and bronze, like those pictured on the arms and necks of young men and necks of women.[95] A popular form of diadem was a wide band made up of two or three rows of beads tied in back with a ribbon; this appears on a number of monuments, worn by both men and women (Fig. 159).[96]

Women wore their hair either short or long and wavy, often tucked into a Greek-style "snood,"$\sigma\phi\epsilon\nu\delta\acute{o}\nu\eta$, or *sakkos*. The figure of Velcha in the Tomba dell'Orco wears it with a garland in front. More often tied into a knot like the krobylos, the hair was held in place by a diadem (Figs. 83, 159) which allows some locks to fall before the ears in front, this being the hair style which regularly accompanied the fringed chiton and heavy mantle of the fourth century.[97] Women never appear without some kind of diadem or headband, either the wide beaded band (Figs. 87, 159, 84, 85) or a simpler crown or band (Fig. 160).

With this costume were worn necklaces (large, beaded necklaces worn at the throat, or *torques*, Figs. 82, 87),[98] bullae (Figs. 85, 92, 93), bracelets, and large earrings, particularly an elaborate cluster-type known to us from monuments and from actual examples found in tombs of this period, or else a pendant type, also rather elaborate (Fig. 160).[99] These cluster earrings and wide, elaborate crowns reflect the fourth-century taste for heavy, solemn forms, in contrast to the lighter, more lithe forms of the Hellenistic period.

Stylization   The typical fourth-century stylization of the hair, for both men and women, consists of long, snaky rounded curls or locks, well adapted to the softness of the medium in which many are carried out (either terracotta or soft stone) but also done in incision (Fig. 160), painting (Tomba dell'Orco, Tomba degli Scudi), and even in bronze.[100] There is also a variety of other stylizations.

PHASE IV: HELLENISTIC PERIOD   Though the boundary line between fourth and third centuries and the change from Classical to Hellenistic dress is uncertain, certain features of Hellenistic fashion are clear. Some developed from Classical costume, and new ones were adopted in this time of change and restlessness. We can thus attempt to draw up a picture of the fashion of the period, between the third and first centuries B.C., even though there is much more to learn about the chronology of the Hellenistic period.

Real Styles for Men   Men still wear short hair. On the more realistic heads it is usually less curly than in the preceding period, while on idealized heads it appears as the lion mane made popular by Alexander. A great change is the total disappearance of beards—except for old men, philosophers, and older gods—in the wake of the enthusiasm with which the "youthful look" of Alexander was imitated from the end of the fourth century on.[101] Portraits of deceased men on funerary urns of this period often show them wearing on their heads a thick, rounded wreath, of the same consistency as the necklace which hangs down the chest like a *lei*.[102]

Real Styles for Women   A group of bronze votive statuettes from the Latin colony of Carsóli (Carseoli), founded in 298 B.C., gives us a securely dated group within the third century.[103] The female figures, slender, narrow-shouldered statuettes, dressed in light Hellenistic chiton and heavy mantle, wear their hair loosely brushed back and held in place with a ribbon, with three locks hanging along the shoulders. In front, the face is framed by a crescent-shaped diadem or *stephane*.[104] Other figures of the third and second century with similar hair styles have a high ogival diadem worn like a coronet, hair parted in the middle and combed back from each side, or billowing locks springing up from the forehead, Alexander-style.[105] Instead of the beaded necklace of the earlier fourth century the jewelry often includes a Gallic torque or necklace with pendants and pendant earrings.[106]

Stylization   Hair styles vary, as one would expect in this eclectic period. Styles found in Greece on Hellenistic monuments are also illustrated in Etruria: we find the love-knot arrangements familiar from statues of Aphrodite or Apollo, as well as simple hair styles with the hair waved, curled, and tied back.[107] On locally made incised mirrors and cistae the stylization of the hair ranges from the full-bodied locks of the earlier period to a more decorative, simplified, linear rendering of short curls (Fig. 91).[108]

Direct Near Eastern influence for dress in Etruria in the early period is not limited to artistic models. Some fashions adopted by artists from Syrian monuments in the seventh century were actually worn, especially hats: the "feather crown" hat of the men (Figs. 10, 150),[109] the women's conical hat, and perhaps even the women's flower hat (Fig. 62), though the last seems less likely.

Most Etruscan hats and hair styles of the seventh century correspond to Greek Orientalizing fashions, and Near Eastern motifs at first imitated directly were probably later copied from Greek Orientalizing models. The back braid, long thought to be of Oriental origin, can be seen now more in the context of the Orientalizing period in the Mediterranean than as an exclusively Syrian and Etruscan fashion.[110] The hair style of the bronze bust from Vulci in the British Museum, dating from about 600 B.C. (Fig. 58), is still very close to that of a North Syrian ivory from Nimrud[111] with separate single curls in front and a flat mass of long curls in back. The fashion for single locks on each shoulder became popular in Etruria later in the sixth century (Fig. 60), at which time it looks very much like that illustrated on Greek works of the Orientalizing period; see, for example, the widely exported bronze "siren" attachments (cf. Figs. 152, 22).[112] The same is true of the short bobbed hair style worn by Etruscan male figures of the seventh and sixth century; originally Near Eastern, it appears to have become conventional in Greece in the eighth and seventh centuries.[113]

The Orientalizing long back braid and the tutulus of the women were also both adapted from Greek fashions and changed almost beyond recognition. Basically Etruscan, too, is the number and variety of hats, contrasting with the Greek tendency to go bareheaded except for special circumstances, such as mourning or travel. Hats were never common in Greece. The continuing Etruscan fondness for hats seems to reflect earlier Near Eastern influence, reinforced by the direct importation of Ionian fashions in the mid-sixth century, as well as, perhaps, the colder climate of Etruria.

As for the adoption of male fashions as predominantly female fashions—pointed hats were originally for men but were used for women in Etruria—this, too, is an Etruscan custom we have already noted.

After 500 B.C. or so the influence is purely Greek, yet we note the continuation of local styles. Hair styles and jewelry in the fourth century show a number of peculiarly Etruscan features which make up a special, recognizable "Etruscan look."[114] Later the Hellenistic period also brings with it special fashions—diadems and torques for women and garlands for men—as well as certain stylizations in art centered in particular local schools, such as Praeneste.

7

FOREIGN INFLUENCES AND LOCAL STYLES

The comparative table (pp. 8–10) listing in chronological order the various types of chitons, mantles, shoes, and hair styles worn in Etruria and summarizing Greek fashions, shows the difference in contemporary dress in Etruria and Greece. A striking feature of Etruscan development, in styles of dress as in art style, is its discontinuity. Styles come on the scene, explode into sudden popularity, and die out, to be replaced with a fresh "Etruscan look."

Differences of date between Greek and Etruscan fashions are apparent. Some seem to come earlier to Etruria than to mainland Greece, for example, the proto-Ionic chiton of the seventh century or the Ionian dress style of the sixth, adopted directly from the Ionian cities. Other fashions imitated from Athens, like the krobylos hair style, appear in Etruria later, with a considerable time lag, as "retarded" features.

There are other differences. Most remarkable is the debt real Etruscan fashion owed to the Near East in the latter half of the seventh century: plumed hats, back braid, "proto-Ionic" and three-quarter-length chiton.

Also in the seventh century, the Dedalic style of the Orientalizing period was more varied in Etruria than in Greece. A number of common Etruscan fashions appear in Greece only rarely, or not at all: the plumed ornaments and three-quarter-length chiton and such local dress as the back mantle and back braid. Etruscan artists who represented these real garments also represented "conventional" features of Greek Dedalic fashion, adopted as artistic motifs: the short chiton of the hero, the *etagenperücke*, the polos. This Dedalic style lasted longer in Etruria than in Greece. Some features of it even survived into much later fashion, for example, the perizoma and the shorter chiton. In fact, other elements of seventh-century Etruscan fashion adopted in northern Italy were still being represented (and probably worn) as late as the third century B.C.[1]

In the second half of the sixth century the Etruscans took from the Ionians a whole outfit—Ionic chiton, diagonal mantle, pointed shoes, and hats.

It is sometimes difficult to tell just when local fashions represented adaptations of foreign models. I can find no certain origin for the rounded shape of the mantle, the back mantle and back braid, the tutulus and the fringed chiton. Some of these are exaggerated renderings of fashions worn elsewhere but particularly popular in Etruria. This is

REAL FASHIONS

certainly the case for the plaid renderings of the seventh century or the calcei repandi of the sixth. The draping of the mantle back to front, in Greece an occasional, conventional rendering of archaic art, flourishes and develops into a full-fledged fashion in Etruscan art, and apparently in real life as well.

ARTISTIC CONVENTIONS Artistic conventions include depictions of costumes which were never worn in Etruria or of real fashions pictured according to a stylized, conventional rendering, which the Etruscan artist was imitating from a foreign artistic model. Costumes not worn in Etruria, but represented in Etruscan art, are listed in the comparative table. Many are special costumes, like the Phrygian hat, the calcei repandi, and the animal-skin mantle or loincloth, which are identified with mythological figures. Some of these garments were originally really worn; later, no longer in daily use, they nevertheless continued to be represented in special cases, as archaic artistic survivals.

Stylized representations of actual dress and textiles involve special renderings of folds, textures, and patterns. For the plaid pattern of seventh-century garments, the heavy Dedalic chiton, or the "transparent chiton" of the sixth century and early fourth century, artists in Etruria used conventional, widely accepted stylizations. In the representation of the finely textured "proto-Ionic" chiton of the seventh century, on the other hand, they seem to have developed their own "realistic" convention of showing the folds of the skirt.

The "Ionic style" of the mid-sixth century brought with it a real change in fashions of dress and their representation in art. Ionic chitons were shown with fine folds, often with a "pouch" at the waistline. Ladies held them up with one hand, though their shorter length in Etruria rendered this gesture unnecessary. Likewise, mantles, shown according to conventions of Corinthian art in the first half of the sixth century, later follow some of the motifs of Ionian art, and eventually reflect Attic models, imitating the manner of the Brygos Painter, for example, or the contrast with the thin chiton as in Attic art of around 400 B.C.

The form of the perizoma of the Barberini lion-jumper and the Egyptianizing loincloth of the Busiris vase also reflect foreign models, as does the frequent representation of nude male figures without the perizoma, a foreign convention which does not correspond to reality. It did not correspond to the reality of everyday normal dress in Greece either, but there it was more than an artistic convention. It was a representation of a young man as the Greeks saw him, not only in art and in their own minds but in real life at the gymnasium and the games.

ORIGINS AND ORIGINALITY Peculiarly Etruscan features noted in preceding chapters must be placed in a broader context in order for us to see their relation to other, "foreign" customs, costumes, and artistic tendencies. For this reason, we must trace foreign sources as well as local originals. For an understanding of Etruscan history and culture, the picture of Etruria's commercial and cultural contacts which emerges from a study of the original models for Etruscan dress and its representation in art is important. Some costumes were reinvented in different times and places, like the perizoma or the simple cap which was the ancestor of the pilleus. Most of the time, however, specific influences from abroad determined both actual fashions in Etruria and their artistic representations.

The earliest influence, that of the Near East, appears as early as the eighth century, as we see from very early monuments whose dress fashions seem inspired by Near Eastern models. These include the plaid pattern, various types of hats and hair styles such as the "plumed" hat, the three-quarter-length chiton, and the wide, fine-textured, "proto-Ionic" chiton. Some of these fashions, like the plaid pattern, were commonly used and represented; others were apparently unknown in mainland Greece. A few, like the three-quarter and "proto-Ionic" chitons, were sometimes represented, but as exotic rather than normal garments. Their use in Etruria is evidence for lively commerce with the Near East in the eighth and seventh century. Actual costumes, and some of the people who wore them, both Phoenicians and Ionian Greeks, surely came to Etruscan cities, and Near Eastern fashions were a familiar sight to Etruscan artists. Worn by Orientals and by the Greek inhabitants of the coast of Asia Minor, who borrowed and adapted various elements of Oriental dress, were the linen chiton, a shorter chiton for men, conical and pointed hats, and various hair styles.

Such costumes were also pictured on artistic monuments. Various surviving objects still testify to imports into Etruria from the Near East—the decorated tridacna shell from Vulci, ivory figurines of northern Syrian style, and "Phoenician" bowls found in Etruscan tombs of the seventh century B.C. It was from such monuments that the Etruscans imitated costumes which they might never have seen, like the tightly pleated garments shown on a number of ivory carvings (Fig. 43; cf. Fig. 56, the "Master of Animals").[2]

As for the two motifs often given as examples of direct Near Eastern influence, the back braid and pointed shoes, one of the principal conclusions of this study is that they had no direct connection with Near Eastern costume, nor should they even be lumped together, since their appearance was widely separated in time. The back braid was the normal hair style in Etruria during the Orientalizing period, by at least the mid-seventh century, while pointed shoes are to be found only a hundred years later, ca. 550 B.C., as part of Greek influence from either Ionian Greeks or Greeks of Magna Graecia. Their Etruscan form is in fact much closer to Mycenean fashions than to any Near Eastern counterpart. We can imagine that Near Eastern fashions, adopted by the

Near Eastern Influences

Myceneans in the second millennium B.C., survived into the Greek period and were *then* brought into Etruria, each through a different route and at a different time. The back braid and the pointed shoes of Etruria might thus indirectly reflect a much earlier Near Eastern contact with Mycenean Greeks, rather than any direct contact between Etruria and the Near East during the Orientalizing period.

During this earlier contact, certainly, the Myceneans adopted the straight shirt-like chiton which became the mainland garment. This garment, which appears on the Haghia Triada sarcophagus in Crete by the fifteenth century B.C., replaces the flounced skirt and bare breasts of the Minoan female figures[3] and takes its place alongside the Minoan perizoma of the men. Eventually it developed into the Dedalic chiton, which survived in Crete and elsewhere, and which the Orientalizing world inherited, along with the perizoma.[4]

Orientalizing Origins   Etruria formed part of the Orientalizing world. Etruscan fashion of the seventh century therefore shared with Greek dress various features characteristically represented on so-called Dedalic figures: hats and hair styles, the perizoma of the men, the long straight chiton of the women, and the plaid fabric.

The differences, however, are at least as interesting as the similarities. Some typically Orientalizing costumes seem never to have been adopted in Etruria: the short chiton, the *etagenperücke*, the polos, which appears only on a few female figures of the seventh century, and the short Dedalic "Cretan" capelet, represented on a single monument of the sixth century. On the other hand, some distinctive Etruscan fashions of the eighth and seventh centuries appear only rarely, or not at all, in Greece. The origin of several of these Etruscan garments is difficult to reconstruct. Some, like the early mantles, for which I can find no obvious parallels, seem to be "native." The long braid worn by clothed female figures, which eventually becomes "naturalized" in Etruria, and the knee-length pants of bronze male figures in Siena (Figs. 36–38) might be traced back, perhaps through a Mycenean source, to Near Eastern fashion. Etruscan costume is thus of special interest because of its conservatism, which preserves for us traces of two "international" periods, the Mycenean world of the mid-second millennium and the later Orientalizing unity.[5]

Cretan-Etruscan connections may be attested by scattered but insistent reminders of Cretan fashions in Etruscan art,[6] as well as Cretan influences on Etruscan art. These, however, may be more apparent than real: so much of Orientalizing art is known to us from Cretan examples that there has been a tendency to speak of "Cretan" art or costume, rather than, say, of Mycenean survivals in the Orientalizing world. The route of this influence may not always have been direct. The perizoma was undoubtedly a development of a Mycenean garment worn universally, in Crete as elsewhere, throughout the seventh century. Very popular in Cyprus, it is often spoken of as typically Cypriot.[7] It may well have come to Etruria from Cyprus rather than arriving in both Etruria and Cyprus at the same time. The long back braid, perhaps a heritage of the Mycenean past, continues to be represented in Crete,[8] though it probably did not come to Etruria from Crete. Many such Mycenean influences and motifs came to Etruria indirectly, by way of North Syrian or Ionian ivories (Figs. 44, 64).

The comparative table shows how much longer the Orientalizing Dedalic dress style of Phase I was represented—and, probably, worn—in Etruria than in Greece.

It is often said that in Etruria the Dedalic fashion was immediately followed by the Ionian. On the whole we have seen that this is true. The whole-hearted manner in which the Etruscans adopted the new Ionian fashions hard on the heels of the long-lasting Dedalic marks a new phase in their art and in their dress. Between Phase I and Phase II—the period between ca. 550 and 475 B.C.—there is a sharp, clear break. Every element of Etruscan dress changes. New costumes make their appearance by the last quarter of the sixth century, when adaptations of these styles become standardized as a typically "Etruscan look," a fashion totally different from the contemporary Attic styles of dress. By 525 we see everywhere the Ionic chiton, usually white, with soft folds; the diagonal drape of the mantle, adopted from Ionian models; the Ionian form of the pointed shoe; the pointed or rounded Ionian hats, and long, loose Ionian hair styles.

Ionian Influences

There are other differences, in Etruria, between Phase I and Phase II. It makes more sense to call Phase II "Ionian" than to call Phase I "Orientalizing" or "Dedalic." In spite of the characteristic way in which Orientalizing elements are represented in Etruscan art and adopted in Etruscan fashion, the elements of the fashion of Phase I are more varied, the influence more scattered. The Ionian influence around the middle of the century is overwhelming, and most of it comes directly, rather than by way of Athens or of Magna Graecia.[9]

Finally, Ionian fashions were translated into typically Etruscan forms such as the tutulus or the diagonally draped rounded tebenna, and new fashions crystallized, with combinations of garments which had not existed before but which marked a definite "style."

Various other sources of Greek influence in the sixth century B.C. can be traced through details of dress and style.

Other Greek Influences

In the second quarter of the century (ca. 575–550) the artistic style of black-figured Corinthian vases was widely imitated in Etruria. A number of peculiarities, particularly in the representations of the women's mantles, can be traced to this influence.[10]

Connections with Laconian art are particularly striking. In the seventh century, there are strong similarities with certain figures from Artemis Orthia: the gesture of grasping locks of hair and the three-quarter-length chiton are features found, within the Orientalizing world, in Etruscan and Laconian art.[11] Then, around the middle of the sixth century, there seems to have been an important phase of Laconian influence, corresponding to the large-scale importation of Laconian vases into Etruria.[12] The calcei repandi seem to be the equivalent of the later Attic shoes called *laconicae.*

Remarkable too, is the fact that the costume of the Vix statuette (Fig. 97) coincides with what was high fashion for women in Etruria around 550–540 B.C.: the mantle worn over the head, the chiton with back folds, and the pointed shoes, illustrated on Laconian vases and Etruscan monuments of the years around 550 B.C. and slightly later on monuments of Magna Graecia. Laconian influence in fact perhaps came in by way of these Greek colonies in southern Italy. If the Vix statuette is not of Laconian workmanship, as has been claimed, it might well be Tarentine.[13]

Contacts between Etruria and Magna Graecia and Sicily soon after 550 B.C. may explain the appearance of the Ionian calcei repandi in Etruria. Sicilian and South Italian monuments of around 530–520 B.C. show remarkable similarities to Etruscan art and costume. A metope from Selinus shows Europa wearing a Cretan capelet very like the one on our Chiusi relief (Fig. 98); the seated terracotta cult statue of Zeus from Paestum (Figs. 111–112) wears a long white chiton, purple mantle, and traces of purple shoes or sandals; fragments of riders illustrate high boots astonishingly similar to Etruscan laced calcei repandi (Fig. 141).[14] Lack of sufficient evidence makes it difficult to be precise as to the nature of this contact. A similar problem exists in attempting to evaluate the importance or the date of Greek influence in early Roman history at the end of the sixth century.[15]

As for Cyprus, a comparison with Etruscan art and fashion seems to confirm what we deduce from Etruscan imports of Cypriot art—the closeness of Etruscan relations with Cyprus. Two phases can be recognized. Surviving monuments imported into Etruria from Cyprus[16] prove that there was direct contact during the Orientalizing period in the international world of the Mediterranean. Near Eastern influences were at this time no doubt brought into Etruria by way of Cyprus. Then in the sixth century Etruria and Cyprus seem to have maintained or renewed their contact—or was their development parallel? How else can we explain such startling similarities in costume as the mantle worn back to front, the conical hat, and the special fitted perizoma?[17] During the last quarter of the sixth century, it has been suggested, the Etruscans even borrowed the particular type of representation used for cult statues of Hercules and of Jupiter directly from Cyprus.[18]

Peculiar Etruscan Features   Two particularly creative periods, the seventh century and the end of the sixth, brought local developments in costume and gave rise to a distinctive Etruscan profile. In the early period, two fashions for women appear—the long back braid and the back mantle—which are rarely or never found outside Etruria. The back mantle we are bound to consider a native fashion until proved otherwise. A type of back braid, in contrast, can be traced to Near Eastern and Mycenean models by way of Asia Minor, in the context of the Orientalizing period, though the resulting fashion is most visible in Etruria.

In the course of the sixth century, certain features of dress were adopted which combined to form another characteristic "Etruscan look." These are the rounded form of the tebenna, its diagonal draping, the short mantle draped back to front, the calcei repandi, and the women's high tutulus. At first most of these fashions were worn by men and women, rich and poor, gods and mortals. Then, apparently by the end of the sixth century, several kinds of Etruscan figures dressed in these costumes become special types: male figures dressed in rounded tebenna and calcei repandi; dancers with the light, short mantle; fashionable ladies wearing tutulus and pointed shoes; and soon after, at the beginning of the fifth century, youths wearing a longer rounded mantle draped back to front, with a wide sweep in front. Underlying the many changes and modifications in fashions was a persistent preference for tailored forms, for garments shaped and sewn according to a specific pattern rather than hanging free like the Greek garments.

One might well ask, to repeat a question frequently asked of Etruscan art, whether there is such a thing as Etruscan dress. The answer seems to be "sometimes." Though the whole range of fashions at any one time is not peculiar to Etruria, some special garments stand out as "native," while others are conspicuous by their absence from the local scene. In original, individual periods such as the seventh and early sixth centuries, the end of the sixth century, and the fourth century, these special features are so numerous as to allow us to speak of a specifically Etruscan style of dress.

We cannot easily go very far beyond this and speak of regional differences in dress. Further study might discover interesting exceptions, but we have seen how hard it is to separate the history of the actual costume from that of its artistic representation. When we say that certain series of bronze kouroi with perizoma seem to be localized in northern Etruria, that archaic korai in the Ionic diagonal mantle are characteristic of southern Etruria, and that the dress of the female demons on late Etruscan urns of the Hellenistic period finds its prototype in the world of earlier south Italian vase painting—Campanian, Apulian, and Tarentine[19]—we are dealing with artistic motifs rather than real costumes. We are saying, in fact, that the art of the southern Etruscan cities is more open to Greek influence, that it accepts Greek conventions more completely than that of the north. The art and costume of the northern cities appears to be more distinctive for this reason: it is less Greek—this explains the persistence of the perizoma fashion—and, later, it continues to represent fashions of earlier times. In the Alpine regions, certain costumes actually become fossilized until a late period, and we have the peculiar fashions of the situla art and of the bronzes from Este, as late as the fourth and third century B.C., which continue to represent the broad lozenge-shaped Villanovan belt, for example. There do seem to be certain garments which are specialties of the northern regions, however, like the pointed hats of charioteers and jockeys on friezes from Poggio Civitate, to be found also on several situlae, and the broad hat of the Poggio Civitate akroteria, so like those of the seated figures on situlae from Bologna and Este, but other than this we cannot really speak generally of a northern or a southern fashion.

Can we, however, make certain other broad generalizations from the evidence at hand? What identifies "peculiarly Etruscan" elements of fashion as "Etruscan"? One marked feature of Etruscan fashion is that women, in the archaic period at any rate, wore clothes which were elsewhere reserved for men. This peculiarity has been noted in regard to a number of garments. According to literary sources, in the early days women wore the toga. The archaic statue of Cloelia, for example, was apparently dressed in the diagonally draped tebenna; in Roman times the tebenna or toga was restricted to male citizens, and women who wore it were marked out as prostitutes. Yet the tradition still remained that the toga had once been worn by men and women alike. The three-quarter-length chiton, too, which in the Near East and in Greece appears only on male figures, may be represented in Etruria on female figures like the seventh-century statuette from the Tomba del Duce in Vetulonia. Women as well as men wear their hair short in the Tomba del Triclinio. The laced calcei repandi were, in Etruria, worn by men and women, and continued into Roman times as the attributes of a goddess, Juno Sospita. Elsewhere similar shoes were reserved for men, both in their original form as a Greek Orientalizing fashion and in their later development as the Roman calcei.

The colder climate of Etruria may account for this custom by making dainty slippers and sandals, for example, impractical for outside wear. Perhaps weather also explains the taste for warmer clothes reflected in Etruscan costume: the popularity of thick plaid fabrics, of heavy woolen mantles, sturdy calcei repandi, a variety of hats, especially women's hats in the late sixth century, and, perhaps, long sleeves.

The Etruscans' greater use of mantles, hats, and covering in general also contrasts with Greek simplicity of clothing and heroic nudity and is closer to the "barbarian" (specifically, Oriental) habit of expressing respect for a figure by dressing it with more garments: "The Asiatic costume . . . was based on a conception of the human body which was completely at variance with that of the Greeks. . . . the latter placed high on their scale of values the idea of the body beautiful—an idea held in abomination by the Orientals. . . . The Oriental . . . sought to inspire respect not by his strength, but by his dignity and wealth; he cared little for muscular symmetry; instead he preferred to cultivate a portly figure . . . and to wrap himself in ample robes. A man of importance, even if he were young, would try to look old, in order to impress others with his appearance of wisdom. Oriental gods are never naked; all the Carthaginian idols were clothed, with the exception of a few lewd examples [which were] fertility charms rather than real figures of divinities."[20]

References to the Etruscans in Greek and Roman literature are concerned mostly with their wealth, their clothes, the freedom of their women, and the looseness of their morals, symptoms of that phase of civilization Greeks called *truphe*, the *luxuria* or *otium* of the Romans.[21] In the fifth century this was a common theme of Greek authors like Herodotus, to whom we owe, for example, the detailed descriptions of luxurious Ionian clothes. Herodotus also reports Croesus' advice to Cyrus: dress the Lydians in trailing robes and boots, in order to make them effeminate and unfit for war.[22] It was in the context of this motif that Theopompus in the fourth century and his sources in the fifth paid so much attention to the place of women in Etruscan society and to Etruscan sexual customs. The Etruscans had *truphe*; so did other barbarians, the Lydians, for example. Herodotus' intriguing tale of the background of the "migration" from Asia Minor to Etruria by the Lydians—who had previously tried to alleviate the horrors of famine by inventing games and other frivolous pastimes—fits into this context. It does seem that Etruscan women at various times had special attributes or wore clothes, like hats and laced shoes, reserved for men in mainland Greece. It may be that the way Etruscan women dressed reflected the greater freedom which they enjoyed in public and social life.[23] The most complete account of this freedom comes from Theopompus,[24] according to whom Etruscan women exercised with the men naked or *gymnai*, that is, wearing only a perizoma. They reclined at dinner, even with men other than their own husbands, and took part in the toasting, traditionally reserved for men. Etruscans did not practice the exposure of infants, as did the Greeks: they raised them all, whether or not they knew who the father was.

The shock and distaste felt by a sixth- or fifth-century Greek at seeing respectable Etruscan ladies reclining at dinner publicly with men, wearing what looked to him like men's garments, undoubtedly accounts for some of less credible reports of Etruscan sexual freedom, as well as for Greek misunderstanding of the real situation.

Etruscan men and women did not exercise together, from what we can see. Even after scandal-mongering details have been partly discounted, however, enough remains in Theopompus' treatment to make us think that there was indeed a contrast between the position of women in Greece and in Etruria during the archaic and classical periods. Later Etruscan funerary inscriptions identifying the deceased by means of the matronymic as well as the patronymic may relate to greater legal and social importance of women, though they need not.

If Etruscan women, unlike Greek women, had the right to raise or recognize the child of a husband who was not a citizen, this would mean, for a Greek, not knowing who the father was. Etruscan women were literate, as witness the many bronze mirrors inscribed with the names of divinities and mythological figures, made for their use and buried with them with their cistae after their deaths.[25] But the proper interpretation of our sources, both the literature and the archaeological finds, may depend on religious beliefs or ritual observances not now known to us. For the moment, we can only say that it does seem that the behavior of Etruscan women and the attitude of Etruscan men toward them was different from that of the Greeks. There is the added problem of the Greek idea of barbarian interrelationships, within the "pre-history" of their own Hellenic groups and of the barbarian peoples they knew. What made Herodotus connect the Etruscans with the Lydians, in this "historical" scheme of relationships?[26]

Etruscan wealth, in any case, was a reality. Roman literature still reflects the experience, in the archaic period of Roman history, of finding themselves across the river from one of the richest people in the Mediterranean. Our survey of the clothes Etruscans wore and represented in their art confirms in part this motif of wealth, lust, and private luxury, though the motif was, as noted, a common one. The interest of the Etruscans in details of apparel, fashion, and luxurious living—as shown by excavations at Acqua Rossa, which uncovered remains of Etruscan houses as elaborately decorated as temples[27]—shows the logic of such a concept of the Etruscans on the part of the Greeks. Because of their wealth the Etruscan upper classes were perhaps more privileged, and women more at leisure, than their Greek counterparts. Perhaps that is why they dined publicly with their husbands, in contrast with the poorer Athenians of the fifth century. Women and clothes, the most evident motifs of *truphe*, are in fact what we know best about the Etruscans.

From their taste in dress and their representations of their own dress and other people's costume, we can perhaps deduce certain further characteristics of Etruscan civilization. Etruscans appear to have been practical where Greeks were inventive. Their "provinciality" in respect to Greek civilization was symbolized in real life by their attitude toward male nudity.

In artistic style, Etruscan taste is also in a way "provincial." It is generally more fussy and at the same time more realistic[28] than the Greek. The Etruscan artist enjoyed depicting details of dress and ornament; the Etruscan tailor shaped and sewed the parts of the garments; and the individual Etruscan adorned himself with a profusion of jewelry and accessories, judging from representations on cistae, mirrors, and urns of the Hellenistic period. The "Etruscan look" which prevailed at various times was due in each case as much to differences in artistic style as in actual dress. Etruscan art tended to accentuate and exaggerate certain features of Greek art, while Etruscan fashion accentuated and exaggerated certain elements of Greek costume. In addition, Etruscan taste injected peculiarities of its own, such as a decided preference for rounded forms and a general love of luxury, in contrast to the simpler contemporary Greek taste. It was probably true, as was recorded in antiquity, that in Etruria even slaves dressed more splendidly than would have been appropriate for their status elsewhere,[29] and we have seen that Etruscan clothes were generally more colorful and complicated than those of contemporary Greeks.

Much of our literature on Etruscan dress, of course, comes from Roman sources. Here, too, the context is a special one. In the later republic Roman antiquarians began to collect material about the origins of their own rituals, laws, and customs. Because of the symbolic and legal meaning of Roman costumes worn by magistrates, priests, and the various classes of citizens and age groups, much of these "antiquities" concern the origins of specific garments. In fact, the religious and ritual costume of Rome retained much of what had been normal Etruscan dress in the late sixth and early fifth centuries B.C. Much the same situation has been noticed in the case of archaic statues in Rome which preserve types from the turn of the sixth century.[30]

Of the information about Etruscan dress which comes to us from Roman sources, much of it is accurate, though it is focused, of course, on what was of interest from the point of view of Roman ritual dress, not on what the Etruscans used to wear. We are never told that the toga was adopted from the "Etruscan kings," only that the toga praetexta was the specific garment of magistrates, with its connotation of regal power. Similarly, Roman antiquarians often equated "archaic" or "ancient" with "Romulus," "Etruscan kings," or "kings of Alba," so that the *trabea*, the high calcei and other costumes were attributed to any of these in turn.

Some basic contrasts between Greek and Etruscan as well as between Roman and Etruscan dress are listed below. Some of these reveal characteristics of Roman dress which may be tied to Etruscan influence.[31]

1. Greek patterns are basically simple; Roman and Etruscan patterns are complicated. Greek garments are commonly based on a rectangular pattern; exceptions such as the rounded Hellenistic chlamys are few indeed. Romans and Etruscans used a variety of forms, rectangular, polygonal, rounded, elliptical, or cross-shaped patterns, often with separate pieces or curved edges.

2. Greek textiles tended to be thin and soft, Roman cloth heavier and more thickly woven. In the Hellenistic period in both Greece and Etruria, especially for clothes for women, certain finely woven, thin fabrics—fine linen from Kos or wool from Tarentum—became fashionable. As a rule Romans preferred heavier wool and the resultant

fuller folds of the cloth, in contrast with the softer, supple, more varied folds of Greek drapery, which were only occasionally adopted in Etruria.

3. The fact that Greek garments were woven in one piece, while Etruscan and Roman clothes were often made up of separate parts, fitted, sewn, and stitched together, also accounts for the difference between the free-flowing Greek and the heavier Etruscan and Roman drapery.

4. Decoration on Greek and Etruscan clothes was purely ornamental; on Roman garments it was symbolic. Among the Romans, details of dress and ornament were formalized as symbols of rank: the tunica laticlava, the calcei, the gold ring, the tunica palmata, and the toga picta each had a specific legal connotation. It is not clear when the Etruscans began to adopt the Roman symbolism of costumes—not before the third century, at any rate.

5. Greek and Etruscan dress therefore usually expresses an individual choice, while Roman dress marks the social class of the wearer. In Greece men and women, aristocrats and "bourgeois," dress much the same way. In Etruria, there were at various times, especially from the fifth and fourth century on, special costumes for priests, priestesses, and divinities. In Rome, a woman could not wear a man's toga or calcei, and senators, consuls, "knights," or priests were recognized by their "uniforms."

6. Unlike Greek and Etruscan dress, Roman dress was used to distinguish different ages. A young girl wore a toga, a woman did not. A man wore a toga praetexta as a boy and a toga pura as a citizen, when he came of age.

7. Greek and Etruscan dress was pretty much the same for all activities. It varied with the mood or intention of the wearer; he decided when to put on his party clothes or his traveling outfit. Roman dress was more rigidly specialized for different functions, for each of which formal dress was required. It was bad form to wear anything but the proper dinner dress, the *synthesis*, at a party. A magistrate had to wear the toga praetexta—or, if awarded a triumph, triumphal dress—at the official opening of the games, the *cinctus Gabinus* for the opening of the Temple of Janus; and the *laena*, if he was a flamen, at certain specific sacrifices. His costume defined his capacity and his function.

8. Within these strictly defined limits, and especially starting from the early empire, Roman dress (as distinct from costume), like Etruscan dress, was more receptive to foreign influences than earlier Greek dress had been. A Greek would never wear barbarian dress, as was made clear by the difficulties Alexander had with his men.

9. Normal Greek dress was plain, Etruscan and Roman costume more luxurious. Etruscans and Romans always made more use of ornamented garments and complicated accessories—shoes, hats, belts, and jewelry.

10. The Romans, like the Etruscans, tended to wear more clothes than the Greeks: they had a greater variety of mantles, some worn on top of each other; they always wore a tunic; and they wore calcei rather than sandals.[32]

Several of the features of Roman dress listed above derive from Etruscan dress: (1) complicated patterns, with separate pieces or rounded edges; (2) a preference, especially in the archaic period, for heavier woolen textiles; (3) a preference for fitted models, made of separate pieces sewn together—on Etruscan monuments, the stitching is often in evidence; (4) receptivity to new fashions, and a practical approach to dressing for warmth; (5) a preference for clothes more luxuriously decorated than equivalent Greek garments; (6) a tendency to wear more clothes than Greeks, to cover their bodies more completely, to wear a greater number of accessories: mantles, chitons, shoes, hats, jewelry, etc. Etruscan influence is clearest, however, in garments denoting civil rank, magistracies, or priesthoods; other Etruscan costumes preserved in the religious tradition; and the costume connected with the institution of the triumph.

Roman conservatism in dress accounts for the preservation of elements of everyday Etruscan dress in religious and ritual Roman costume. Connected, of course, are the conservative tendencies of religion. Since religion in Rome was relevant in every area of public life, there was no real difference in kind between the dress of a priest and that of a magistrate. In each case, it was a formal costume, a uniform, a "habit," which did not change according to the vagaries of fashion but remained official and immutable. This tendency helps to explain the numerous originally Etruscan elements of Roman costume. Just as the Church today retains certain ordinary fashions of the Middle Ages,[33] the religious and ritual costume of Rome preserved much of what had been everyday Etruscan dress in the late sixth and early fifth centuries B.C. Linguistic evidence shows that the names of many garments, too, as well as words connected with religious ritual, apparently came into the Latin language before the end of the sixth century or the early part of the fifth.[34] Roman antiquarians were, as it turns out, generally correct in equating "ancient" with Etruscan, since direct contact between Greece and Rome came relatively late.

STRANGE COSTUMES AND SPECIAL PROBLEMS

A survey of Etruscan dress represented in the art of Etruria includes some puzzling costumes, for which it is difficult to give an adequate explanation. I have included these in the appropriate chapters, even when a description of the original clothes is uncertain, whenever the type of garment fits into a certain chronological or artistic context: the perizoma or the Barberini "lion-jumper" (Fig. 43), the "Cretan capelet" (Fig. 98), the long sleeves of the female figures on the Monteleone chariot (Fig. 61).

The present chapter singles out certain other special problems. Some strange costumes can be explained. For others an answer may not be found at this time, but focusing on these problems may lead to their solution. Sometimes the sex of a figure is wrongly identified from its style, costume, or attributes. Bronze statuettes have been identified as female (Fig. 119), or at least androgynous (Fig. 107), because of their plump limbs, rounded breasts, and soft features. The style of the later sixth century, however, influenced by the Ionian style with its curves and softness, accounts for these features of the statuettes, whose mantles otherwise fit male figures.

A bronze statuette of a cloaked figure in the British Museum (Fig. 95) has usually been identified a male figure and thought to represent an "augur" or priest because of the *lituus* it is holding. Remove the *lituus*—which does not seem to have been part of the image originally[1]—and the figure fits into the context of late seventh- and early sixth-century figures of women dressed in mantles draped over their heads.

A much more puzzling case is that of three terracotta statuettes from Cerveteri (Figs. 14–16). These statuettes, with arms held out in a ritual position, were found in a tomb in Caere (Cerveteri) in 1863, sitting on "seats carved out of the living tufa."[2] They are all dressed alike, in a short-sleeved, unbelted chiton reaching down to their ankles and a mantle worn like a chlamys, fastened on the right shoulder with a large, butterfly-shaped brooch. Both mantle and chiton have a plaid pattern incised in the fabric and a border marking the edges, the hem of the chiton, and the sleeves. All are barefoot.

The coloring is especially well preserved on one of the British Museum statuettes (D219). Flesh parts on face, arms, and feet were covered by a light orange slip. There are traces of a dark red color on the hair. The chiton was painted the same orange color as the flesh, with a dark red border at the edges; the cloaks were dark red. Probably "ancestors," or figures of the deceased from the tomb, they have been called portraits, but the faces are too much alike (they are apparently mold-made, with details added by hand).

After being excavated in 1863, one of the statuettes was acquired as part of the Castellani collection by the Museo del Palazzo dei Conservatori, in Rome. The other two found their way to England and were acquired by the British Museum in 1873.[3] All of them had been "restored," though it was impossible to tell how much. Helbig, the excavator who first published these three statuettes in 1866, reported that there were other statuettes in the tomb, but that they were broken so badly that he did not even bother to pick up the pieces. He thought that they all represented female figures.

This was the beginning of a long controversy over the sex of these statuettes. Because of the bun hairdo and earrings of the two in the British Museum, they were generally identified as representing women; the one in the Capitoline museum, with a different hairdo and no earrings, was said to be male.[4] The latter statuette was also, however, mistakenly said to come from Montalto di Castro because Castellani had declared that as its provenance, forgetting they all were from the same tomb. This fact helped to isolate this statuette even more from the other two.[5]

In 1955 R. A Higgins, the curator of Greek and Roman antiquities at the British Museum, washed off the two statuettes. Like almost all of Castellani's objects, they had been imaginatively reconstructed, with a good deal of plaster. The most important reconstruction was found to be the bun hairdo which had caused such surprise. Most important of all, the necks and heads did not join. The necks had been built up with new plaster, painted over to match the rest of the statuette, and joined to the heads; the heads were probably originally not meant for these particular bodies.

The bodies were made in piece molds, with the heads made separately. Castellani's restorer was apparently given several of the larger fragments, from which he put together three "complete" statuettes. The missing backs of the heads of the two British Museum figures, together with the large, feminine earrings they wore, inspired him to give them Victorian "chignon" hair styles. The left earring, missing in both, was easily copied from the original right one. From a piece of the back of the neck, still preserved on one of the figures (D219), we see that the hair *did* end smoothly on the neck at this point. There was no question of its having had bobbed hair like its companion in Rome.

The breasts on all three figures are quite prominent, but female and male figures in this period often have "extra adipose tissue," like the bronze statue of "Vertumnus," long called androgynous because of the developed breasts.[6]

The statuette in the Capitoline museum was cleaned in March of 1959. It too was discovered to be in a very fragmentary condition. All of the original back is missing, from halfway up the right thigh to the level of the left shoulderblade in back. As in the other statuettes, there is no join between head and neck. Head and bobbed hair, however, are genuine; only a small piece of the hairdo is broken off in back.

The head did not necessarily belong to this body, any more than the other two did, but while this male head had a bobbed hair style and no earrings, the other two had earrings (cf. Fig. 56)[7] and smooth hair representing a long braid seen from the front. Two female heads have apparently been put on male bodies. All three bodies are dressed in identical fashion, with long plaid chitons and plaid mantles covering both shoulders and fastened on one shoulder with a brooch.[8] The mantle has curved edges; otherwise it is reminiscent of the seventh-century cloak represented on male figures from the Chiusi ziro vases (Fig. 6).[9] The brooches, carefully simulated in relief and painted with silver paint to look like the original, are typically seventh century, as are the hair styles[10] of the figures.

If the rounded edges of the mantles were a realistic representation of the actual shape of the mantle, then this would be the earliest instance of the rounded mantle in Etruria:[11] there are no other examples before the second half of the sixth century. On the other hand, the rounded edges and also the diagonal, rather than squared, plaid pattern were probably the result of the artist's attempt to express the folds and the draping of the mantle. This manner of showing the draping of the mantle without any folds is a convention in Near Eastern art, where it is also often difficult to reconstruct the actual shape of the garments represented.[12]

No less hard to place are costumes which might represent single examples of a variant fashion not otherwise attested. In some cases the singularity of the dress[13] is due to a misunderstanding. The artistic monument used as a model was misinterpreted, either by an Etruscan artist (Figs. 43, 98, 132; supra Chapter 4, n. 31) or by a modern forger. The misunderstanding of dress is, in fact, a sign of a copy, whether ancient or modern.[14]

With misunderstood or unclear representations of strange costumes, we are at a loss when the original which was copied is not available. Occasionally, a missing link may turn up to guide us. This is perhaps the case for a strange, hitherto unexplained feature of the costume illustrated on an Etruscan bronze relief from the Bernardini tomb (Fig. 156) and on a retarded monument of northern Italian art, the fifth-century Arnoaldi mirror from Bologna.[15] The objects hanging from the waist of the figures have been called at various times "tails," "wings," or "snakes." They might be wings. On the other hand, they might be connected with certain "tails" which originally seem to have represented locks of hair and belonged to a Mycenean funerary costume.

Such strange-looking fancies, to our unaccustomed eyes, are the "snakes" or "tails" hanging from the waist of Mycenean figures on the Haghia Triada sarcophagus, as well as on a peculiar series of Mycenean representations dating around the time of the Warrior vase, ca. 1200 B.C., on painted terracotta *larnakes* or sarcophagi. Emily Vermeule describes these figures as follows: "Both women have attachments which blow straight out from their robes at hip level, looking like a pair of tails or flames. This feature is common to many of the larnakes and occurs also in a few other Aegean religious scenes. It has never been clearly interpreted. It may be a shorthand version of the floating animal tails worn by persons performing the ceremony on the Hagia Triada sarcophagus; similar reduced animal tails are worn in fresco scenes of worship at Tiryns and Pylos. Perhaps it represents locks of hair cut off in mourning and attached to the girdle. This larnax illustrates a welcome stage in its representation between the Hagia Triada sarcophagus and late survivals in Crete after the Dark Ages. A well-known figure of a female on a Geometric vase from Fortetsa is a direct descendant of the type. Her 'tails' have sometimes been interpreted as snakes, lowered from where the old Minoan snake goddesses used to wear them, but the larnax in Germany shows that such tails are not alive, whatever else they may be."[16]

These hanging ornaments survive in Orientalizing art[17] to make a surprising appearance in a monument of Etruscan art of that period (Fig. 155), allowing us perhaps to trace an eighth- and seventh-century element back beyond the Dark Ages to an original Mycenean model.

Another originally Mycenean ritual, perhaps funerary, element of costume may be the snake-like white band winding spirally about the skirt of a female figure on the Boccanera plaques (Fig. 75). An important figure, she stands between two pairs of female figures who, dressed more conventionally and carrying alabastra and pomegranate branches, come toward her on either side. She is not necessarily, however, a "snake goddess."[18] The spiral band looks less like a snake than like the bands or flounces of Mycenean "priest robes." Adopted into Mycenean art from Near Eastern models, these garments are represented in seals, on the Haghia Triada sarcophagus, and on the side of a larnax. In Near Eastern and Mycenean art costumes with such decoration are apparently worn by men, often priests,[19] yet its appearance on this Etruscan female figure need not surprise us. The figure is clearly marked out as a priestess or goddess by her position and by the rest of her dress, and we are familiar with the tendency in Etruscan art to represent women wearing costumes elsewhere reserved for men.

A probable forgery is the "Ossuario Primoli" in the archaeological museum in Florence,[20] a primitive-looking statuette of the type of the ziro burial urns from Chiusi, who wears an odd costume. The mantle draped over the head (if the figure represents a woman, one would expect a back mantle: if a man, it should cover him completely) in an unheard-of "star-studded" pattern, the huge necklace, objects like corn husks hanging from the waist, the "proto-Ionic" chiton worn under the mantle—all these seem to constitute a kind of ignorant pastiche of the dress of figures on ziro burial urns.

I cannot place the hair style of a bronze male statuette reported to have been found at Piombino,[21] whose hair is neither quite bobbed in the early sixth-century style nor long in the Ionian style of the later part of the century. Nor am I sure of the strange mantle of another bronze statuette, in the British Museum:[22] a *capite velato* fashion is otherwise unknown in the fifth century B.C.

Another problem is the actual shape of the predecessor of the Roman laena, the long Etruscan rounded mantle worn back to front. Most representations show it with the two ends thrown back over the shoulders (Figs. 117–120), yet stone relief cippi from Chiusi show another rounded form in back, as though the original garment were a kind of poncho. Is this a misunderstanding, or a stylization, or a different way of wearing a rounded mantle?

The "Capestrano warrior," ca. 500 B.C. (Fig. 27), and the figures found with it are not Etruscan but Italic, and reflect some features of early dress shared by Etruscans and other inhabitants of the peninsula. Perizoma and bullae are familiar to us from a sixth-century Etruscan context. Most of the armament of the warrior—bronze disc-protector, belt, sword, spearhead—can be identified from actual finds in this region.[23] Other features, such as the hat with huge brim and the sandals painted on the feet, still need to be explained. What about the strange sandals with metal "blades" or nails on the soles, found at Capestrano and the nearby region?[24] Considering the climate, which is not cold, the suggestion that they were made to walk on ice is not convincing. Perhaps, like the "elevator shoes" on the later Greek *kothornoi*, the framework under the sole added height to the wearer, as the statue's hat added to his dignity and the armor to his awesomeness.

The costume of the female figure, one-third life size, of which unfortunately only the torso survives, is very difficult to interpret,[25] yet some features, like the gesture of the left hand to the throat, are reminiscent of small-scale Etruscan statuary. The bracelets on the upper arm match those on the Cerveteri terracotta statuettes (Figs. 14–16). Neckline and sleeve edges just above the bracelet indicate the top of the chiton, interrupted at the waist by a broad belt, as on Etruscan female busts of ca. 600–575 B.C. The border running below the breasts is, frankly, puzzling.[26] Over the chiton a short mantle is worn, which one is tempted to reconstruct as the back mantle of seventh-century Etruscan dress: the pins and straps which hold it up over the shoulders are there, and the top part of this mantle looks familiar, even to the fragment of back braid which lies on it. Unfortunately, it is much too short. Has the back mantle been abbreviated on this figure, for some external reason? Do the fringe-like decorations hanging on the shoulders from the pins give us a clue as to the origin of the fringe of Etruscan fourth-century ceremonial dress? These questions remain open. Until more evidence can show us the context in which these figures are to be studied, it may be worthwhile to try to see them within the context of early Etruscan or Italic dress fashions.[27]

VOCABULARY

Because of our ignorance of the Etruscan vocabulary for clothes and fashions, Greek and Latin terms are used to describe Etruscan dress. This vocabulary for Greek, Etruscan, and Roman dress brings up some interesting questions. Often word and fashion have the same origin. Emilia Masson's recent work on Semitic words in Greek assembles some of the evidence for Greek. (Especially useful for us is the grouping in a separate section of words dealing with textiles and garments.) The author's conclusion is that Greek words of Semitic origin most often refer to real objects used in everyday life, garments, textiles, containers, names of food and of plants: κάννα ("reed"), κασία ("cassia" or *cinnamomum iners*), κιννάμωμον ("cinnamon"), κύμινον ("cumin"), κύπρος ("henna color"), μύρρα ("myrrh"), νάρδος ("nard"), σήσαμον ("sesame"), σοῦσον ("lily oil"), χαλβάνη ("juice of all-heal"). Of these, some had entered the language in Mycenean times: σήσαμον, χρυσός, χιτών ("sesame," "gold," "chiton"), etc. Technical terms entered the language at a later time: δέλτος ("writing tablet"), musical instruments (possibly τύμπανον, σαμβύκη), etc. All these borrowings reflect a commercial relationship between Greeks and the speakers of these Semitic languages (cf. μνᾶ, "mina," or 100 drachmae, and σίγλος, "shekel"). Many of the Semitic words in Greek refer to objects actually imported (χρυσός, ἔλεφας ["gold," "ivory"]), to types of linen (βύσσος, σενδών), and to clothes, like the originally Semitic words χιτών, κρώβυλος (?), κόθορνος (?), and σάκκος. Such words and objects entered Greek culture either during Mycenean times or later, through Phoenician commerce. Masson emphasizes the commercial or trade aspect of the relationship reflected by these borrowings: there are no abstract notions, no political, philosophical, or artistic vocabulary.

The Iranian-related μίτρα and συκχίς, "hat" and "shoes," respectively, with effeminate connotations, and κυπάσσις, a Persian long-sleeved chiton, were adopted by the Phrygians and Ionian Greeks during the period of Persian rule. Herodotus (1.155) ascribes the adoption of Persian chitons and kothornoi to that period, along with other customs of a higher civilization, such as playing stringed instruments and taking part in commerce, καπηλεύειν. This agrees with Erbacher's comment about the large number of shoe types brought in around the time of the Persian wars and before and with the strong Ionian influence apparent in mainland Greek and Etruscan art in the second half of the sixth century B.C.

There was much less borrowing after these two "international" periods of Mycenean and Phoenician trade and the Ionian influence of the later sixth century. Except for a temporary enthusiasm for luxurious foreign items in the fifth century, in the period following the Persian wars (cf. the στρεπτός, "twisted" necklace or torque) the Greeks did not borrow much in the way of clothing fashions until the Hellenistic period. Later, with the rise of Roman power, Roman terminology was adopted either by using the Roman name, as in τήβεννα, "tebenna," by translating it (φοινικοπάρυφος for *praetexta*), or by transliterating it (κάλτιος, "calceus").

Greek reaction to nudity in art and in language is unique; yet the condition of being naked is always a special one. The Greek word for "naked" is the most changed of all the related Indo-European words; it is so far differentiated as to be unrecognizable, except to a linguist. This fact is at first surprising. Why should the Greeks, apparently the only people in the Mediterranean to break through the barrier of male nudity and expose their sex—even if only on special occasions and, eventually, in art—be so emotionally touched by the word to want to change it beyond recognition? Of course, one possibility is that the word was changed in an early period of the language, at a time when, in fact, the Greeks *were* still bound by the taboo—when one of Homer's characters, Thersites, could still be threatened with exposure before his own comrades as a shameful, humiliating punishment. But perhaps there is more to it than that. The original reason for which the Greeks first started to practice public or "heroic" nudity is discussed by ancient authors (see supra Chapter 2); the explanation given, however, is a rationalization which cannot be taken seriously. Athletes could not really run that much faster without a perizoma, and even if they had run faster and won, such a practical advantage would not have been important enough to change an immemorial tradition, whose religious connotations would outweigh any practical considerations. Nor could it have been an "accident." More probably, the Greeks felt so strongly about nudity that it was thought to have a magical effect (cf. the apotropaic use of the *phallos*, gestures against the evil eye, etc.). Their athletes were thought to be protected in some way by their nudity. Then too, when they competed in the games, in the holy sanctuaries of the gods, they were in some way sanctified (in the Near East, priests appear naked before the god).

In Latin, borrowings of clothes and their names also reflect foreign relations. The Latin debt to the Etruscans is considerable. Possibly Etruscan, or by way of Etruscan, are *tutulus, laena, tunica, lacerna,* τήβεννα. The fact that these words often have Latin or Greek equivalents shows that the object, originally adopted from another culture, had become familiar, and was no longer felt to be foreign: *tutulus = sex crines; tunica = chiton; toga =* τήβεννα. We might add χλαῖνα =*pallium,* but *laena* and *pallium* eventually represented two very different garments, after a long process of specialization had taken place: the *laena* became a religious costume and the *pallium* became the Roman name for the Greek *himation,* contrasting with the toga.

Contact between Etruscans and early Romans (Latins) seems, in fact, to be comparable to "Oriental" or Semitic-Greek relations in many ways. That it was a superfical one, which merely introduced into the vocabulary terms indicative of greater luxury and higher culture (*perso-na* [*phersu*], *taberna, lacerna, laena, histrio, atrium*[1]), has been shown by Ernout in his still-classic article.[2] Etruscan influence on such a native rite as the Roman triumph, too, was apparently limited to externals: music, clothes, temple architecture, type of cult statue.[3] If we except the very doubtful *populus*, there are no words for abstract notions or philosophical or religious ideas which can be shown to have come into Latin from the Etruscan language. This type of influence is strikingly similar to what Masson brings out in her study of Semitic words in Greek. There is even a technical word to remind us that in each case the debt included writing. The Greeks adopted the Semitic word δέλτος for writing tablets; the Latin word *litterae* seems to have come from Greek through Etruscan. Yet the barrier of language effectively separated these cultures. The influence of the more advanced culture in each case was enormous, but it never touched the basis of language or religion—at least so far as we can tell from our limited knowledge of the Etruscan vocabulary.

A single Latin word for a garment, *balteus*, is stated by Varro to be Etruscan. His assertion[4] has been taken at face value, though scholars have occasionally expressed puzzlement about it. There does not seem to be any linguistic reason for *balteus* to be Etruscan. Not only is it closely related to German *balz* and English "belt," but the presence of "b," which is not an Etruscan sound, is definitive evidence against the notion. The group to which this word belongs, however, even if not Etruscan, is interesting in itself, and should be studied further. Though Ernout sharply distinguishes the noun ending in *-eus* (which *balteus* shares with a number of other words concerning dress—*clupeus* and *calceus*; cf. the nouns *pluteus, puteus,* and *cuneus*) from the adjectival ending, *-eus*, this ending is also frequent in words relating to dress, e.g., *purpureus, trabea* (**toga trabea,* *trabeus).

The majority of foreign borrowings in Latin are, as is to be expected, Greek. Even when the garments were not originally Greek, the force of Greek cultural influence caused a Greek name to be adopted —though a Latin name was also often preferred, in line with the "national" character of Roman dress: cf. *soleae* for σανδάλια, *pallium* for *himation*, etc.

Other relations are also reflected in the Latin vocabulary relating to dress. *Sagum, hosa,* and *bracae* are northern names for northern garments, more or less "barbarian" dress. The distinction of clothing in the vocabulary thus parallels the "symbolic" use of clothes in descriptions of ethnic groups. Scythians wore long pants, Gauls *bracae* and *torques*; "Orientals" were a bit more loosely characterized by Phrygian hats and pointed shoes.[5]

Many words, identified as Etruscan in "glosses" by Greek authors, are actually not Etruscan at all: δέα and κάπρα are Latin: δέα could not be Etruscan, since there are no voiced consonants—"b," "d," or "g"—in the language. (τήβεννα would have come from Etruscan *tepenna.) The word ἰταλός is not Etruscan: ἰταλός (vitellus), from which the word Italia derives, was originally an Oscan word, which the Greeks of southern Italy adopted. Later Greek authors mistakenly attributed to the Etruscans in Italy this word, which they knew was not Greek, though it was used by some Greeks.[6]

In fact it was evidently because the Greeks thought of the Etruscans when they thought of Italy that they erroneously identified as Etruscan a large number of words with voiced consonants, many of them Latin (e.g., baltea),[7] and words written in Greek ending in -ουμ (in Latin, -um) or -αμ (in Latin, -am).[8] That leaves only a few genuinely Etruscan words out of all the glosses that have come down to us. Of Etruscan origin is the name of the entrance hall of the Roman house, the atrium; ἄριμος, "monkey" (cf. ἐναρίμη and πιθεκοῦσσα, the name of Ischia, TLE No. 811), αἴσοι, "gods" (θεοί, TLE No. 804; cf. aesar, TLE No. 803). Nefts ("grandson," cf. "nephew") seems to have come into Etruscan from the Umbrian, or the Latin nepos.

Laena and triump[h]us are Greek words which came into Latin by way of the Etruscan language, and reflect Etruscan influence on Latin culture in the seventh and sixth century B.C.

INTRODUCTION

1. Heurgon has a chapter on dress, with valuable references. Still useful is Solari, with an appendix by Aldo Neppi Modona.

2. *Griechische Kleidung* and *Entwicklungsgeschichte*, as well as a forthcoming book on Greek and Roman dress in collaboration with the author.

3. See Bibliography.

4. See "Nuovi studi sul problema delle origini etrusche (Bilancio critico)," *StEtr* 29 (1961) 3-30, with previous bibliography; *Etruscologia* 81-116.

5. See Bibliography.

6. Vergil *Aen.* 8.722-723: *gentes/quam variae linguis, habitu tam vestis et armis.* Cf. Polybius 2.17; A. S. F. Gow, "Notes on the *Persae* of Aeschylus," *JHS* 48 (1928) 143-152.

7. See Bonfante Warren, *AJA* 75 (1971) 277-284, esp. 277. To the bibliography quoted there, add B. Goldman, "The Dura Synagogue Costumes and Parthian Art," in J. Gutmann, ed., *The Dura-Europos Synagogue, a Reevaluation (1932-1972)* (American Academy of Religion, 1973) 53-78; "Origin of the Persian Robe," *Iranica Antiqua* 4 (1964) 133-152.

8. *AJA* 75 (1971) 277-279. Lamb (108) is, however, mistaken in considering the costume of Bibl. Nat. 1040 a misunderstanding of the himation drape: see infra Fig. 106. Other possible misunderstandings—feather hats, short chitons, wings—are discussed in the text.

9. Bonfante Warren, *AJA* 75 (1971) 278. On forgeries, see M. Pallottino, *The Meaning of Archaeology* (London 1968) Figs. 52-54, esp. 53; G. M. A. Richter, "Newcomers," *AJA* 74 (1970) 334, Pl. 84, Figs. 14-17; and supra Appendix I, n. 14.

10. Pfiffig, *Etruskische Sprache* 7-9; Harris 179. These phases coincide with those Emeline Richardson distinguishes in her forthcoming book on Etruscan bronzes.

11. Banti[2] 46-29.

12. See Hencken, *Tarquinia*; Camporeale, *Tomba del Duce*; Cristofani, *T. Monte Michele*; Ström; and my reviews in *AJA* 77 (1973) 100-102, 73 (1969) 484-486, and 75 (1971) 440-441.

13. A similar distinction between purely local, imported, or generally contemporary material was effectively used by G. Camporeale in *Tomba del Duce* and in *Commerci di Vetulonia*.

14. Forthcoming article on Etruscan influence in northern Italy.

15. For the idea of *truphe*, see my articles in *Arethusa* 6 (1973) 91-101 and in *Archaeology* 26 (1973) 242-249. For references to shoes, see infra Chapter 5.

16. *AJA* 62 (1958) 241; cf. A. Rumpf, *AJA* 60 (1956) 75.

17. This chapter has appeared in *ANRW* I₄ (1973) 584-614 (a Festschrift in honor of Joseph Vogt).

18. The subject of the Romans' attitude toward Etruscan culture is worth further study. Domenico Musti (*Tendenze nella storiografia romana e greca su Roma arcaica. Studi su Livio e Dionigi d'Alicarnasso*, in *Quaderni Urbinati di Cultura Classica* 10 [1970]) discusses the pro- or anti-Etruscan bias of the sources.

19. Maecenas proudly claimed them as his ancestors (Heurgon 317-328); Horace *Od.* 1.1.1, 3.29.1; cf. *Sat.* 1.6.1-4 and others. On the Cilnii, to whom he was related, see Harris 320-321.

20. See my articles in *JRS* 60 (1970) 49-66, esp. 58-62, and *Kerns Studies.*

21. On the Capitoline wolf, see Riis, "Art in Etr. and Lat.," and O.-W. von Vacano, "Vulca, Rom und die Wölfin. Untersuchungen zur Kunst des frühen Rom," *ANRW* I₄ (1973) 523-583. For its interpretation, see Bickerman. For monuments used as sources by Roman historians and Etruscan statues in Rome, see Momigliano; Fraccaro; and Richardson, *MAAR* 21 (1953) 110ff.; Pliny *HN* 34.21-23; Propertius 4.1.5; 4.2.1-6, 61-64.

1. FABRICS AND PATTERNS

1. Wild, *Textile Manufacture*, lists the finds. He also points out the importance of the northern provinces—e.g., Gaul—for Roman textiles. See S. Mazzarino, "Sociologia del mondo etrusco," *Historia* 6 (1957) 116, on Rome as an economic center in the sixth century B.C. and the survival of the Etruscan textile industry in Rome. Traces of actual garments (and in general precious information about the life and commerce of the Orientalizing period in Etruria) have been found in the course of recent excavations in Latium, especially at Castel di Decima, near Rome. F. Zevi, the excavator, described the finding of skeletons with dark spots at the shoulders representing the bunching of the cloth where the pins had held it: the men had the pin on the right shoulder, evidently fastening a woolen mantle like the one described infra Chapter 4. Another spectacular find in a tomb containing a chariot (dated to the late eighth–early seventh century) is that of a woman buried in a robe sewn with carved amber and glass beads, wearing a gold and amber pectoral and gold spiral hair-rings. Nothing in this excavation was later than 600 B.C. (F. Zevi and A. Bedini, *StEtr* 41 (1973) 27-44, 457). Further discussion and bibliography are found in D. Ridgway, "Archaeology in Central Italy and Etruria, 1968-73, Archaeological Reports for 1973-1974," *JHS* (1974) 45-46, nn. 22-29. (I have not dealt with the jewelry, except very incidentally; for that, see Higgins.)

For the mantle from Gerömsberg, Sweden, dated by pollen analysis to the Danish Bronze Age, ca. 1200 B.C., see L. von Post, *Bronsåldermanteln från Gerumsberget i Våstergötland*, K. Vitterhets Hist. och Antiqv. Akad. Monografien-Serien no. 15 (Stockholm 1925); Broholm-Hald, *Costumes*; J. Brönsted, "Bronze Age Clothing Preserved in Danish Graves," *Archaeology* 3 (1950) 16f. The weave is illustrated in Singer 443, Fig. 279. Cf. Forbes 188. Wild writes: "The Gerum mantle . . . is the earliest evidence both for the weaving of 2-over-2 twill and for the most advanced form of it, diamond (lozenge) twill" (*Textile Manufacture* 48). Further references and bibliography are found in Gullberg-Åström.

2. Cristiana Morigi Govi, "Il tintinnabulo della Tomba degli Ori," *ArchCl* 23 (1971) 211-235. The tomb belonged to a woman, evidently a wealthy matron, around thirty or forty years old (228). For northern textiles in Rome, see Pliny *HN* 8.191; see also above, n. 1. For evidence of decorated and plaid colored textiles in the Early Bronze Age, 1800-1600 B.C., in Europe and Italy, see Peroni 100-107.

3. Chamber tomb from Poggio della Sala, in the Museo Archeologico, Florence. See Levi, *Mus. Chiusi* 94-95; Gempeler 240. The bronze figure, now headless, sat on a bronze throne before a bronze table. The gold was probably originally attached to the cloth in thin gold plaques (H. H. Scullard, *The Etruscan Cities and Rome* [Ithaca, N.Y. 1967] 154: the linen was "covered with gold leaf"). Unfortunately there are not enough fragments of either linen or gold to check, since the flood of 1965 in Florence reduced them all to an unrecognizable mass. Another figure was provided with a bronze belt; see Gempeler 240-241.

Covering the figure with real cloth was, of course, the easiest way of "representing" a garment. Statues of divinities were often dressed: "The ritual clothing of the images is an important and very old feature of the Mesopotamian cult which has never been made the subject of a special investigation" (A. Leo Oppenheim, "The Golden Garments of the Gods," *JNES* 8 [1949] 172). Cf. the garments offered to Athena at Troy (*Iliad* 6.289f.) and at Athens in the Panathenaic procession (J. A. Davison, "Notes on the Panathenaia," *JHS* 78 [1958] 25). On the ancient image of Fortuna in the Forum Boarium, see Livy 10.23.3f.; Dion. Halic. 4.40.7, Ovid *Fasti* 6.577f., Pliny *HN* 8.197, and Dio Cassius 58.7.2; O. J. Brendel, "Two Fortunae, Antium and Praeneste," *AJA* 64 (1960) 44; and H. Lyngby, "Fortunas och Mater Matutas Kulter," *Eranos* 36 (1938) 47ff. The bronze statue of Hercules Triumphans was dressed in triumphal clothes whenever a triumph was celebrated in Rome (Pliny, *HN* 34.33). Cf. also the custom of dressing someone in the honorary clothes of the deceased, putting the funerary mask on him, and parading him in the funerary *pompa* (Polybius 6.53).

There is ample evidence for the ritual use of linen in connection with religious and funerary rites in Etruria and early Rome. In the Tomba del Duce at Vetulonia were found the bones of a cremated corpse, wrapped in a linen cloth; see Camporeale, *Tomba del Duce* 14. Cf. also the mummy of Zagreb (though this was an Egyptian ritual) and the famous *libri lintei* of Rome, the *legio linteata*, etc. (Bonfante Warren, *ANRW* I₄. s.v. *"linum"*).

4. An Etruscan bronze bowl found at Veii, now in the Newark Museum, bears "the imprint of a textile with three or four areas, totaling approx. 26 sq. cm., containing the fossilized fragments of a cream-colored textile," dating probably from the sixth century B.C.; see Diane Lee Carroll, "An Etruscan Textile in Newark," *AJA* 77 (1973) 334–336. The fragment appears to be part of the front of a woman's chiton with belt. The threads of the material have been identified as spun in Etruria rather than in Egypt, where a more sophisticated process of wet spinning was used. The problem of where the flax was grown is left open. That it was expensive to grow, since it depletes the soil, was a fact of which the ancients were aware: Columella, Virgil, and Pliny are quoted. Columella specifically warns that flax should not be grown unless it fetches a good price.

5. On fancy patterned textiles, see F. von Lorentz, "βαρβάρων ὑφάσματα," *RM* 52 (1937) 165–222. On decoration of Etruscan houses, including richly ornamented rugs and blankets and pillows, which have been lost, see T. Dohrn, "Zwei Etruskische Kandelaber," *RM* 66 (1959) 45–64; Heurgon 239.

6. See infra Chapters 3–4 below.

7. Wild, *Textile Manufacture* 23, 53; Bonfante Warren, *ANRW* I₄, s.v. *"scutulatus."* Pallottino (*Etruscologia* 337) thinks the early seventh-century "net-patterned textiles" were embroidered, but A. Wace, in *Artemis Orthia* 280, points out that such designs "could easily be rendered in weaving and do not imply embroidered or applied ornamentation." See, for example, *Iliad* 6.289f. (of the robe woven by the women of Sidon, which Hecuba offers to the goddess), where ποικίλος is often erroneously translated as "embroidery." See Wace, "Weaving or Embroidery?" *AJA* 52 (1948) 51–55, for the frequent Homeric references to ποικιλία, "many-colored garments." Bieber (*Entwicklungsgeschichte* 10f.) contrasts the traditionally soft, pliable textiles of the Greeks with the stiff fabrics of the Near East, decorated by applying other elements to the surface (embroidery, plaques, etc.). See Peroni 100–107.

8. A bell-shaped figurine from Boeotia, ca. 700 B.C., has a plaid zone down the front of the chiton like that of some Orientalizing Etruscan bucchero statuettes; see F. R. Grace, *Archaic Sculpture in Boeotia* (London 1939) 10f.; Louvre C 18, Hoernes 396. Cf. the plaid or otherwise ornamented zone on the skirts of Dedalic figures from Crete, for example on a gold plate from the

Idaean Cave (Levi, "Arkades" 536f.); and also the chiton of the figure on the tridacna shell, infra Fig. 22.

9. Vatican, seventh century B.C.; see Magi, *StEtr* 11 (1937) 95–105, Pl. 10. Cf. also a late example, on a bronze cista dating from ca. 480 B.C., imitating Greek red-figured style, where the costume of the (barbarian?) Gorgon is shown in a plaid pattern. The seventh-century lead figures from Sparta frequently have this kind of relief decoration (infra Fig. 19).

10. Barnett, in the text to Pls. 16–17, 83, "Pyxides from the S. E. Palace at Nimrud, in Syrian style," describes the goddess as wearing a quilted dress, which is unlikely (infra Fig. 20).

11. Ducati ("Laminette eburnee" Pl. 3) dates them 600–550 B.C. (closer to 600 than to 550) because of the absence of Orientalizing elements, which have been replaced by the Ionian influence of the following phase, "Ionic-Etruscan." Huls (177f., No. 66, Pl. 31) dates them at the beginning of the archaic period in northern Etruria, ca. 565 B.C., and certainly later than the Pania figures. Mühlestein (158f.) feels that Ducati's date is too low and dates them 625 B.C. at the lowest, perhaps 650 B.C., apparently on the basis of the early Etruscan hair style, with a lock on each shoulder.

Huls (178), wrongly, in my opinion, implies that the original dress of the Bologna ivory plaques was embroidered. Her list of Etruscan examples of the plaid pattern in Etruria contains several inaccuracies. 1. Not all the bucchero figures from the Regolini-Galassi tomb have a plaid pattern. (Why does she say there are thirty of them? Ducati Pl. 54, No. 164, gives the number as thirty-three, but Ducati incorrectly shows figures from two different types, 233 and 317, as well as one not from the Regolini-Galassi tomb.) See Pareti 272–273, Pl. 28, No. 233. 2. The wrong provenance (Montalto di Castro) is given for the statuettes from Cerveteri (infra Figs. 14–16). 3. The bronze figure from Rapino (infra Fig. 128) has lines indicating folds (cf. the stitching on the seams), *not* a plaid pattern. 4. The bronze plaque from Castellina in Chianti (*NSc* 1905, 235, Fig. 30) shows a pattern, on a figure of Athena, which is not plaid, though it is a zoned decoration like the ivories: such a patterned decoration often indicates armor. See infra Chapter 3, "Penguin Women," for the manner of wearing the mantle in the Corinthian fashion, held out by both hands in front, a stylization which dates the figures ca. 575 B.C. See infra Chapter 4, n. 11.

12. Athenaeus *Deipn.* 12.525 c–d, quoting from the book by Democritus of Ephesus, *On The Temple of Ephesus*, whose date is unknown (see *RE*, s.v. "Ephesus"); the temple of Ephesus referred to is the sixth-century building. "Woven in a lozenge pattern": ῥομβοῖς ὑφαντά. Heuzey (206f.) thought this kind of material was a very fine cloth, the weave of which formed lozenge shapes as it was stretched in one direction or another: "On a pensé d'abord, sans en trouver d'exemple, que ces *rhomboi* étaient des métiers d'une forme particulière. D'autres commentateurs ont vu là une disposition en losanges de couleurs différentes . . . qui distinguaient ces tuniques; mais le mot est lié trop étroitement au verbe ὑφαίνειν pour ne pas se rapporter au tissage même."

The description of borders with figured decoration agrees with the representation on the famous vase in Bologna showing Penelope weaving a piece of cloth with a figured border above and vertical and horizontal designs below (Furtwängler-Reichhold Pl. 142; Bieber Fig. 5). For similar colors in Mycenean dress, see L. Stella, *La civiltà micenea nei documenti contemporanei* (Rome 1965) 104–5 (supra n. 7).

13. See Bieber, *AA* (1973) 425–430, with full references, for wool and linen and for the weaving of textiles in antiquity.

14. Akurgal Fig. 10. Cf. gold disc from Toprak Kale, near Van: R. D. Barnett, "Excavations of the British Mus. at Toprak Kale, Near Van," *Iraq* 12

(1950) Fig. 18, ca. 700 b.c.; A. Leo Oppenheim, *JNES* 8 (1949) 172–193, with refs. Fragments of a lead dress inlaid with ivory, from Toprak Kale, are illustrated in Barnett Pl. 130, W.8. Cf. Barnett, "Excavations" 29, Fig. 18, "eighth to seventh century b.c."

15. Gullberg-Åström 23; Bellinger. This was true even for the rounded Etruscan tebenna and the Roman toga; as we saw (supra n. 1), the Scandinavian woolen cloak was woven in an oval shape. The graceful draping of Greek, Etruscan, and Roman cloaks was due to the fact that there were no seams to disturb the fall of the folds.

16. Painted sarcophagus from Haghia Triada, Crete, Heraklion museum, fourteenth century b.c. (Matz, *Kreta, Mykene, Troja* Pl. 47; Vermeule 205).

17. See Chapter 3.

18. Otto J. Brendel, review of G. Becatti and F. Magi, *Tarquinii III–IV: Le pitture delle Tombe degli Auguri e del Pulcinella* (Rome 1955), in *AJA* 62 (1958) 240f., for the *praetexta pulla*. For the use of purple, see M. Reinhold, *History of Purple as a Status Symbol in Antiquity* (Brussels 1970); L. B. Janssen, "Royal Purple of Tyre," *JNES* 22 (1963) 104–118.

19. Mark I. Davies, "The Suicide of Ajax: A Bronze Etruscan Statuette from the Käppeli Collection," *Antike Kunst* 14 (1971) 149. The figure is not a cista handle. There are no archaic Praenestine cistae, as G. Battaglia, who is preparing the corpus of cistae, kindly reminds me. See M. Renard, "A Small Bronze from Cerveteri," *Studies in Honor of D. M. Robinson* (St. Louis 1951) I 753, n. 26. Cf. Elba statuette, supra Chapter 4, n. 20.

20. On a number of fourth- and third-century Praenestine cistae and mirrors, see K. Schumacher, *Eine praenestinische Ciste im Museum zu Karlsruhe* (Heidelberg 1891) Pl. 2, cited in M. Cristofani, *DialArch* 1 (1967) 186–219.

21. Bonfante Warren, *JRS* 60 (1970) 64, Pl. 8, Fig. 3.

22. Gullberg-Åström 11, 16.

2. PERIZOMA AND BELTS

1. Pausanias 1.44 also uses the participle (ἀνὴρ) περιεζωσμένος. "Perizoma" refers as well to later garments, or to Roman equivalents: see Plutarch *Romulus* 21 (περίζωσμα), *Aem.* 33, Arr. 4.8.16, Polyb. 6.25.3.

2. Ath. *Deipnosophistae* 13.607C.

3. Thucydides 1.6. Lucian *Alexander the Oracle-Monger* 13.

4. Homer, e.g., *Iliad* 23.685; ζώννυσι is often translated by the general term "gird one's loins," and a ζώστηρ is a metal belt, a protective piece of armor: see S. Karouzou, *Deltion* 16 (1960) 60ff., for a list of Homeric passages. Cyrus Gordon ("Belt-Wrestling in the Bible World," *Hebrew Union College Annual* 23 [1950–51] 131–136) interprets this passage and *Iliad* 23.710 as meaning that the contestants put on a belt for wrestling (cf. 23.684, boxing). On the other hand, Dionysius of Halicarnassus (7.72.3) cites the same passages (and *Odyssey* 16.66–69, 18.74f.) as evidence that the Greeks did not compete in the nude in ancient times. In his own time this ζῶμα would seem to have signified pants or loincloth, since a plain belt would hardly keep the contestant from being naked.

5. Wilson 73; Isid. *Orig.* 18.17.2. For *licium*, see *Gai. Inst.* 3.192–193: "qui quaerere velit, nudus quaerat, licio cinctus, lancem habens . . . quid sit autem licium, quaesitum est; sed verius est consuti genus esse, quo necessariae partes tegerentur." E. Peruzzi, "La *quaestio cum lance et licio*," *La Cultura* 6 (1966) 161–166, and Peruzzi, *Origini* I 77–83. J. G. Wolf, in *Sympotica Franz Wieacker* (Göttingen 1970) 59–79.

6. The term "bathing trunks" is used to describe the perizoma of Cypriot statues; see Myres, *Cesnola Collection* 154; H. A. Tubbs, "Excavations in Cyprus, 1889," *JHS* 11 (1890) 92.

7. D. Levi, "Le Cretule di Hagia Triada e di Zakrò," *ASAtene* 8-9 (1925-26) 156, gives a summary of different types of Minoan loincloths. Vercoutter (243-287, 303) distinguishes types of short pants, loincloths, and kilts represented on Egyptian figures of foreign Keftiu, and compares them to Cretan examples. His observations on the construction of the original models and their artistic representation, illustrated with patterns and comparative drawings, make it clear that, in spite of the difference in representation, we are dealing with a few traditional, basic types of garments which were handed down to the Orientalizing world practically unchanged.

8. Elsewhere, too, women used the perizoma when they performed as acrobats. For Egyptian examples, see the limestone fragment in the Egyptian museum in Turin, end of Eighteenth Dynasty; Ranke, *Anc. Egypt* Pl. 268 (Twentieth Dynasty, *ca.* 1180 B.C.); Hanfmann, *Altetr. Plastik* Fig. 1; and Smith, *Anc. Egypt* 16, Fig. 3. Cf. infra Fig. 24. In Greece, they often wore it when performing the *pyrrhic*, or armed dance (Fig. 52), when they did not appear completely naked: see J.-C. Poursat, "Les représentations de danse armée dans la céramique attique," *BCH* 92 (1968) 550-615, 587ff., "Danses armées féminines" (for women wearing the perizoma, see Poursat Figs. 24, 51-52, 53-55). The bikini-clad girls in the mosaics at Piazza Armerina (supra, text) belong to this same tradition (Gentili 47ff.).

9. Fresco from Knossos with bull-jumping scene, Crete, Heraklion Museum, ca. 1500 B.C.; Evans, *PM* 213, Fig. 144; Matz Pl. 51; Marinatos Pl. 17. Cf. Vercoutter 253-255: "composé d'une pièce d'étoffe coupée en forme et maintenue en place par la ceinture." The pattern illustrated, however (Figs. 27, 30, 109), does not take into account the "slip" section, hiding the sex in front.

10. Pallottino, "Fond. miceneo" Pl. 4, Figs. 13, 14, a bronze figure from Olympia in the Berlin Antiquarium. On the "conservative transmission of athletic customs and equipment from the Mycenean into the Classical period," see Mark I. Davies, "The Oresteia before Aischylos," *BCH* 93 (1969) 223; Heurgon 262.

11. F. Poulsen, "Eine Kretische Mitra," *AM* 31 (1906) 343f., Pl. 23. D. Levi (*ASAtene* 8-9 [1925-26] 536f.) describes the costume as a chitoniskos and warns that Poulsen's drawing is inaccurate for various details: cf. Hoffman-Raubitschek Pls. 1-3, 5. On other monuments of the period the drawing of chiton or perizoma is ambiguous, e.g., Kunze 225.

12. Berlin Inv. Misc. 7477; Greifenhagen, *Staatl. Mus.* 41, Pl. 8. Lamb 84, Pl. 25b, recognizes the connection with the Minoan perizoma but claims that "its folds are less clearly understood." It was, in fact, a Cretan fashion, which the Cretan artist renders perfectly clearly in Orientalizing form. For a similar form of perizoma on a statuette from the Acropolis, ca. 700 B.C. (de Ridder I No. 696) and the connection of this Cretan garment with the Cretan *Etagenperücke* hair style, see Georg Kaulen, *Daidalika* (Cologne 1967) 8, n. 7, 13, Figs. 1-3; and especially David Mitten's review in *AJA* 74 (1970) 108.

13. See the aryballos in Berlin (Pfuhl Fig. 58); the Chigi oinochoe, Rome, Villa Giulia Museum (Pfuhl Fig. 59; Arias-Hirmer 28, No. 16f., Arias Pl. 20b [color]). Both are attributed to the Macmillan painter, ca. 640 B.C.

14. For an example of a beautifully detailed "diaper" type of perizoma of the Orientalizing form on a bronze statuette found at Corfu in 1965 and a list of similar perizomas in Greek art, see G. Dontas, "Λάκων Κωμαστής," *BCH* 93 (1969) 39-55.

15. Pausanias 1.44: Orsippus of Megara "won the footrace at Olympia by running naked when all his competitors wore the perizoma according to ancient custom"; cf. Isid. *Orig.* 18.17.2.

On the sacral, magic character of nudity in the games (cf. also the costume of the *nudi luperci*), see A. Bernardi's review of M. Meslin, *La fête des kalendes de janvier dans l'empire romain*, Coll. Latomus 115 (Brussels 1970), in *Athenaeum* 49 (1971) 189, and E. J. Bickerman's review of G. Dumézil, *Les Mythes romains: Horace et les Curiaces*, in *CP* 41 (1946) 122: "In a 'clothed' society, where garments are a social obligation, nakedness is an exception and, as such, a monstrosity."

16. Richter, *Kouroi.*

17. For the distinction, see Thuc. 1.6.5, and Herodotus' comment (1.10) on the story of Gyges: "for among the barbarians it is considered shameful *even for a man* to appear naked" ("καὶ ἄνδρα ὀφφῆναι γυμνὸν ἐς αἰσχύνην μεγάλην φέρει").

The distinction did not hold true in all cases. Greeks in real life often did use a kind of perizoma or loincloth; and conversely Etruscans, even in the early period, sometimes represented nude male figures. Wrestlers, especially, regularly stripped naked before performing and were so represented on Etruscan monuments, for example, in the Tomba degli Auguri or in the Tomba della Scimmia, where their clothes are laid on a stool. Cf. the Providence situla, where they are placed on the ground. G. Colonna, in a review of Lucke-Frey, *Die Situla in Providence*, in *Gnomon* 36 (1964) 192f., suggests that the form on the Benvenuti situla, formerly interpreted as a "headless man" seated on a throne, represents a similar bundle of clothes.

18. Isid. *Orig.* 19. 31.17: "fibulae sunt quibus pectus feminarum ornatur, vel pallium tenetur a viris in humeris, sed cingulum in lumbis." In other words, women used the fibula only as a piece of jewelry, while for men it had a practical use. Cf. Juvenal 6.73 and 379, where "keeping his fibula fastened" is equivalent to "keeping his pants on."

19. For the fibulae, see Higgins 144-148; J. Sundwall, *Die älteren italische Fibeln* (Berlin 1943); H. Hencken, *AJA* 62 (1958) 268-272; Richardson 35, 37; Wilson 32 (fibulae); 34 (buttons). The rich documentation and conclusions of Hencken in *Tarquinia* are summarized in his *Tarquinia and Etruscan Origins*, Ancient Peoples and Places (London 1968), 30-31, in which he distinguishes between men's and women's fibulae. In graves dating from Villanovan I, most fibulae "were found in the urn upon the ashes as though they had fastened the cloth or garment in which the cremated bones had been wrapped. . . . These fibulae often have rings on their pins. In one case a string was still attached to such a ring and perhaps even to the surviving edge of a garment. This suggests that the pins of the fibulae were not always stuck through the fabric but through rings attached to it by strings." See also infra Chapter 4, n. 2.

20. On a bronze figurine in Kassel (*Antike Bronzen* 23-24, No. 30, Pl. 11), the lozenge-shaped sections front and back are incised in imitation of the decoration of the original. This is true of a number of examples, including a bronze nude female figure from the Barberini tomb; Curtis, *MAAR* 5 (1925) No. 78, Pl. 25. The perizoma of the figure in Kassel is in the shape of a stiff short skirt: perhaps the garment represented was actually a short leather chiton. On the Villanovan belts, see especially Kossack. For the hinged model, see Curtis, *MAAR* 5 (1925) No. 83, Pl. 34. For further examples, see M. T. Falconi Amorelli, "Tomba Villanoviana con bronzetto nuragico," *ArchCl* 18 (1966) 15, No. 24, Fig. 4; Amorelli, *Coll. Massimo* Nos. 27-29 (Vulci, ninth to eighth

century B.C.); J. Close-Brooks, *NSc* (1963), 239, Fig. 101 (Veii). Richardson ([*MAAR* 27 (1962] 175) calls them "willow-leaf belts," Hencken (*Tarquinia* 551–552) "broad bronze girdles." The bibliography is copious. See L. Laurenzi, *Civiltà del Ferro* Nos. 4, 5, Pl. 3; C. Hopkins, "Oriental Elements in the Hallstatt Culture," *AJA* 61 (1957) 334–335, and "Oriental Evidence for Early Etruscan Chronology," *Berytus* 11 (1955) 75–84. I see no similarity in either form or decoration (nor does Hencken, 552) between the Villanovan belts and some Hittite models represented on reliefs from Carchemish cited by Hopkins (*Berytus* 11 [1955] 78). Part of the original leather backing has in some cases survived: see A. Talocchini, "Le armi di Vetulonia e Populonia," *StEtr* 16 (1942) 33f., No. 3. Cf. holes for attaching a leather or cloth backing on broad bronze belts, in *Abruzzo* 47, Pl. 15; and in Boardman, *Anatolia* 6 (1961–62) 180. For such a belt found in Greece, see J. Close-Brooks, "A Villanovan Belt from Euboea," *University of London, Institute of Classical Studies* 14–16 (1967–69) 22–24.

Such belts remained in use in North Italy: see examples from Este, in *Mostra delle Situle* Nos. 30–31, Pl. 23 (fifth century B.C.; here the bronze back section, which has been preserved, is straight, not lozenge-shaped); and a bronze relief plate with figure of a woman wearing a lozenge-shaped belt with incisions imitating the geometric ornament of the original (*Mostra delle Situle* No. 59, Pl. 43; Bianchi Bandinelli-Giuliano 51, Fig. 52). The question of their use as protective belts or armor remains open in view of the fact that so many were used by women. P. Perdrizet ("Sur la *mitré* homérique," *BCH* 21 [1897] 169) thought the Homeric *mitré* was a broad bronze belt; but see Hoffmann-Raubitschek, and C. Rolley, *BCH* 93 (1969) 673–678. I have suggested (*ANRW* I₄ 588–589) that the bronze protective belt, part of the armor of the Roman priesthood of the Salii, might, however, go back to such a Villanovan type.

21. This type appears on figures of the eighth and seventh century B.C., on a bronze belt buckle from Marsiliana d'Albegna, on bronze figures of acrobats, on a youth in a wall painting in the Campana tomb, and on figures on the bronze cart from Bisenzio: see Moretti, *Mus. V. G.* 61, Fig. 43; Vighi, *Mus. V. G.* 40–41, Pl. 8. It also appears on a bronze decoration from Praeneste, in the Tomba Bernardini; see Curtis, *MAAR* 3 Nos. 90–91, Pls. 65–66. On this heavy belt, see Hanfmann, *Altetr. Plastik* 60; Richardson, *MAAR* 27 (1962) 175 and Fig. 79.

The type is not peculiar to early Etruscan art, however. Nude figures wearing thick belts about their waists were common in early or proto-historic times in the Near East (Cyrus Gordon, "Belt-Wrestling in the Bible World," supra n. 4), and the thick belt continued to be represented in the Mediterranean—for example, on the Minoan and Mycenean perizoma—down to the archaic Greek period. For the ridge, see Boardman, *Anatolia* 6 (1961–62) 180. A later local Etruscan fashion, a belt like a heavy roll of cloth which appears on funerary urns of the Hellenistic period, may be connected: see Brunn-Körte I 22–24, Pl. 46 and *passim*.

22. F.-W. von Hase, *JdI* 86 (1971) 1–59. See also *Schimmel Coll.* No. 76, and G. Bartoloni, *Le Tombe da Poggio Buco* (Florence 1972) Pls. 10a, 19a.

23. On the Ionian belts, see Boardman, *Anatolia* 6 (1961–62) 179–189. On a broad bronze belt of a type found also in Italy (infra Fig. 26), see S. Karouzou, "Χαλκίνος Αρχαϊκὸς Ζωστήρ," *Deltion* 16 (1960) 60–71. On the decoration of bronze plaques probably serving as the terminal clasps of narrow belts, closely related to Phoenician and western Asiatic metalwork, see W. Culican, "A Foreign Motif on Etruscan Jewellery," *BSR*, n.s., 26 (1971) 1–12.

24. A bronze belt buckle from Sovana is shown in Mühlestein 84, Fig. 154 (erroneous provenance); Richardson, *MAAR* 27 (1962) 181, Fig. 79; F. W.

von Hase *JdI* 86 (1971) 8, Fig. 6b. This apron type is a form for which no Mycenean parallels can be found. It is not clear whether the bronze statuette from the Ortiz collection wears such an apron perizoma, perhaps made of leather, or a bronze mitre: *Master Bronzes* No. 12; C. Rolley, *BCH* 93 (1969) 673-678. For the skirt-like perizoma, see the bronze in Kassel (*Antike Bronzen* 23-24, No. 30, Pl. 11) and in Richardson, *MAAR* 27 (1962) 187, Pls. 16-18 (Bernardini tomb).

The strange perizoma (sometimes called *mitré*) of the warrior from Capestrano seems at first sight to have such an "apron" panel in front, but in fact the perizoma does go between the legs: the top of the garment appears in back just above the buttocks (infra Fig. 27; *Abruzzo* 18, Figs. 1-2, Pl. 91).

25. Bronze statuettes of male figures with "sex sacs" are found in Paris, Louvre, Inv. No. MND 2122, and Florence, Museo Archeologico, Nos. 55, 132. Provenances are not given. They are dated to the seventh century B.C. M. F. Briguet, "Deux groupes de figurines étrusques archaïques," *Revue des Arts* 9 (1959) 134f., Figs. 3, 4, lists ten examples. The "sex-sac" type of perizoma has as its predecessor the Minoan-Mycenean-Cretan type illustrated on paintings from Knossos such as the bull-jumper fresco (supra n. 9). The garment is similar to the modern athletic support. The belt is visible on the back of the early bronzes; see Richardson, *MAAR* 27 (1962) 189. Provenances, though they cannot be established in every instance, seem to be mostly North Etruscan.

26. The fitted and sewn Orientalizing perizoma is shown in Fig. 23 and in Vercoutter, Figs. 30, 109 (supra n. 9).

27. See Riis, *Tyrrhenika* 144-45, and Hus 133, who dates them, respectively, 635-625 and 625-610. Cf. also the discussion in G. Camporeale's review of Hus, in *Gnomon* 35 (1963) 294.

28. The original discussion of this series, which now includes over twenty bronze statuettes similar in dress and pose, was that by G. M. A. Hanfmann in 1935: *Altetr. Plastik* 88-90, "Die Schwert-Träger." For further bibliography, see A. Hus, *MélRome* 71 (1959) 7-42. Many new examples are added by Neugebauer, "Gladiatorentypus," and J. C. Balty, "Un centre de production de bronzes figurés de l'Etrurie septentrionale (deuxième moitié VII-première moitié VI s. av. J. C.): Volterra ou Arezzo?" *Bulletin de l'Institut Historique Belge de Rome* 33 (1961) 1-64. Discussion of these figures, erroneously called by Magi and Hanfmann "skirted kouroi," is also found in the following publications: F. Magi, *StEtr* 9 (1934) 415, n. 1; Riis, *Tyrrhenika* 120, 141, 164; Neugebauer, "Gladiatorentypus" 7ff.; Briguet (supra n. 25) 132-35; Hus 129; Richardson 13, Pl. 15.

29. For the Louvre kouros, see de Ridder I 22, No. 105, Pl. 12; Lamb 83, Pl. 25C; Neugebauer, "Gladiatorentypus" 8, No. 6, n. 1.

30. Neugebauer ("Gladiatorentypus" 7f.) thinks they represented gladiators in fencing position holding swords in both hands. Briguet (supra n. 25) Fig. 2, illustrates an example in a private collection still holding a fragment of an object resembling a cymbal, suggesting that they may have represented musicians. Cf. the example from Boğazköy, showing the two musicians, cited infra n. 42.

31. Examples come from Perugia, Cortona, Arezzo, Volterra, etc.; see Hus 129, n. 4. G. Camporeale (*Etruria Interna* 112, Pls. 36, 37) also attributes to Chiusi, in the north, both the bronze statuettes from Brolio (infra Fig. 39), and the stone torso with kilt from Marciano (infra Fig. 42).

32. Riis, *Tyrrhenika* 164.

33. Luisa Banti (letter of November 1970). Emeline Richardson points out, in her forthcoming book on Etruscan bronzes, that a number of these statuettes are contemporary with female figures whose pointed shoes date them

in the second half of the sixth century, in spite of their archaic appearance and early sixth-century costume (infra Chapter 4, n. 40 and Fig. 96). As Briguet (supra n. 25) points out: "le réalisme naif . . . des *couroi* en font de bons exemples de la production artisanale de l'Etrurie centrale et septentrionale." See also a small bucchero statuette from Tarquinia in Berlin (Hanfmann, *Altetr. Plastik* Fig. 11a), wearing a tiny perizoma without sex sac below a thick belt, whose similarity to the northern bronzes seems due to the primitive style they share.

34. Riis (164) characterizes it as sub-Dedalic. Two specimens exist, one, better preserved, in Florence, the other in Copenhagen. F. Magi published the photographs of the figure in Florence after cleaning (supra n. 28). Magi's Fig. 1 incorrectly shows the pattern of this garment as a short skirt wrapped about the figure.

35. Cf. especially the mantles of the statuette from Rapino (Fig. 128) and of a statuette in the Museo Archeologico in Florence (Fig. 130), infra Chapter 4.

36. For techniques and materials of sewing among the Romans, see Wilson 31.

37. Peruzzi, *Origini* II 72.

38. Limestone statue from Cyprus, in the Metropolitan Museum. New York, Inv. CS 44 (24.51.2479), shown in Myres, *Cesnola Collection* 154 (550–525 B.C.). Even the long hair and the rigid stance of the figures are similar. The Cypriot figure wears a short-sleeved shirt above the perizoma, however, while the Etruscan style is to wear the perizoma alone. G. Camporeale ("Le figurine di Brolio," *BdA* 45 [1960] 193f.) tends to deny the similarity between the Etruscan and the Cypriot model. The rosette on the Cypriot perizoma is traditional. See J. L. Benson, *AJA* 75 (1971) 339, for the rosette and cable on the thigh of male figures in Protoattic vase painting, originally transferred from textile patterns; rosettes continue to be found in this position, or rather on perizomas, throughout the Orientalizing period.

39. Hus 129, with bibliography.

40. The longer, knee-length "Bermuda shorts" may have their earlier counterparts in Cretan models such as those of the acrobat on the sword-handle from Mallia (Marinatos Pl. 69) or the god on the Idaean shield (Kunze No. 74, Pl. 49). Of the latter, J. Boardman (*The Greeks Overseas* [Baltimore 1964] 84) notes that "the god wears non-Oriental (though perhaps Cypriot) bloomers." I disagree with Kunze (224), who calls the belt Oriental.

41. This vase from Monte Abatone, tomb 279, now in the Museo Archeologico at Cerveteri, has not yet been properly published. For references, see infra Notes to Illustrations.

42. For Samos, see D. Ohly, "Frühe Tonfiguren aus dem Heraion von Samos I," *AthMitt* 65 (1940) 63; Demargne Fig. 502. A stone relief from Boğazköy, found in 1957 in the forecourt of the city gate, shows a female divinity with two musicians, who wear the perizoma; see K. Bittel, *Antike Plastik* (1963) 10, and cf. Fig. 4; Akurgal Pls. 56–57. Bittel compares the Cypriot perizoma, ignoring the Samian examples. Actually, the musicians' costume is closer to the Greek or Etruscan than to the Cypriot, since the perizoma is quite plain and worn without a shirt.

43. Hanfmann, *Altetr. Plastik* 21, Figs. 9–10.

44. The same motif exists in three fragmentary examples from the Barberini and Bernardini tombs. The one illustrated, from the Barberini tomb, is in Rome, Museo Villa Giulia, No. 13233 (Curtis, *MAAR* 5 [1925] No. 54). Banti (298, Pl. 26) dates it to the last quarter of the seventh century, while Brown (32f.) places it 675–650 B.C. On the example illustrated two right hands clutching at the lion's mane are still visible.

45. Curtis (*MAAR* 5 [1925] No. 54) identified the group as a victorious lion with several male victims, an identification which has been generally accepted. The motif of a human limb dangling from a lion's mouth is typically Etruscan (P. Bocci, *Studi Banti* 69-79) and may have influenced this representation. But this is a strange position for a victim. In Near Eastern and Egyptian representations, the victorious lion stands over his victim and straddles him menacingly; it does not carry him on his back. See, for example, the ivory from Nimrud in the British Museum with a lioness mauling a Nubian (Frankfort Pl. 169A).

46. Matz, *Kreta, Mykene, Troja* Pl. 21; Marinatos Pl. 14; from a vaulted tomb of Mesara, Early Minoan II to Middle Minoan I, 2300-1900 B.C. The terracotta vase in the form of a bull shows a male figure lying on his back between the horns, while two other figures clutch at the bull's horns on either side. By coincidence or distant influence, this is exactly the original scheme of the Etruscan ivory group, with the "lion-jumper" in the center and a partner on either side grasping the lion's mane. Cf. a bronze bull and acrobatic figure from Crete, wearing the perizoma, in Evans, *PM* III 220, Fig. 155, Middle Minoan III.

47. Barnett S 72, Pls. 42-43, from the Southeast Palace.

48. Banti 298. Poulsen (58, Fig. 58) considered the piece to be Cypriot. Brown (5) feels it is "very likely [among the] imports or works of an immigrant oriental from Syria," and T. Dohrn, in Helbig⁴ 2864, is sure that it is Syrian work, though the treatment of the man, especially in the hair and peculiarities of the lion's mane, speaks against this, as Brown notes.

49. Banti 298. For the hair style, cf. the lion's mane on another locally made, contemporary ivory group with two men and a lion: Helbig⁴ 2867; Banti 296, Pl. 26B, and *Etruscan Cities* 252-253, No. 58c. For the belt, see supra n. 20.

50. Scholars have suggested a variety of origins for it: Ducati (119, Pl. 31, Fig. 106) says Minoan-Mycenean, Poulsen (58) Hittite or Syrian, Brown (4, 32) Syrian, and Huls (52) Egyptian *schenti*. All these elements are present, but the immediate model is Syrian. The pleats are Egyptian: see H. Bonnet, *Die altägyptische Schurztracht* (Leipzig 1916). The form of the short kilt is Cretan: see Bossert, *Altkreta* Pl. 257; Vercoutter Figs. 90-94, 110; but cf. Barnett S 1.

51. Cf. Bonfante Warren, AJA 75 (1971) 277-284.

52. Bronze statuette of a centaur, Hanover, Kestner museum, Inv. 3097, height 11.5 cm., early sixth century B.C., in G. Q. Giglioli, *StEtr* 4 (1930) 360, Pl. 27; von Vacano Pl. 64.

53. See the bronze statuette of Hercules, Berlin, Staatl. Museum, Inv. 7773, late sixth century B.C. E. Galli, "Hereklu," *StEtr* 15 (1941) 27-71, Pl. 6, 1 lists other examples of the type, and cf. Colonna, *Bronzi umbrosabellici* 26, No. 2, Pl. 3. For Hercules and other youths with mantles draped about their loins, see G. A. Mansuelli, *StEtr* 15 (1941) 101, Fig. 1; and Rebuffat-Emmanuel Pl. 46.

54. Vercoutter 252, Fig. 29. It was shaped like a triangular diaper, draped with the short end pulled up between the legs and the longer ends tied over it in front.

55. Romanelli (26) describes this costume as "un giubbetto scuro e corte braghe." The same author calls "perizoma" the garment, probably a mantle, tied about the waist of one of the figures shown fighting on this same right wall; but this is not, strictly speaking, the perizoma. See Brendel, *AJA* 62 (1958) 241, on the nomenclature of Etruscan dress and the inadequacy of such a current expression as *"giubbetto"* for a short chiton; cf. A. Rumpf's review of Pallottino, *Etr. Painting*, in *AJA* 60 (1956) 75.

56. In the Tomba dei Tori, Achilles wears a red perizoma; on the bucchero oinochoe, all three male figures—Theseus, the minotaur, and an

armed hoplite—wear the perizoma. On a Roman bronze oinochoe with Egyptian-style decoration, dancing mimes wear such a perizoma; see infra Chapter 6, n. 22.

57. The five Negro slaves running to the aid of their master wear white or red perizomas; the colors show up brightly against their dark skins.

58. Wall painting from Thebes, Eighteenth Dynasty, Metropolitan Museum photograph (from a painted copy). See also Davies, *Rekh-mi-Re* Pls. 6, 7, 17.

59. See infra Chapter 7, nn. 17, 20. The Ionian fashion, too, was modified by this compromise of Greek perizoma and Eastern shirt.

60. See infra Chapter 7, n. 20.

61. Supra n. 53. The primitive animal-skin perizoma of the Roman *lupercus* can be similarly traced to an early period, in the eighth and seventh century. A. W. J. Holleman ("Ovid and the Lupercalia," *Historia* 22 [1973] 264) misunderstands the implication of the word *nudus*: it means wearing only the perizoma.

3. CHITON AND TUNIC

1. In Homer the term is used only for the costumes of the men, while the women's garment is called *peplos*. When Athena arms herself, she removes her own peplos in order to put on her father's chiton (*Iliad* 5.734). The François vase, on which the women are pictured in the peplos, is often used to illustrate Homeric costume, but the Homeric peplos did not have the same form as the later, Classical peplos (Studniczka 13f. and Bieber 12f.).

2. *RE*, s.v. "chiton," χιτών (Amelung); Daremberg-Saglio, s.v. "tunica" (G. Blum).

3. Ernout-Meillet, s.v. "tunica." Cf. *laena* from χλαῖνα.

4. The Roman form of the tunic was actually the same as the archaic chiton, with the openings for the arms at the sides: see infra Fig. 53.

5. Bronze statuette from Cortona, male figure, Cortona, Mus. dell'Acc. Etr. 1624, ca. 600 B.C.; see Richardson, *MAAR* 27 (1962) 194–195, Figs. 98, 99. On many figures from the Chiusi vases, on the other hand, the garment represented is obviously a cloak fastened at the right shoulder and left open at the sides (Figs. 8, 9); see infra Chapter 4.

6. S. Ferri, in his reconstruction of the Pietrera female statue (Fig. 57), "Tentativo di ricostruz." 442f., misinterprets this seventh-century motif as a cloak which forms a V on the skirt in front. (See infra n. 8 for misunderstanding of the tight-fitting chiton top.) Another characteristic feature of the Dedalic chiton is the stylized curve of the front hem, exposing the feet of the figure: see the bracelet from the Regolini-Galassi tomb, Fig. 56 (cf. Figs. 60, 61, 96, 97).

7. This decoration is often confused with the neckline of the garment (Hus 121). On most statue-busts from Chiusi it appears to represent a necklace with pendant lobes like that of the Vetulonia bust. Cf. Higgins Pl. 39D; Hus 262: "collier ou broderie à languettes pendantes." The first seems more likely: a necklace was a typical ornament of Syrian and Phoenician figures (Hus 121, 213). See B. Segall, *AJA* 60 (1956) 169, Pl. 65, Fig. 13, for a Syrian-type necklace worn dog-collar fashion; Frankfort Fig. 157A, for one with pendant beads (or embroidery?). For an eighth-century B.C. stele from Zinjirli see Bossert, *Altanatolien* No. 953; Frankfort 185.

8. Because the nipples are emphasized and neckline and sleeve edges obscured, the fragmentary torso from Vetulonia has been erroneously described as bare-breasted, as has the bronze bust from the Tomb of Isis, infra Fig. 58 (Richardson 93; Haynes 13ff.; and drawing in Dennis I 460). Camporeale (*StEtr*

35 [1967] 567) correctly describes it as dressed in chiton and back mantle, like the ivory caryatids which inspired it (infra Fig. 63). The convention of showing the nipples or other forms of the body through the garment is not unknown in Etruria: Ferri, "Tentativo di Ricostruz." 445. (Cf. the discussion of the "transparent" chiton skirt, a convention of Greek vase painting, on p. 38.) Nude figures, which rarely appear in early Etruscan art, are mostly direct imitations of Near Eastern figurines: see Hus 262: "L'Étrurie répugne à la représentation de la femme nue, chérie par l'Orient." For examples, see Andrén, *Antike Plastik* 7 (1967) n. 1; Richardson, *MAAR* 21 (1953) 145, Figs. 100-102.

9. For the long-sleeved chiton, see *RE*, s.v. "χειριδωτὸς χιτών" (Amelung).

10. Luisa Banti believes the Monteleone chariot to be later than the statuettes from Brolio because of the seated centaur, a motif found only in the last quarter of the sixth century (*StEtr* 34 [1966] 371-379). Certainly this monument exhibits a mixture of motifs and styles which should be studied further.

11. See the Attic *kore* in the Lyons museum and in Athens, Akropolis museum, ca. 540 B.C. The oldest Attic kore wearing Ionian dress wears a chiton with long, tight sleeves; Payne-Young 14f., Pls. 22-26; Richter, *Korai* 57-58, No. 89, Figs. 275-281 (bibl.). For Near Eastern long-sleeved chitons see Frankfort Pl. 71. For the Mycenean "Warrior vase," in Athens, Nat. Mus., ca. 1200 B.C., see Vermeule 208, Pl. 33B; Matz, *Kreta, Mycene, Troja* Pl. 109; G. Becatti, "Interrogativi sul vaso dei guerrieri di Micene," *Studi Banti* 33-46.

12. See a bronze relief plate found at Olympia in 1957, *Deltion* 17B (1961-62) 107, Pl. 114; G. Daux, *BCH* 84 (1960) 720. See Kunze 227 for references to the "Faltenstil," or representation of folds at this time. Cf. the Gorgon on a relief pithos from Thebes, Boeotia (Paris, Louvre, C.A. 795), representing Perseus and the Gorgon, of the sixth century. Hampe Rl, Pl. 36, 1; Matz 415, 492, Pl. 251.

13. Etruscans always wore their chitons shorter, even the long Ionic chiton of the sixth century. This is why the women's gesture of holding up the long, trailing chitons, so typical of Ionic art, is unnecessary for Etruscan women, and becomes a meaningless convention in Etruscan art.

14. See also a lead plaque for a brooch from the Argive Heraion, probably Laconian, ca. 650 B.C., in Alexandris, *BCH* 88 (1964) 525-530. Lorimer (358) attributes the three-quarter-length chiton on the Olympia cuirass and on some Melian amphorae—an exception to the usual short chiton of the men—to Near Eastern influence. It was often represented together with the "*Etagenperücke*" style, or with hair hanging loose over the shoulders: see Poulsen 148. This chiton length is normal in Asia Minor and the Near East; see, for example, a stone relief from the palace of Sennacherib at Nineveh, ca. 700 B.C., British Museum, in *BMMA* 13 (1955) 240, and Frankfort, Pl. 98. In the first centuries of the Christian era it still appears on statues of princes of South Arabia: see L. Legrain, *AJA* 38 (1934) 329-337; Pritchard 65, 66.

15. Several archaic figures wearing this three-quarter-length chiton have recently been reinterpreted, thus clearing up some of the previous confusion as to its identification. B. S. Ridgway (*AJA* 69 [1965] 3, Pls. 1-2) explains the central figure on the pediment of the Siphnian treasury at Delphi as Zeus, not, as was formerly thought, Athena. In Greek art the men's Ionic chiton was, as she points out, usually shorter than the women's. Jucker, in *Art and Technology* 199, Fig. 6, publishes a statuette from Populonia, in the Museo Archeologico in Florence, also previously interpreted as female; but the knee-length "minichiton" is too short for a woman, and the shoulder-length hairstyle is that of Ionian kouroi. He therefore identifies the figure as male and dates it ca. 530 B.C. A scene on the lid of a seventh-century cinerary urn from Montescudaio, also in Florence, has recently been reconstructed by F. Nicosia, *StEtr* 37 (1969) 369-401,

with interesting results. The small attendant figure is now definitely proved to be a female by the long braid hanging down the back (387, Pls. 93C, 94B). The faulty restoration had led most scholars to consider the figure a man (except for H. Jucker, *Kunst und Leben d. Etr.* [Cologne 1956] 37, No. 12, Fig. 2; followed by Pallottino, in *Mostra* 7–8, No. 14, Pl. 4).

16. For the procession frieze, see T. Gantz, *RM* 81 (1974) 1–14; for the banquet, J. P. Small, *StEtr* 39 (1971) 25–61. Timothy Gantz' identification (*StEtr* 39 [1971] 3–24) of the seated figures as divinities, holding their attributes, makes sense. The seated personage with *lituus* could be Jupiter. I do not, however, see the figure behind him as Jupiter's child Minerva. Minerva, a warrior goddess, does of course wear men's clothes; but the servile position of this figure, standing in attendance behind the master, and its smaller size do not seem to fit such an important goddess. The shorter, unbelted chiton characterizes a male attendant. I would suggest husband with male attendant, wife with female attendant, then the group of three male figures with male attendant. The sarcophagus from Vulci in the Boston Museum (Fig. 85) shows the standard grouping of husband with male attendants and wife with female attendants. See *Poggio Civitate* 53–61, pls. 36–39, and J. MacIntosh, *RM* 81 (1974) 15–40, for the furniture. I have discussed the interpretation of the second figure from the right in *JRS* 60 (1970) 60, n. 69; cf. O.-W. von Vacano, "Vulca, Rom und die Wölfin," *ANRW* I₄ 537; M. Cristofani, *Prospettiva* I (1975) 9–17; Pfiffig, *Religio etrusca* 36. Neither Cristofani nor Pfiffig believe that the figures represent divinities. Cristofani suggests a family group: the master, his wife (the couple of the procession frieze), and other members of the family seated behind them. For the difficulty in distinguishing representations of men and gods from their costumes, see my article in *AJA* 75 (1971) 280–282.

The armchair of "Juno" is used by men and women: see infra Fig. 2. See the discussion in Prayon (infra Appendix I, n. 11).

17. Hus (128) calls the garment on one of the fragments of male statues from Vetulonia (Hus No. 12) a short chiton, rather than a perizoma. On this short tunic ("maillot-tunique") and its history, see Hus 128–129, with bibliography.

18. The monument is so close to Eastern models that it was at one time thought to be the work of an Oriental artist. See Poulsen 129 and cf. Gjerstad, *Swed. Cyprus Exp.* IV 2, 128, Fig. 41; Huls 137–139, 210; and Brown 32. Cf. the lion-jumper from the Barberini tomb infra Chapter 2, Fig. 43.

19. Brommer, *Vasenlisten* 226ff., with additions by D. von Bothmer, *AJA* 61 (1957) 109; C. Dugas and R. Flacelière, *Thésée, images et récits* (Paris 1958).

20. The figure is heavily restored, however.

21. Richardson 129; see the discussion of Hercules in Chapter 2, n. 53.

22. The representation of the short chiton was influenced by the change in style: see, for example, the pouch at the waist of the chitons on the Loeb tripod. A. E. Akurgal (*Schriften zur Kunst des Altertums, Arch Inst d. deutsches Reichs* [Berlin 1942] III 112) calls this pouch an Ionian characteristic. Cf. infra Fig. 67, a relief from Isinda in Lycia. R. Ross Holloway points to an instance of an artist's "modernizing" the representation of the short chiton by adding stacked folds in "The Reworking of the Gorgon Metope of Temple C at Selinus," *AJA* 75 (1971) 435–436.

23. Represented for perhaps the first time in Etruscan art in one of the Boccanera slabs in the British Museum, representing the Judgment of Paris: Hera pulls up the material of her outer chiton, modestly letting the pleated

Ionian chiton hang free; Aphrodite bares her legs to the knee: Roncalli 61, 72. See also T. Gantz, *StEtr* 39 (1971) 11, n. 27.

24. Louisa Bellinger's drawing (Fig. 53) illustrates how such a type was woven all in one piece, with the sleeves and neck opening already formed on the loom. Cf. Richter, *Sculpture* 88f.; Bieber, *AA* (1973) 433, with refs.

25. Bieber *AA* (1973) 427, 430–434, Figs. 4, 10 (from a vase by Makron, on which the chiton has a peplos-like overfold).

26. The earliest appearance of these points at the elbow seems to be on the Loeb tripods (infra Figs. 76–80). In Greek art they appear ca. 530 B.C. on the Ionic chiton of a seated divinity of the frieze of the Siphnian Treasury at Delphi (Richter, *Sculpture* Fig. 419), and in South Italy, on one of the Ionian-inspired metopes from the larger temple of the Heraion at the Foce del Sele, in the Paestum Museum: P. Zancani Montuoro and U. Zanotti Bianco, *Heraion alla Foce del Sele* I (Rome 1951) Pls. 55–59.

27. For the change to the Ionic chiton as represented on Etruscan monuments, see Banti, *StEtr* 28 (1960) 277ff. 285. On a relief from Chiusi (infra Fig. 101), the lower pleated edge represents the edge of an Ionic chiton worn under the Dedalic model.

28. Riis, *Tyrrhenika* 172: "On the background of the receptivity of the Etruscan artists in archaic times, the tenacity of the ancient types and the infrequent occurrence of new types in the subsequent period is remarkable."

29. Riis, *Tyrrhenika* 172. Richardson 104, Fig. 246.

30. Roncalli 61.

31. Bonfante Warren, *AJA* 75 (1971) 279–280. To the bibliography, add Banti, "Div. fem. a Creta" 26; Schefold, *JdI* 49 (1934) 32f.

32. See an ivory statuette from Asia Minor, Berlin, Staatl. Mus., ca. 575 B.C., in A. Greifenhagen, *JBerl Mus* 7 (1965) 125–156; K. Schefold, *Propyläen* I, 167–168, No. 32, Fig. 7. Bonfante Warren, *Brendel Studies*, discusses a statuette in the Istanbul museum considered the earliest representation of the Ionic chiton (Lorimer 353, Pl. 29, 1; Matz Pl. 702, "ca. 650"); though Akurgal (210–211) has shown that, in spite of the statuette's Dedalic elements, the costume cannot be earlier than ca. 570–560. See Boardman, 43–45, Pls. 38–41: "580–570 B.C.; the earliest of the chiton-korai by Ionian artists." These korai wear a thin chiton but not the diagonally draped mantle which forms part of the new Ionic "outfit" in Athens: see infra Chapter 4, n. 18. Cf. a bronze relief plate from Olympia, in the Olympia museum, showing Orestes killing Klytemnestra, and Theseus and Antiope, ca. 570 B.C., in G. Daux, *BCH* 84 (1960) 720, Pl. 18, 2; K. Schefold, *Frügr. Sagenbilder* (Munich 1964) Pl. 80. For the controversy as to the priority of the Near Eastern (e.g., Phrygian) or Ionian form of costume, with veil tucked in at the waist, see Akurgal 56; K. Bittel, *Antike Plastik* 2 (1963) 9f.; B. Goldman, supra, Introduction, n. 7.

33. Herodotus (5.87) explains the change from the woolen peplos pinned at the shoulders to a sewn linen chiton as a result of the war with Aegina and Argos. Unfortunately, the date of this war is very uncertain: see T. J. Dunbabin, *BSA* 39 (1936–1937) 83–91, who thinks that "it is unlikely the change of dress is rightly associated with this defeat." In fact there are two changes involved, the one from sewn chiton to pinned peplos occurring much earlier—long bronze dress pins (*peronai*) appear in the proto-Geometric period; see J. N. Coldstream, *Greek Geometric Pottery* (London 1968) 339; cf. 361; and M. S. F. Hood and J. N. Coldstream, *BSA* 63 (1968) 210–212, Fig. 4. (I am grateful to Evelyn Harrison for discussing this with me.) The later change from pinned garment to chiton, which took place gradually, was completed at the same time as the

change from black- to red-figure vase painting: See Richter, *Red-Fig. Vases* 39, 174, n. 8; Rumpf, *Chalk. Vas.* 134; Langlotz, *Zeitbestimmung* 28–31; van Ufford, *Terrescuites sicilennes* 20; Payne-Young 16; Richter, *Korai* 9–10.

34. For the gesture of holding out a fold of the skirt, see Riis, *Tyrrhenika* 170f.; Ducati, *Pontische Vasen* 11, nn. 22–23; Richardson 124. The "transparent" chiton appears in a tomb painting from the Tomba del Colle at Chiusi (but these are heavily overpainted, as Luisa Banti informs me) and in a relief, also from Chiusi. The relief preserves traces of blue on the "jacket"; on the painting, the jacket is red with a blue border. See Duell 23. Johnstone, *Dance in Etr.*, discusses the dancer in the Tomba delle Leonesse, Tarquinia, 530–520. For the dancer in the Tomba dei Giocolieri at Tarquinia, see Banti[2] Pl. 35.

35. Richter, *Red-Fig. Vases* 62, 83, Fig. 63: this is typical of the style of Euthymides, or of Makron. See L. Lawler ("The Maenads: A Contribution to the Study of the Dance in Ancient Greece," *MAAR* 6[1927] 86) on the problem of the representation of transparent garments on vases, and Richter (*Sculpture* 100) on the transparent chitons of later fifth-century sculpture. See supra Chapter 1.

36. On the dancer's *ependytes*, see list and discussion in B. Neutsch, *AA* 71 (1956) 413, and cf. Duell 23. Other examples of the ependytes (or overgarment) worn by *crotalistrae* or castanet-playing dancers in late archaic Etruscan art of the early fifth century are a bronze mirror from Bomarzo, in Gerhard 98 (cf. 99); a black-figure vase, in R. Herbig, *StEtr* 7 (1933) 359, Pl. 17, 5; cf. *AA* 71 (1956) 414, n. 378; a wall painting from the Tomba del Colle, Chiusi (red ependytes with blue border over "transparent" skirt), in Pallottino, *Etr. Painting* 66, 131; also from Chiusi, a relief from a funerary cippus, evidently copied from the former, in *Mostra* No. 275, Pl. 49; Greek ependytes portrayed on a castanet-playing maenad on a vase by the Andokides Painter, in D. von Bothmer, *BMMA* 24 (1965–66) 201–212 Figs. 4, 11; see also Lawler, *MAAR* 6 (1927) 85; a terracotta architectual sculpture (antefix) from Paestum, fragmentary, also representing a maenad, ca. 500 B.C., in A. W. Van Buren, *AJA* 58 (1954) 325, Pl. 67, Fig. 3; B. Neutsch, *AA* 1956, 413f., Fig. 137; P. C. Sestieri, *BdA* 48 (1963) 212–220, color pl. 2; M. Gj⊘desen, in *Art and Technology* 159, Figs. 28–29.

37. Richardson Pl. 43. Emeline Richardson first drew attention to its special significance (Richardson 134). Other examples, worn with pointed shoes, are cited infra Chapter 5, nn. 26–28. Cf. the group which Sybille Haynes dates to the late fourth century (*Art and Technology* 187); and G. Muffati, *StEtr* 37 (1969) 264–266, Pl. 55. The chiton of the female figure, so thin that the nipples show through, would seem to place the bronze candelabrum group from Marzabotto around 400 rather than 450 B.C., as it is dated by S. Doeringer and G. M. A. Hanfmann, "An Etruscan Bronze Warrior in the Fogg Museum," *StEtr* 35 (1967) 645–653, Pl. 141. An examination of the costumes of the figures studied in this article confirms the authors' conclusions: of the three groups compared with the Fogg statuette, this group from Marzabotto, in which the woman wears the characteristic Etruscan tassel, is indeed Etruscan; the others, wearing more normal Greek dress, show South Italian influence.

An interesting modification can be seen on a bronze statuette of Athena (Minerva?) of this date in the Berlin Museum, Inv. 3964 (Richardson Pl. 246, with bibliography) wearing an archaizing peplos, its overfold modified into a kind of aegis, and such "antique" touches as a rising hemline over the feet in front and a patterned zone down the front of the skirt. Although when seen from the front the figure seems to wear such tassels, from the side one can see that the artist has rendered in this way two locks of hair emerging from the helmet. Evidently a divine figure was at this time expected to wear these honorific tassels. In order to remain true to his archaizing model, however, the artist "explained" the tassels by making them look like locks of hair.

Some figures on Etruscan urns appear to combine the fourth-century tassel with the high belted Hellenistic chiton: see Laviosa, *Sc. Volterra* 42, 51(?); Florence. Museo Archeologico, Inv. 5511.

38. Sprenger 69–70; M. Cristofani, "La 'Mater Matuta' di Chianciano," *Nuove letture* 87–94, Pls. 45–51.

39. These funerary representations may show the deceased in "idealized" costume rather than ordinary, everyday dress, as seems to be the case with the male figure appearing together with the lady with tassels on the Vulci sarcophagus (infra Fig. 85): see Pallottino, *Etruscologia* 336. For the himation as "heroic" dress, see my article in *AJA* 75 (1971) 282–284. An idealized Hellenistic portrait figure of a man on an urn from Volterra (Laviosa, *Sc. Volterra* 39, Inv. No. 119) is bare-breasted, in contrast to his colleagues, who wear a chiton under the mantle. See also the couple from Chianciano (infra Fig. 159) and a bronze statue in Leningrad, published by Alexandra J. Vostchinina, "Statua-cinerario in bronzo di arte etrusca," *StEtr* 33 (1965) 317–328; Bianchi Bandinelli-Giuliano (294, Fig. 338) date it ca. 300 B.C.; infra Chapter 6, n. 98.

40. Richardson 169–170. On the difficulty of dating material from the fourth to the first centuries B.C., see my article on "A Latin Triumph on a Praenestine Cista," in *AJA* 68 (1964) 35ff., and *Roma Medio Repubblicana* 3ff. and *passim*. A rare example of a dated portrait is that of the sarcophagus of Larthia Seianta, dated by a coin to around 150 B.C.: *NSc* (1877) 142.

41. For the torque, see infra Chapter 6, n. 98; for the diadem, especially a lunate tiara, see Richardson 169, Pl. 47B, and Bieber, *Entwicklungsgeschichte* Pls. 39, 41. For "body jewelry," see Laviosa, *Sc. Volterra* Nos. 41, 48, 51, Pls. 33, 11, 50, 15.

42. For "local color" on cistae and mirrors, see Dorothy K. Hill, unpublished paper delivered at a symposium on Etruscan Art at the Worcester Art Museum, Worcester, Mass., May 1967.

43. For Hellenistic urns, see A. Piganiol, *Recherches sur les jeux romains* (Paris 1923) ch. 3, "Le décor théatral d'après les reliefs des urnes étrusques," 32.f.; P. Mingazzini, "Su una fonte d'ispirazione dei rilievi di alcune urne etrusche," *Archaeologia. Scritti in onore di Aldo Neppi Modona* (Florence 1975) 387–393. For mirrors, see O. Vessberg, *Medelhavsmuseet Bull.* 4 (1964) 62: "The source of the inspiration is the classical stage." Other references are collected by J. P. Small, "Aeneas and Turnus on Late Etruscan Funerary Urns," *AJA* 78 (1974) 49–54 (who erroneously, however, takes the Pasinati cista to be genuine).

44. Laviosa, *Sc. Volterra* 104, No. 19, Pl. 41. Cf. infra Chapter 4, note 56. For an isolated and puzzling instance of long sleeves on a terracotta statuette, see F. Johansen, "Cinque figure fittili etrusche," *StEtr* 34 (1966) 381–383; *Mostra* No. 346, Pl. 68. Johansen dates these figures at the beginning of the first century B.C. The authenticity of the male figure, the so-called Negro, as well as the female figures, is doubted ("n.d. Redattore" to Johansen's article). Bianchi Bandinelli-Giuliano 376–377.

A bronze mirror in the British Museum (Gerhard 389), apparently of the fourth century, shows a male figure wearing a most interesting costume: a kind of plaid underwear, the long sleeves and knee-length pants of which appear below his chiton. He wears a helmet and chlamys and is adjusting his greaves, while Athena comforts him with a hand on his shoulder and a winged Nike or Lasa looks on. Is he a soldier going off to war, wearing warm clothing? The knee-length pants are like those worn by Roman soldiers on the frieze of the column of Trajan, the warm *feminalia* Augustus also wore (Suet. *Aug.* 82).

45. Otto J. Brendel, "Der grosse Fries in der Villa dei Misteri," *JdI* 81 (1969) 232; Mingazzini (supra n. 43) 387, n. 2. Cf. the Siren on a tomb at

Sovana, published by Joseph Carter, *AJA* 78 (1974) 136, n. 33. F. De Ruyt long ago (*Charun, démon étrusque de la mort*, Brussels 1934) identified this figure as Vanth, rather than Lasa, as she is often called. See F. De Ruyt, review of G. R. Orsolini, *Il mito dei sette a Tebe nelle urne Volterrane* (Florence 1971), in *AntCl* 41 (1972) 768–769.

46. Harris; Pfiffig, *Einführung* 42–56.

47. J. Heurgon ("La place de Rome dans la *koiné* étrusco-romano-campanienne," paper read at the *Colloquio su Roma medio-repubblicana*, Rome, April 1973) interprets a fourth-century inscription from the Tomba Golini in Orvieto (*TLE* 233) in which a man is called *lecate*, and lists among his honors that he has held this title *Rumitrini* "at Rome," "among the Romans," as showing that at this date, a noble Etruscan was proud of his title of *legatus* and his connection with Rome. In such a context, the wearing of the toga might also take on similar honorable connotations as Roman symbolic costume.
The decoration of the François tomb can be understood as a cycle celebrating the triumph of Vel Sathies over the Romans (F. Zevi). For triumphal statues and paintings, see M. Torelli, "Il Donario di M. Fulvio Flacco nell'area di S. Omobono," *Studi di Topografia Romana* (Rome 1968) 71–75; *Roma Medio Repubblicana* 103–104, No. 89, Fig. 10.

48. Richardson 167, "ca. 100 B.C."; T. Dohrn with M. Pallottino, "Nota sull'iscrizione dell'Arringatore," *BdA* 49 (1964) 115–116; Dohrn, *Arringatore* and review by D. K. Hill in *AJA* 74 (1970) 116–117, "90–80 B.C."

49. Cf. a beautifully colored example in the British Museum, an Etruscan terracotta cinerary urn from Chiusi, of the Hellenistic period (D795). On the cover, the figure of the dead man wears a tunic with bright red stripes and a bordered mantle. Inscribed *"thane ancapui thelesa;"* second century B.C.(?)

50. Richardson 167.

51. For the Roman triumphal "tunica palmata," which originally had a border one handspan, or *palma*, in width, according to Festus (s.v.), see my article on "A Latin Triumph on a Praenestine Cista," in *AJA* 68 (1964) 37; and also *ANRW* I₄ 610, 614; it probably derived from Etruscan dress.

4. MANTLES

1. The right arm emerges in a traditional gesture of mourning, with the hand held to the head: cf. Poulsen, *Etr. Paintings* 11. Sometimes the arm does not emerge, and the mantle seems to muffle the figure entirely.

2. Dohan 203–204. Bronze and iron pins and brooches or fibulae are found in eighth- and seventh-century graves, often still in place on the skeleton, where they were fastened on the garment when the dead man or woman was laid in the grave. Their use is thus often clear. See, e.g., C. Hopkins, "Syracuse, Etruria and the North: Some Comparisons," *AJA* 62 (1958) 259–272, who studies the metal objects from graves at Syracuse dating from the eighth century to ca. 600 B.C. when, he notes, metal objects become extremely rare. This last observation fits in with our awareness that a change of dress style occurs in the early sixth century, and that mantles are then more likely to be draped than pinned. On the three terracotta statuettes from Cerveteri the brooches, reproduced in clay and originally silver-colored (Figs. 14–16), are of a type characteristic of the seventh century, the "comb fibula": see Higgins Pl. 38B. Gold specimens of the "comb fibula" type have been found in seventh-century contexts: see Curtis, *MAAR* 3 (1919), 22f., Pls. 4–5; *MAAR* 5 (1925) 17f., Pls. 2 (16), 3(1–4). Another type, also dating from the seventh century, with several long narrow tubes coming out at right angles from a central bar, is known to us from several examples; one (Higgins Pls. 38A, B.M.

1371) was found at Caere in the same tomb where the three statuettes wearing this type of brooch sat on rock-cut chairs. See infra Appendix I. For a silver specimen recently found in Vetulonia, see *StEtr* 25 (1957) Fig. 17. Other provenances are Praeneste, Villa Giulia No. 13211 (*Mostra* No. 114, Pl. 24), and the Campagna, B. M. 1370. See also P. Marconi, *MonAnt* 35 (1935) 317.

3. Plaid mantles represented on travelers of the eighth and seventh century are seen in the proto-Attic vase in the Metropolitan Museum, New York: see B. Schweitzer, *Greek Geometric Art* (London 1971) 47, 49ff., Fig. 51; and in a terracotta statuette from Jordan found at Tell es-Saidiyeh in 1967 (J. Pritchard, *Expedition* 10 [1968] 26-29).

4. See infra Chapter 6 for the back braid. Ferri ("Tentativo di ricostruz.") erroneously reconstructs the mantle of the fragmentary bust from Vetulonia as covering the lower part of the body in front. For brooches at each shoulder, originally perhaps fastening such a mantle, in seventh-century tombs, see C. Hopkins, *AJA* 62 (1958) 261, 263.

5. See infra Chapter 6.

6. The figure has often been dated much earlier: in the seventh century by Solari (101, Fig. 28), and ca. 600 B.C. by Goldscheider (No. 80); more correctly, in *Mostra* (No. 79, Pl. 17), to ca. 550 B.C.

7. M. Gjødesen, "Greek Bronzes. A Review Article," *AJA* 67 (1963) 335f., a review of Charbonneaux, *Br. grecs*. Note the long nose of the figure and "primitive" or provincial elements, such as the large hands. Cf. Joffroy, *Vix*; P. Amandry, *RA* 43 (1954) 125-140; A. Rumpf, "Krater Lakonikos," in *Charites, Festschrift E. Langlotz* (Bonn 1957) 127-135.

8. Gjødesen (340), citing comparisons with Corinthian works of the early sixth century, assigns the statuettes from the Vix crater to a date ca. 575 B.C. and to a Corinthian workshop. Corinthian influence in this period is ubiquitous, however and cannot be used as evidence for establishing exact date or origins. See G. Colonna, "La ceramica etrusco-corinzia . . . ," *ArchCl* 23 (1963) 24: "problema destinato a restare in sospeso è quello del rinnovato influsso corinzio in Etruria nel secondo quarto del VI secolo a. C."

9. Greek metope relief from Selinus, Palermo, Mus. Naz., Europa on the bull, ca. 540 B.C., in Kähler, *Metopenbild* 97, Pl. 22. On this capelet, see Bonfante Warren, *Studi Banti* 81-87; add now Canciani 124-125. On a bronze statuette in Naples, Mus. Naz. Inv. 5543, this Dedalic mantle is worn with the panel decoration of the chiton skirt, in Colonna, *Bronzi umbro-sabellici* 142, No. 429, Pl. 103.

10. The representation, which is, of course, very stylized, might simply not show the folds which would form on the shoulders and upper arms. Greek himatia were sometimes draped about the neck and formed this pattern in front; see e.g., a bronze statuette from Olympia showing an old man with a staff, late sixth century B.C., in R. Hampe, U. Jantzen, *Olympia-Bericht, JdI* (1937) 77, Pl. 22, Fig. 39. Cf. a Laconian statuette in *Propyläen* I, 42A, B; also Apollo and the Berlin maiden in Richter, *Sculpture* Figs. 267-269. Luisa Banti (*StEtr* 28 [1960] 248, nn. 30, 34) compares the fashion to triangular mantles for men represented on Greek monuments; see, e.g., the François vase (Furtwängler-Reichhold II 13; drawings in Tilke 51, Figs. 87-88) and the Moschophoros from the Acropolis (Payne-Young Pl. 2). Cf. Roncalli 71, n. 1.

Emeline Richardson suggests that the mantle consisted of a long rectangle with added panels (cf. infra Fig. 61): "it appears in a perfectly readable form on too many . . . little votive bronzes to be a misunderstanding of a Greek himation with the corners pulled over the shoulders" (letter to the author, September 1970).

11. Cf. Huls No. 58, Pl. 25, Fig. 2; the female figure on the Monteleone chariot (infra Fig. 61); and a bronze plaque from Castellina in Chianti (Ducati

207; Krauskopf 14–17, Pl. 1). Huls erroneously ascribes this point to another figure on the relief from Castellina in Chianti.

12. See Beazley, *Dev.* 46, with reference to an amphora by Lydos (Pl. 46 *top*); the motif disappears in Greece after 550 B.C. Cf. Banti, *StEtr* 28 (1960) 282, n. 27, and examples in Gjødesen, *AJA* 67 (1963) 335, Figs. 7, 14.

13. For this gesture, which is found from the seventh century on, see Beazley, *Dev.* 24; Roncalli 73, n. 5. It occurs on the figure of Hera on a plaque from Poggio Civitate; see T. Gantz, *StEtr* 39 (1971) 11–12; infra Fig. 72.

14. *Tebenna*, τήβεννος, τήβεννα ("*toga*"); τηβεννοφόρος ("*togatus*"); -εννα is an Etruscan ending. The Greek word, regularly used in referring to the Roman toga, is probably a transliteration of the Etruscan name for the rounded mantle; it first occurs in Polybius (10.4.8, 26.10.6) who seems to have learned in Italy, and taken to Greece, the original name. The Romans, who adopted this Etruscan garment for their own use, soon gave it a Latin name, *toga*, and forgot its origin: see Artemid. Dald. *Oneirocrit.*, who said it was named after its Arcadian inventor, Temenos.

Varro, in Non. 867 L: "Praeterea quod in lecto togas habebant; ante enim olim fuit commune vestimentum et diurnum et nocturnum et muliebre et virile." He obviously derives the word toga from *tego*, "to cover," and perhaps refers to the Etruscan custom, which seemed strange to a Greek or Roman, of showing men and women reclining together, "under the same blanket," as Aristotle is quoted as saying (*Ath.* 1.23d). See Heurgon, 100ff.; Bonfante Warren, *Arethusa* 6 (1973) 91–101 and *Archaeology* 26 (1973) 242–249.

15. The custom of covering the couple under a single mantle seems to derive from the symbolism of the marriage ceremony, represented in relief on a cippus from Chiusi; see Pallottino, *Etruscologia* 325, Pl. 68; Giglioli 142.

16. Fig. 106 represents one of a group of figures resembling in dress and pose the male "togati." See the female figure in the Louvre, close to the bronze from Isola di Fano (Fig. 107), in de Ridder No. 240, "Aphrodite, from South Italy, beginning of the fifth century." See also L. Banti, *StEtr* 16 (1942) Pl. 33, Figs. 3–4. There are a number of similar examples, listed by Richardson, *MAAR* 21 (1953) 117, n. 168, Fig. 40, and T. Dohrn, in Helbig⁴ 701 (where the reference to C. Albizzati, "Un'ambra scolpita d'arte Ionica nella Raccolta Morgan," *Rassegna d'Arte* 19 [1919] 183–200 should be corrected). As Dohrn points out, the closest model for these statuettes is a male figure, an Ionian statuette, E. Buschor, *Altsamische Standbilder* (Berlin 1934–1935) III, Figs. 160–162. Were these Etruscan female figures in fact shown wearing male dress?

17. See D. Haynes, "Mors in Victoria," *BSR* 15 (1939) 29–30, with refs., for the rounded tebenna worn on horseback. Richardson, *MAAR* 21 (1953) 112f. (Cloelia).

18. See the Ionian terracotta statuettes from Rhodes wearing, over a short-sleeved chiton, a mantle covering the shoulder and right breast, in Greifenhagen, *Staatl. Mus.* 43, Inv. 30732, 30733, Pl. 35. Cf. the British Museum terracottas Nos. 1610 and 1617, made in Rhodes, found at Vulci. Athens, Nat. Mus. D. Ohly, *AM* 66 (1941) 28f., Nos. 387, 748, Pls. 25–27; Matz 166, Pl. 76; W. Darsow, *Festschrift für A. Rumpf* (Krefeld 1952) 43f.; Helga Herdejürgen, *Untersuchungen zur thronenden Göttin aus Tarent in Berlin und zur archaisch und archaistischen Schrägmanteltracht* (Waldsassen-Bayern 1968) 37, n. 188.

For a female figure on a seventh-century painted stamnos from Lemnos, see infra Fig. 164: Della Seta, "Lemno" 644, Fig. 4; Riis, *Tyrrhenika* 174; Banti, *StEtr* 28 (1960) 282, n. 31. There are also a number of earlier Near Eastern models: see Moortgat 35, Pls. 61, 63, 93–94, 96, 99–100 (women); Pl. 153 (Naramsin). For cloaks of a Semitic caravan, both women's and men's, pictured on Egyptian paintings, see P. Newberry, *Beni Hasan* (London 1893) tomb 3, 31, details.

19. Richardson, *MAAR* 27 (1962) 110ff., and "Libation-Bearer." The author places the series in northern Etruria.

20. *Mostra* No. 254, Pl. 42, 530–510 B.C. Emeline Richardson would date it ca. 500 B.C. H. Jucker ("Etruscan Votive Bronzes of Populonia," in *Art and Technology* 207) says: "we see from the Greek style that it can hardly have been made before 520 B.C." He adds, "its rustic nature is not a matter of its date but of the place where it was made." Luisa Banti agrees with the latter remark, and would accordingly date it well within the fifth century (conversation with the author). G. Hafner ("Etruskische Togati," *Antike Plastik* 9 [1969] 23–45) collects a number of later statuettes of this type, but does not always recognize the difference between togati and palliati; see the review by R. Winkes in *AJA* 75 (1971); Bieber, "*Romani Palliati*"; and K. Polaschek, *Untersuchungen zu griechischen Mantelstatuen. Der Himationtypus mit Armschlinge* (Berlin 1969). For a recently published bronze togatus in Cleveland, see J. D. Cooney, *Bulletin of the Cleveland Museum of Art* 58 (1971) 213–215: "520–500 B.C. . . . but a date a few decades later is possible."

21. Pliny *HN* 34.11.23 (see notes in Sellers' ed.). Cf. Asc. on Cic., *Pro Scaur.* 30; Pallottino, *Etruscologia* 336. Richardson (129; cf. 134) points out that in the early period, the toga with tunic was characteristic of Etruscan (never of Greek) divine figures, such as the Zeus of the Pyrgi group and the Apollo of Veii; but see B. S. Ridgway, *AJA* 69 (1965) 3.

22. Roncalli 20–22, No. 5, Pl. 5.

23. Mazzarino 69–75; in contrast, see Banti 315f., Pl. 52; M. Pallottino, *StEtr* 20 (1947) 321–326. Cf. P. de Francisci, "Intorno all'origine etrusca del concetto di 'imperium,'" *StEtr* 24 (1955–56) 19f., with previous literature; T. Gantz, *StEtr* 39 (1971) 3–24. For the calcei repandi, see infra Chapter 5.

24. The folding stool, the ancestor of the Roman *sella curulis*, is the Greek δίφρος ὀκλαδίας (used by Athena; see infra Fig. 115 and cf. 78). See Banti 299 and Pl. 28; Richter, *Anc. Furn.* 37f., 107, Figs. 109–121, 155, 160; *NSc* 1915, 83. Judges at funeral games are equipped the same way, e.g., the judge in the Tomba degli Auguri followed by a servant lad carrying his folding stool.

For other judges at funeral games, see Levi, *Mus. Chiusi* No. 2284, Fig. 17a; Banti Pl. 104; Heurgon 258. On the *lituus*, see T. Gantz, *StEtr* 39 (1971) 8–9. A. Ernout (*Philologica* II [Paris 1957] 234) says "Etruscan word?" Though none of the literary sources explicitly claim an Etruscan source for the *lituus*, archeological monuments from Etruria show its origin to be there. It appears on archaic reliefs of the later sixth century and early fifth century, and a votive or funerary model has recently been found in a tomb in Cerveteri (Rome, Villa Giulia Museum; see *Arte e civiltà degli Etruschi* 14, Pl. 2, early sixth century). Eventually, it developed into the pastoral staff or crozier.

25. For the use of this fashion on sacrificing figures of emperors of the first and second centuries, see H. Oehler, "Eine kleine Beobachtung—Zur Diskussion Gestellt," *Opus Nobile. Festschrift Ulf Jantzen*, ed. P. Zazoff (Wiesbaden 1969) 121–124; H. G. Niemeyer, *Studien zur statuarischen Darstellung der römischen Kaiser. Monumenta Artis Romanae* 7 (Berlin 1968) 101ff., 107ff.; and review of Niemeyer by G. Koeppel, *AJA* 75 (1971) 229–230. Another good example is in A. M. McCann, "Portraits of Septimius Severus," *MAAR* 30 (1968) 162, No. 62b, Pl. 63, "mid-second century."

26. See the relief from Chianciano, "Cippo Barracco," in Bianchi Bandinelli, "Clusium" Fig. 81, and the bronze statuette of Hermes, Paris, Louvre, in de Ridder Pl. 24, No. 269, infra Fig. 119.

27. Cf. also an Etruscan black-figure hydria attributed to the Micali painter, ca. 520 B.C., in von Bothmer, *Anc. Art* No. 261, Pl. 96; the bronze relief plaque from Bomarzo, Vatican, Mus. Greg., Alinari 35611, in G. Bovini, *StEtr* 15 (1941) 73–79, and in Ryberg 12, Fig. 6; and a Pontic amphora, in de Ridder No. 178.

28. The draping of the himation across the shoulders in back is far more frequent, see, e.g., the Attic red-figure kylix by the Panaitios painter in the Boston Museum of Fine Arts, Inv. 00.499, in Pfuhl Fig. 409. For this reason, no doubt, G. M. A. Richter (*Perspective in Greek and Roman Art* [Phaidon 1970] 22, Fig. 83) misunderstands the figure of a dancer in the Tomba del Vecchio at Tarquinia, who wears the mantle front to back. The figure is no more distorted than that of Zeus on a Chalcidian hydria in Munich; see Rumpf, *Chalk. Vas.* 12, No. 10, Pl. 25, Arias-Hirmer color plate. Examples in Greek sculpture are rare. The fashion closest to the Etruscan mode occurs on a male nude figure from the sanctuary of Artemis Orthia at Sparta; see Dawkins, *Artemis Orthia* 275, Fig. 127 (drawing), p. 198, 17 (photographs), 600–500 B.C. Cf. a marble kore, 520–510, in D. M. Brinkerhoff, "Greek and Etruscan Art in the Rhode Island School of Design," *Archaeology* 11 (1958) 152. The fashion is illustrated especially on black- and red-figure vase paintings of the last third of the sixth century. See the black-figure amphora from Gela, Syracuse, Mus. Arch. Naz., Sopr. Ant. Photo No. 4670 B; cf. the black-figure plate attributed to Psiax, in Richter, *Red-Fig. Vases* 47, Fig. 36. The Attic red-figure kylix in the Vatican museum has on the reverse Aeneas and Anchises; see Pareti No. 522a, Pl. 65. See also a red-figure amphora by Andokides in the Louvre, in von Bothmer *Amazons* 149, No. 34. Most of these vases come from Sicily and southern Italy—Gela, Syracuse, Taranto (and see the Chalcidian hydria mentioned above). Possibly the fashion was favored in Italy and Greek vase painters were satisfying a special taste, for export to Italy. See T. B. L. Webster, *Potter and Patron in Classical Athens* (London 1972) 291–292.

29. Jacques Heurgon (218 and n.) has adopted the name *lacerna* for this, the most conspicuous form of Etruscan mantle next to the tebenna. The Latin word *lacerna*, whose ending in *-na* seems to identify it as Etruscan, might have been used in Rome to refer to a mantle originally Etruscan, but that tells us next to nothing about its shape or the way it was worn by the Etruscans. (The suffix *-erna* is Etruscan; see A. Ernout, *BSL* 30 [1929] 94f.; Palmer 51f. Cf. Ernout-Meillet s.v. "*lacerna.*" Festus [in Paul., 105.4] derives the word from "*lacer,*" not in the popular sense of "ragged" but because it had no hood: "quod minus capito est," as if implying the hood was torn off. Cf. Wilson 117f.)

"Laena: quidam appellatam existimant Tusce, quidam Graece, quam χλανίδα dicunt" (Fest. Paul. 104.18). The Latin word probably came from the Greek χλαῖνα by way of Etruscan; but see de Simone 283. The form of the mantle worn over the toga in Rome, where it is used as a ritual garment, is originally Etruscan, going back to the rounded mantle draped back to front. In Rome the *laena* proper is the official dress of the augur and of the *flamen* when he is sacrificing; then he wears it with the *apex* and calcei, as illustrated on the Ara Pacis. It is a heavy mantle (often called *duplex*), draped over both shoulders, hanging in a curve in front and back, and fastened with a fibula: "proprie toga duplex, amictus auguralis. alii amictum rotundum, alii togam duplicem, in qua flamines sacrificant infibulati" (Serv. *ad Aen.* 4.262; cf. Cic. *Brut.* 56). Cf. perhaps χλαῖνα διπλῆ, Od.19.226. The designation of it as "*duplex*" is puzzling: Varro (*LL* 132) explains the "*ricinium*"; "idquod eo utebantur duplici, ab eo quod dimidiam partem retrorsum iaciebant, ab reiciendo "*ricinium*" dictum." The heavier, full-size himation was worn by less active figures, those shown at banquets, etc. See B. Shefton, *Hesperia* 31 (1962) 356.

30. Gjerstad, *Swed. Cyprus Exp.* II 706, Pl. 205, 2; 205, 12–13; late sixth century. Cf. No. 1141, Pl. 212, 6–7. E. Sjövquist ("Cypriote Art, Ancient," in *EWA* IV 189, Pl. 99) says the costume is typical of Cypriote dress. Although sculptured representations of the fashion in Greece proper are rare, the aegis of Athena and of Zeus is sometimes shown like this in Greek art, e.g., in the Aegina pediment.

31. For Vulci figures, cf. *BMMA* 20, 2 (1961) 52; the tripod stand in *Etruscan Culture* Fig. 414; the bronze statuette in the Minneapolis Institute of Arts, Acc. No. 47.39; and Arndt-Amelung pt. 2, 3509–3510. The scarf on the figure of the flute player in the Tomba del Triclinio is draped in a complicated manner which is difficult to reconstruct. The artist seems to have repeated incorrectly the draping of the left arm on the right arm. The explanation given by Houston, *Anc. Greek, Rom. Byz. Cost.* 85, Fig. 93, is unconvincing, and in general this author's treatment is unreliable.

32. This triangular version is also illustrated by an engraved bronze mirror in Berlin, in Gerhard 99. Emeline Richardson kindly informs me the so-called Athena statuette (Figs. 119–120: Paris, Louvre, Br. 269, J. Charbonneaux, *BMF* [1946] 16, gift, Nanteuil Collection) is actually a male figure, with excess adipose tissue as on some male figures of this period, such as the "Vertumnus" statuette. There is an almost identical figure in Munich; see R. Lullies, *AA* (1957) 402–404, Figs. 22–23.

The longer form, closer to the Roman laena, had already been reserved for men immediately after 500 B.C. The only exceptions, except for the possible one of the statuette of "Athena," are the women pictured in the Tomba Francesca Giustiniani (470–450 B.C.), where a provincial artist was repeating Etruscan models of several decades before (Pallottino, *Etr. Painting* 87; Romanelli, *Tarquinia* 29, Fig. 42; Heurgon 214f. and Fig. 46).

33. Palermo museum, Gábrici, *StEtr* 2 (1928) e.g. Pl. 8a.

34. Supra n. 26, Cippo Barracco.

35. M. F. Briguet, *Mélanges de philosophie, de littérature et d'histoire ancienne offerts à Pierre Boyancé*, Coll. de l'École Française de Rome 22 (1974) 124. Roncalli 70, n. 11; on his 71, n. 1, different mantles are confused. A mantle with a hole in the middle is pictured held out by four girls on some of the terracotta relief plaques from Locri Epizefiri, in the Museo Nazionale di Reggio Calabria; their date is more or less contemporary with that of the cippi from Chiusi; see P. Zancani Montuoro, *ArchCl* 12 (1960) 37ff., Pl. 2.; B. S. Ridgway, R. T. Scott, *Archaeology* 26 (1973) 43ff.

36. Varro's description of the Roman *laena* as *duplex* can be interpreted as meaning either "heavy" or "double weight," actually doubled over (supra n. 29). For the Roman ritual *laena*, see Bonfante Warren, *ANRW* 1₄ 594–595. Cf. also two archaistic reliefs, the "Four Gods Base" in the Villa Albani, in E. Harrison, *Archaic and Archaistic Sculpture*, Athenian Agora II (1965) Pl. 64a; and the relief from Nemi with the murder of Aegisthus, in F. H. Pairault, *MélRome* 81 (1969) 425–472; correctly dated by J. Heurgon, *La Magna Grecia e Roma nell'età arcaica, Atti VIII Convegno Magna Grecia* (Taranto 1968) 28–81. See infra Appendix I, n. 14.

37. See for example the figure in the extreme lower left, in the Tomba Stachelberg (called the Tomba delle Bighe in Weege Figs. 78, 81, 87, Suppl. 4). The fashion is not limited to Etruria: see, for example, a Greek komast on a plate by Skythes in Munich (end of sixth century B.C.), in *AA* (1957) 374, Fig. 4.

38. In Roman times the toga was the mark of a prostitute; Hor. *Sat.* 1.2.63; 1.2.82; Tib., 4.10.3; Mart. 6.64.4. Cf. Pliny's surprise at the fact that the

statue of Cloelia showed her wearing a toga: "ceu parum esset toga eam cingi" (*HN* 34.28).

39. For a pattern similar to that of the rounded back of the mantle of the *Kourotrophos* from Veii, see the back of one of the korai from the Acropolis, Athens, Acropolis Mus. 684, ca. 490 B.C., in Payne-Young Pl. 79; Bianchi Bandinelli, *Storicità dell'arte classica* Pl. 11; Richter, *Korai* No. 684. On the Greek monument it represents an artistic stylization of the back folds of the usual rectangular himation, rendered with a decorative rounded pattern; on the Etruscan figures the artist is faithfully reproducing the folds of the actual garment, which we know to have been rounded, from its appearance on other monuments. So Etruscan realism on the one hand and Greek abstraction on the other produced similar forms from different models of drapery.

40. The fashion of wearing a mantle pulled over the head spanned the whole of the late seventh and sixth century, overlapping both the long back braid of the early archaic period (Fig. 96) and the characteristic high-crowned tutulus profile of the later sixth century (Figs. 146, 147). See infra Chapter 6.

41. The custom of cutting material is relatively recent: the ancients would weave the required shape wherever possible. Despite the variety of shapes of Etruscan mantles, I have not found one which would actually require cutting.

42. Rome, Barracco collection. The meaning of this scene is uncertain. Poulsen (*Etr. Paintings* 55, Fig. 42) interprets the mantle as a shroud for the dead. Pallottino (*Etruscologia* 325) identifies it as a wedding scene and compares it to a similar ritual in the Hebrew wedding ceremony. Cf. a similar relief in the Ny Carlsberg Glyptotek; see F. Poulsen, *Katalog d. Etr. Mus., Ny Carlsberg Glyptotek* (Copenhagen 1927–28) Inv. No. H. 205, Pl. 82; V. Poulsen, *Den Etruskiske Samling* (Copenhagen 1966) 37; Paribeni, *StEtr* 12 (1938) 99, No. 83. Cf. supra n. 35 for the mantle on the plaque from Locri. For another Chiusi wedding scene, see Giglioli 142; Pallottino, *Etruscologia* 325, Pl. 68.

43. E. Galli, "La Dea Madre di Rapino," *StEtr* 13 (1939) 231f., Pls. 14–15, Fig. 3.

44. Mus. Arch. No. 261. The front was illustrated by Elena Baggio, "Impressions of a Costume," *Italy's Life, ENIT Review* 24 (1957) 63. (It is not a "tight-fitting bolero.")

45. See the red-figure Attic cup infra, Fig. 115. Three-dimensional examples include korai from the Acropolis, e.g., Acropolis Mus. No. 594, and Payne-Young 22f.

46. Haynes (*Etruscan Sculpture*) illustrates (see cover and Pl. 8) a bronze statuette of a girl from the neighborhood of Naples, attributed on stylistic grounds to a southern Etruscan workshop; see also the examples quoted by L. Vagnetti, *Il deposito votivo di Campetti a Veio* (Florence 1971) 57, F1-F2, F5, Pls. 24–25. Two statues in Munich (one a mirror handle) imitate Greek types; see Goldscheider Fig. 110, and Ohly, *Antikensamml.* Pl. 54. For the Greek and Etruscan artists' misunderstanding of a costume which they had not actually seen, see Bonfante Warren, *AJA* 75 (1971) 278, n. 8; add to these examples the statuette in the British Museum illustrated in S. Haynes, *Etruscan Bronze Utensils* (London 1965) Pl. 2, and see also a bronze statuette from Sparta, with a smooth back, Berlin, Staatl. Mus. Misc. 7933, in Charbonneaux, *Br. Grecs* 70, Pl. 802, and Greifenhagen, *Staatl. Mus.* 132, Pl. 12. The terracotta statuette in the Ny Carlsberg Museum in Copenhagen is a forgery: see M. Pallottino, *The Meaning of Archaeology* (London 1968) Fig. 53. On the difficulty of dating Etruscan bronzes of the late archaic period, see Richter, *Handbook* 28, Fig. 71.

47. Bonfante Warren, *AJA* 75 (1971) 284; Richardson 144-145.

48. Richardson 144-145, Pl. 43.

49. M. Bieber, "A Bronze Statuette in Cincinnati," *ProcPhilSoc* 101 (1957) 70-92, esp. 90; *"Romani Palliati"* 388f., 404.

50. For the *toga picta*, see L. Bonfante Warren, *JRS* 60 (1970) 64; *ANRW* I₄ 610-611, s.v. *"picta."*

51. H. Dragendorff, ("Rappresentazione di un aruspice sopra un vaso aretino," *StEtr* [1928] 77-83) discusses a number of figures of the Hellenistic and Roman period showing *haruspices* in the act of reading the liver. The dress of these varies: two shown on Arretine vases wear a mantle (toga or himation?) over a long-sleeved chiton, which in one case is definitely short (Pl. 38, 1-2). A statuette in Florence wears a *toga sine tunica* (Pl. 38, 3-4), a figure on a scarab wears only a mantle (181), and a funerary statue on an urn from Volterra has tunic and mantle (Körte, *RömMitt* 20 [1905] 378-379, Pl. 14). Did the "official" dress of the haruspex change, from the mantle, worn *infibulatus*, and pointed hat (Pallottino, *RendLinc* [1930] 49f., 55f., Pl. 2; *Etruscologia*, Pls. 29, 31) to the long-sleeved short chiton, which Dragendorff considers to be so unusual as to constitute an Etruscan or local, Italic element—the only one—in the repertory of Arretine ware? Or must we admit that we do not know what the official dress of the haruspex was? In any case, the special mantle with fibula and pointed hat seems to represent the special costume of some priesthood and to bear a definite religious significance. See Guzzo 157-160, Pl. 28.

52. Serv. *Ad Aen.* 4.262: "in qua flamines sacrificabant infibulati"; Paul. Fest. 113.15: "infibulati sacrificant flamines, propter usum antiquissimum aereis fibulis"; Ernout-Meillet, s.v. "laena." The *trabea* of the knights was also *infibulata*; see *ANRW* I₄ 613.

53. Metropolitan Museum of Art, Acc. No. 08.258.7, found near Andritzena, in P. Perdrizet, *BCH* 27 (1903) Pls. 7-9, p. 300; Richter, *Greek, Etr. and Rom. Br.* No. 58. Evidence for the existence of Arcadian elements in Roman tradition as early as the third century B.C. might be connected with the borrowing of such a costume on the part of the Etruscans. See J. Bayet, "Les origines de l'arcadisme romain," *MélRome* 38 (1920) 63-143.

54. Hes. *Op.* 544-546;
δέρματα συρράπτειν νεύρῳ βοός, ὄφρ᾽ ἐπὶ νώτῳ
ὑετοῦ ἀμφιβάλῃ ἀλέην· κεφαλῆφι δ᾽ ὕπερθεν
πῖλον ἔχειν ἀσκητόν, ἵν᾽ οὔατα μὴ καταδεύῃ.
I owe this suggestion to Prof. Evelyn B. Harrison.

55. See the *capite velato* on a statuette from Carsóli (Richardson 160; E. H. and L. Richardson, Jr., *YCS* 19 (1966) 260-261). Cf. Laviosa, *Sc. Volterra* 43-46, esp. 47 (boy with a bulla); the women also wear mantles over their heads. Notice also the rounded mantle pulled up over the head of the avenger on Fig. 89.

56. Giglioli (*StEtr* 4 [1930] 365f.) has shown that in the scene of Admetus and Alcestis, on the well-known Etruscan red-figure skyphos from Vulci, the white hose with animal feet worn by one of the demons proves that stage costume is being represented. The long sleeves on many of the figures on the Hellenistic urns from Volterra also seem to represent stage costume: for example, Fig. 90, where the figure of Pelops wears a separate sleeve under the chiton; but this, like his heavy, tight-fitting hose or stockings, may be his costume as charioteer. (See supra Chapter 3, nn. 43-44.) A better example is Brunn-Körte 2, 1, 50, Pl. 18, 3, with a scene from the Theban cycle (on these see J. P. Small, *AJA* 76 [1972] 220). Oedipus and King Creon both wear the stage king's dress with long sleeves, as does the older figure on the mirror pictured in Fig. 91, though in fact there is often a contrast between the nearly naked figures of mirrors and cistae of the Hellenistic period and the usually overdressed figures of the urns, presenting scenes as though in a theater.

57. Banti 303–304: "si manifesta nel mantello affibbiato sulla spalla, il quale non è un mantello etrusco e può essere confrontato solo con la clamide greca . . . l'inizio dell'influsso greco nella plastica di Cere."

58. See supra, nn. 10, 13. For other Laconian parallels, see infra Chapter 7.

59. For other Cypriot parallels, see infra Chapter 7.

60. Banti (*StEtr* 28 [1960] and *Mondo degli Etruschi*[2] 309) dates the statue as late as 550, mostly on the basis of her reconstruction of this mantle, which was a *male* fashion in Greece. I think it likely that the mantle was merely an early version of the himation with ends in front. It was worn this way by mourning women in Greece, presumably because they were careless with their appearance. See supra n. 10. On the representation of this fashion on both men and women in Greek art, see B. S. Ridgway, *AJA* 69 (1965) 3.

5. SHOES

1. Traces of red paint are still visible on monuments of the later sixth century, some of the cippi from Chiusi (Fig. 124). On a non-Etruscan monument, the laces, painted on the fragmentary leg of the terracotta cult statue from Paestum, are preserved (Fig. 111). See the votive shoe from Vetulonia in Falchi, Pl. 16, 15.

2. An ivory foot with sandal, in Rome, Villa Giulia Museum, Barberini Inv. 13634, L. 13.5 cm. See the fragment of leather sandal, Barberini Inv. 13653, L. 14 cm., seventh century B.C.; the terracotta vase in the form of a man's right leg with sandal, from Vulci, probably Rhodian, Berlin, Staatliche Museum, Inv. F 1307, H. 28.5 cm., sixth century B.C., in Greifenhagen, *Staatl. Mus.* 45. A similar one (right leg), also from Vulci, is shown in G. Riccioni and M. T. Amorelli, *Tomba Panatenaica di Vulci*, Quaderni di Villa Giulia 3 (Lerici 1968) No. 3.

3. See Mueller-Deecke 254f. for the texts; cf. Heurgon 222. The fullest description is in Pollux 7.22. 92f.: τυρρηνικὰ τὸ κάττυμα ζύλινον, τετρα-δάκτυλον, οἱ δὲ ἱμάντες ἐπίχρυσα. No gilded laces have been preserved.

4. Cratinus frag. 131: the comedy writer, a contemporary of Aristophanes, refers to *Tyrrhenia sandalia* in connection with the statue of Athena by Pheidias.

5. Pallottino, *Etruscologia* 232.

6. V. Ehrenburg (*The People of Aristophanes, a Sociology of Old Attic Comedy* [Oxford 1943] 105, 278) believes it unlikely that "Etruscan sandals" were actually imported into Athens from Etruria, Laconian shoes from Sparta, or Persian slippers from Persia. Even if the name of the shoe does not imply its actual origin, and all these shoes were made in Athens by Athenians, the name "Etruscan" fashion would still seem to be based on some Etruscan primacy of invention, or reputation.

7. In Rome, Villa Giulia Museum: 1, from Bisenzio, tombs 77 and 80, in Helbig[4] 2552, A. Pasqui, *NSc* (1886) 45, Solari Pls. 24, 44, and *EAA* 4, Fig. 622 (some of these are of iron); 2, from Bisenzio, bronze, outer frame; 3, Castellani collection, No. 51832-3, bronze, seventh century B.C.; 4, from Cerveteri, Barberini tomb, fragment, decorated leather; 5, from Cerveteri, wood, in G. Ricci, *NSc* 42 (1955) 592; 6, from Cerveteri, recently found, unpublished, Cerveteri museum; 7, from Trevignano, Villa Giulia Museum, Inv. TR 17, in *Arte e civ. degli Etruschi* Nos. 71–72 (two pairs are shown here, a man's and woman's: the man's preserves the iron framework only, the woman's, leather, wooden, and bronze parts); see also, with the same form, 8, from Corchiano, No. 6499, bronze plates for sole over 4 cm. high, fourth century B.C. There are many

others in Florence, Museo Archeologico, in Cerveteri, Museo Archeologico, in the Museo Etrusco Gregoriano of the Vatican (for these see Helbig[4] 697 with further bibliography), and in the Louvre (for these see de Ridder Nos. 3732-3733). For similar examples from Eretria see de Ridder No. 3731.

8. Women's shoes and men's sandals appear on a black-figure vase from Vulci by the Micali painter (in London, British Museum), with a scene of a wake, ca. 520 B.C., in Beazley, *EVP* 2, Pl. 3, 1; Camporeale, "Le scene etrusche di protesi," *RM* 66 (1959) 36-37, Pl. 18,1. Cf. the sandals in the Tomba dei Rilievi, in G. Ricci, "Necropoli della Banditaccia," *MonAnt* 42 (1955) 899, tomb No. 400, detail of Fig. 211a; Heurgon 224, Fig. 40; *Propyläen* I 384b, third century. Hus (165) is wrong in stating that sandals in Etruria were worn by "gens de condition modeste ou relevant de la tenure quotidienne, les *calcei repandi* étant la chaussure d'apparat." Before 550-540 B.C., everyone wore sandals or other shoes, since calcei repandi did not come into use before then; and even after that date, sandals continued to be worn by the upper classes.

9. Cic. *Nat. D.* I 29 82. Since *"repandus"* is used of snub-nosed dolphins, etc., the German term *Schnabelschuhe* is a fairly close translation. On the calcei repandi, see Bonfante Warren, *AJA* 75 (1971) 279-282.

10. E. M. Douglas, "Iuno Sospita of Lanuvium," *JRS* 3 (1913) 61f., with list; J. C. Hoffkes-Brukker, "Iuno Sospita," *Hermeneus* 26-28 (1956) 161f., reviewed in *FA* (1958) 2274. The representation of Juno Sospita often quoted to illustrate Cicero's passage is a statue in the Vatican, probably of the Antonine period (Reinach, *Rép. St.* I 200, 731; Douglas No. 1), on which the feet, including the pointed shoes, have been restored according to Cicero's description. Add to the list in Douglas a bronze relief in Toronto, Inv. CA 314; Richardson, *MAAR* 21 (1953) 87, Fig. 4; Bayet, *Herclé* 146-148.

11. Walters, *B. M. Bronzes* No. 587; *BMMA* 20 (1961-1962) 52, Fig. 20 (illustration only, no author), 500-475 B.C. Juno and Hercules frequently appear together in early Etruscan art on bronzes from Vulci, vases, and reliefs (Hampe-Simon Pl. 6, 1, 21, and Fig. 3); see Bayet, *Herclé* 53, 146-154, 198f., 217-223. Representations of "Minerva" and "Juno" are often indistinguishable in Etruscan art.

12. *ANRW* I$_4$, 593, 605.

13. I use here the Latin terms referring to the later Roman calceus, based on the form of the early Etruscan shoes: see *ANRW* I$_4$ 605f. The number of these *corrigiae* on the early monuments varies from three to five. The traditional Roman lacing became fixed at four straps: see 19, 34, 4; Isid. *Orig.* 19, 34, 4: "patricios calceos Romulus reperit IV corrigiarum assutaque luna."

14. *ANRW* I$_4$ 609.

15. Perhaps most meticulously shown on a bronze relief from Castel San Mariano, in Perugia, illustrated in Hampe-Simon, Suppl. plate, Pls. 20-21, Fig. 3. S. Haynes (*JdI* 73 [1958] 17) agrees with Riis and others in considering them the oldest of the series of archaic metal reliefs from the vicinity of Perugia, ca. 550 B.C.

16. Roncalli 30-32, Nos. 18-20. Pls. 13-15.

17. Though it apparently continued to be worn and remained part of the warrior's costume.

18. The shoes of Troilus, which are not laced, are closer to the soft soccus worn by figurines of dancers than to the calcei repandi, but both fashions came in at the same time.

19. Phillips, *Poggio Civitate* 26-27, Pls. 6, 7; I. Gantz, *DialArch* 6 (1972) 167-235; K. M. Phillips, *AJA* 77 (1973) 319-331. I have recently suggested (*AJA* 79 [1975] 149) that some of the dress and attributes of figures from Poggio Civitate might be understood in the context of northern Italy (and of the

Villanovan antecedents they have in common?). A number of features are paralleled in the art of the northern situlae, as has been noted in the publication of the akroteria and frieze plaques by I. Gantz in *DialArch* 6 (1972) 203, n. 132, and J. MacIntosh in *RM* 81 (1974) 21, n. 38 (cf. n. 37). T. Gantz finds examples from Bologna closest to the procession represented on one of the frieze plaques (*RM* 81 [1974] 8-9). Bologna was the exchange center between the Etruscan cities and the area of the situla art. The pointed shoes which appear on the enthroned male figure on the Benvenuti situla, dated around 600 B.C. (*Mostra delle situle* No. 11, Pls. 4, 5, A, and O.-H. Frey, *Die Entstehung der Situlenkunst* [Berlin 1969] tomb 126, Pls. 17-19, 31, 47-50) do not fit the chronology I have suggested in the text. Neither do those of the somewhat similar seated akroterion from Poggio Civitate, dated around 570 B.C. (See infra Chapter 6, n. 20.) Does this time difference imply that influences came in independently in the North, from different sources and at different times from the rest of Etruria?

20. D. von Bothmer, "Two Etruscan Vases by the Paris Painter," *BMMA* 14 (1955-56) 127-132; *Propyläen* I 413. See supra Chapter 6, n. 85. A convincing interpretation of this scene as Achilles in Skyros was offered by Otto J. Brendel in "Etruscan Myth," an unpublished lecture given for the Archaeological Institute of New York and New York University, February 1972. The figure differentiated from the others by the hair style, which is a male one on contemporary Caeretan hydriae, would represent Achilles. There are only three pairs of shoes hung up for the three women who recline with him. Hampe-Simon (35f., Pl. 15) instead identify the figure holding a pet bird as Aphrodite at the wedding banquet of Peleus and Thetis: the unfeminine figure would then represent Eris. Cf. Banti, *Etruscan Cities* 247, Pl. 47. For examples of shoes taken off at banquets, see G. Camporeale, "Le scene etrusche di protesi," *RM* 66 (1959) 37f., Pl. 18, 1. On the Boccanera plaques (Figs. 73-75) the figures of Hera (or Juno) and Aphrodite are both represented wearing calcei repandi. For the banquet motif, see De Marinis.

21. Sometimes, especially on female figures where the long chitons cover the tops of the shoes, it is difficult to distinguish the soccus from the calceus repandus.

22. Cf. the figure of Troilus in the Tomba dei Tori, Fig. 46, and supra n. 18. For the Etruscan custom of adding shoes to nude figure types, see P. Bocci, *StEtr* (1960) 118f.; Banti, *Etruscan Cities* 245; *Mostra* No. 351; and the mirror from Palestrina in Gerhard V 12, third century B.C.(?). For other examples on mirrors, cf. R. Herbig, *StEtr* 24 (1955-56) 183f. and *passim*.

23. See Erbacher.

24. See Fig. 139 (models of Greek laced boots, Nos. 10-13) and the Etruscan calcei repandi shown in Nos. 17-18; the latter preserve an earlier form of Greek laced boot which had gone out of fashion in Greece itself.

25. Bonfante Warren, *AJA* 75 (1971) 279-282, and the references for Juno Sospita cited supra n. 10.

26. See Leda, with Tyndareus and others, in Gerhard 5, 77; Bonfante Warren, *AJA* 75 (1971) 281, Fig. 15. See supra Chapter 3, n. 37, on the chiton with tassel. The two fashions of pointed shoes and tasseled chiton do not completely coincide: pointed shoes often appear on figures wearing tasseled chitons, but numerous figures wearing fringed chitons are barefoot or wear blunt-toed shoes.

27. Pallottino, *Etr. Painting* 105. The dating of the Tomba degli Scudi is controversial. Banti (Pl. 98; cf. Pl. 73; *Etruscan Cities* 80, 234, 239, Pls. 38a, 77a) and Richardson (148, 177) date it in the third century, though Richardson points out (177) that the dress is still in the fashion of the fourth century.

Jucker, in his review of Banti in *Gnomon* 37 (1965) 313, believes it should be dated in the fourth century, remarking specifically on the earrings of a fourth-century type (Banti Pl. 110, 1; Banti, *Etruscan Cities* Pl. 42b; and Richardson Pl. 40.)

28. Supra n. 25. Hellenistic elongated figures of priestesses with pointed shoes are shown in *Mostra* No. 344, Pl. 80.

29. Frank Brown and Emeline Richardson ("Cosa II, the Temples of the Arx," *MAAR* 26 [1960] 341, Fig. 33) show the front half of the right foot of a woman wearing a sandal with a thick sole and a double thong between the first and second toes, knotted on top and dividing to pass around the foot: "The form of the sandal . . . is not uncommon and seems to have been in fashion for a long time." See also supra nn. 7–8: the woman's sandal from Trevignano has bronze loops for the laces.

30. De Ridder No. 2293, Pl. 26; Richardson, *MAAR* 27 (1962) 114, Fig. 28, "third century B.C."; Riis, *Tyrrhenika* Pl. 21, 2.

31. App. *Mith.* I.2: ὑποδήματα ἔχων ἰταλικά. The freedman's pilleus showed that the king considered himself a client of Rome: cf. Petron. *Sat.* 40–41, where a roast pig dressed in the pilleus appears at Trimalchio's supper to illustrate one of the host's elaborate puns.

32. There is a good list in Hus 165, n. 2. Cf. also fragments of terracotta plaques from Corinth in the Berlin museum; see *AntDenk* II (1908) Pl. 30, Fig. 30; Richter, *Archaic Greek Art* Fig. 153. Greek sandals are illustrated in Erbacher 73f. Some are inaccurate, e.g., his Fig. 7, from the relief stele from Chrysapha, which is also misunderstood by A. J. B. Wace, in "A Spartan Hero Relief," *ArchEph* (1937) 217–220. Greek models for sandals have been found dating from the late seventh century B.C.; e.g. Payne, *Perachora* Pl. 114, No. 302, and text; cf. Bieber Pl. 64, 7.

33. Bonfante Warren, *AJA* 68 (1964) 39. Cf. situlae represented on the bronze situlae in *Mostra delle situle* Pls. 4, 13, 41, A, H.

34. Heurgon 222–224, nn. 121–128; Pallottino, *Etruscologia* 332.

6. HATS, HAIR STYLES, AND BEARDS

1. Compare the disproportionate interest paid to hats and head-dresses by Cypriot makers of votive terracotta figures, discussed in J. H. Young and S. H. Young, *Terracotta Figurines from Kourion in Cyprus* (Philadelphia 1955) 196.

2. Wind-blown hair was always popular in Etruria; see, in the sixth century, the hair styles of the figures on Caeretan hydriae, in Banti Pl. 26, 625–600 B.C. For the lion with wind-blown hair, see supra Chapter 2, n. 49. For human fashions on figures of animals, see the flower-hat on the monsters in Fig. 150, the perizoma and *etagenperücke* on centaurs, or the long chiton in Fig. 70. See also the sphinx with arms in Camporeale, *Tomba del Duce* 150 (for *reparto superiore* read *reparto inferiore*), Pl. 35b *lower right*; and tritons dressed like humans, in G. Camporeale, "Variazioni etrusche sul tripo arcaico del tritone," *Archaeologia. Scritti in onore di Aldo Neppi Modona* (Florence 1975) 149–163.

3. See, for example, the youth in the Campana tomb or the sphinx or griffin-sphinx in Camporeale, *Tomba del Duce* 150–151, Pl. 35 *below*.

4. Richardson (*MAAR* 27 [1962] 189) says of the bronzes from Orientalizing tombs at Praeneste and Vetulonia, "such details as the long hair and beards of the men are seen here for the first time." For a seventh-century beard, see Cristofani, *Nuove letture* Pl. 10, 2, from Marsiliana d'Albegna, 680–640 B.C. Cf. Gempeler Nos. 92, 102–104.

5. See a "Melian" amphora, seventh century B.C., showing Apollo, Artemis, and the Muses(?), in Arias-Hirmer 22–23A, and a black-figure neck-amphora, ca. 625–600, in Arias-Hirmer 18–20. Spartans shaved their mustaches, we are told, while they let their beards grow: see G. Dontas, *BCH* 93 (1969) 47 (supra Chapter 2, n. 14).

6. Even an occasional kouros (Fig. 31); cf. the Cypriot kouros in Fig. 40 and, in Greece, the Moschophoros and the Rampin horseman. For the beard worn by gods and heroes as a mark of authority in black-figure vase painting, see G. P. Oikonomos, "Miroir grec de la collection H. A. Stathatos," *Mélanges Charles Picard* (Paris 1949) 774f., especially 777f. (cited by Banti in "Tomba dei Tori" 148, for the beard of Achilles).

7. On the overlapping of hat forms and on flexible terminology, see Young and Young, *Terracotta Figurines* 196, 198–199, 206 (Cypriot hats). The pilleus appears on a figure on a large vase from Bisenzio (*Mostra* No. 13, Pl. 3) and on a cinerary urn from Montescudaio near Volterra (*Mostra* No. 14, Pl. 4); see F. Nicosia, *StEtr* 37 (1969) 386, n. 52. It is often called a helmet (e.g., *Mostra* No. 8, Pl. 2; Banti Pl. 11; cf. Montelius, *Civ.* 192). The same form may well have been used for both helmets and hats at first; see Bonfante Warren, *ANRW* I₄ 594, 611, on the flamen's hat. For Villanovan helmets on seventh-century bronzes see H. Hencken, "Horse Tripods of Etruria," *AJA* 61 (1957) 1f.

8. See Fig. 136, a statuette of an Arcadian peasant. On the Greek πῖλος and its variations in Cyprus, see Young and Young, *Terracotta Figurines* 195ff.

9. Frankfort 134, Fig. 135.

10. Frankfort 134: "tall conical felt hats worn to this day in north Syria and Jebel Sinjar, and depicted on Syrian monuments of all periods."

11. C. Albizzati ("Ritratti etruschi arcaici," *Dissertazioni della Pontificia Accademia Romana di Archeologia* Ser. 2, 14 [1920] Pl. 3, 3–4 [560–550 B.C.]) identifies the figure as a farmer and calls the hat a narrow-brimmed petasos. Actually early forms of petasos and pilleus were close and often undistinguishable. For the pilos shape of helmet on a Greek Geometric statuette, see H. Sarian, "Terres cuites Géométriques d'Argos," *BCH* 93 (1969) 651–673. This figure wears armor very similar to that on a relief from the Alpine area, now in the museum at Como, identified and published by F. Rittatore Vonwiller in "Dati sul vestiario e l'armamento dei popoli alpini in età preromana," *Bulletin d'Études préhistoriques alpines* 3 (1971) 5–23; and "Novità attorno all'armamento dei popoli alpini nel fregio di Bormio," 4 (1972) 81–88.

12. See a charioteer in the tomb of the Olympic Games in Moretti 108, the Tomba del Colle in Chiusi in R. Bianchi Bandinelli, *Clusium. Le Pitture delle tombe archaiche* (Rome 1939), and Pallottino, *Etr. Painting* 66, 131. The horseback riders in the frieze plaques from Poggio Civitate (M. C. Root, *AJA* 77 [1973] 121–137) wear pointed bonnets like jockeys and charioteers on the northern situlae (*Mostra delle Situle* Nos. 52, 54, Pls. G, H). For other similarities to the costume on the situlae, see infra n. 20, and Chapter 5, n. 19.

13. For the history and symbolism of the felt pilleus, the attribute of the Dioscouroi, see L. Olschki, *The Myth of Felt* (Berkeley 1949), especially the references in nn. 109 and 122, and R. D. DePuma, "The Dioskouroi on Four Etruscan Mirrors in Midwestern Collections," *StEtr* 41 (1973) 159–170. Cf. Daremberg-Saglio, s.v. "pilleus"; infra Chapter 5, on the pilleus of the client; and Körte, *Göttinger Bronzen* 22f.

14. Daremberg-Saglio, s.v. "*petasus*"; Bieber Pl. 19.

15. Rome, Villa Giulia Museum, Giglioli Pl. 253. Banti dates the figure as fourth to third century B.C. The hat has been explained as a farmer's protection against the sun; cf. the hat represented in the Tomba del Cacciatore

in Tarquinia, in Moretti 152ff. E. Richardson, however, noting the importance of the tradition of tracing the furrow—e.g., Romulus and Roma Quadrata—believes the hat here too marks a divinity or priest.

16. The peculiar form of the hat has led scholars to consider it a priestly attribute: see J. L. Myres, *JHS* 10 (1889) 243f.; Körte, *Göttinger Bronzen* 22f.; Roncalli 71.

17. Florence, Museo Archeologico, 72, 725; Richardson, "Libation-Bearer" Fig. 8.

18. Andrén 449f. Mazzarino and others believe the Velletri plaque to represent magistrates, but see supra Chapter 4, n. 23. T. Gantz (*StEtr* 39 [1971] 7) is probably right to identify the figure with the hat as Hermes (the hat is not, however, a tutulus). Like the pilleus, the early form of the petasos was used for helmets; see I. Gantz, *DialArch* 6 (1972) 202-204.

19. Körte (*Göttinger Bronzen* 22f.) rightly criticizes W. Helbig's identification ("Über den Pileus der Italiker," *SBBayerAkad* [1880] 490f.) of the normal pilleus of early Etruscan art with the *apex* of the *flamines*; but Körte assumes, wrongly, in my opinion, that we must look for the origin of the Roman priestly hat in an Etruscan priestly costume.

20. I. Gantz, *DialArch* 6 (1972) 167-235; K. M. Phillips, *AJA* 77 (1973) 319-320, Pls. 54-55; R. Bianchi Bandinelli, *DialArch* 6 (1972) 236-247. For my suggestion that the figures from Poggio Civitate might fit into a northern context, see supra Chapter 5, n. 19. The broad-brimmed hat of the seated male figures on monuments like the Benvenuti situla from Este or the Kuffarn situla from the Alps (*Mostra delle situle* No. 54, Pls. 40, 41H) was probably the kind Plautus had in mind when he made fun of the wide Illyrian hat that made its wearer look like a mushroom (see infra Appendix I, n. 24). The high peak of the "cowboy" hat, missing on the situlae, does appear on the Capestrano warrior (Fig. 27), but this armed figure seems to wear a helmet rather than a hat, while the seated figures on the situlae wear long robes and pointed shoes, as do the akroteria.

In her publication of these figures from Poggio Civitate (see supra Chapter 5, n. 19) Ingrid Gantz identifies some of the fragments as belonging to female figures. Female figures in this pose and dress seem less usual; cf. the male bodies of the three seated terracotta figures from Cerveteri (Figs. 14–16) and the two similarly dressed seated "guardians," armed with knives (or carrying litui?), carved in relief in the recently discovered Tomb of the Statues near Ceri (Cerveteri: G. Colonna, "Scavi e scoperte," *StEtr* 41 [1973] 540–541, Pl. 115).

21. Hinks, *B.M. Paintings* 4; Körte, *Göttinger Bronzen* 17. For the haruspices, see supra Chapter 4, n. 51; M. Pallottino, *RendLinc* 6 (1930) 49f.; *StEtr* 10 (1936) 463.

22. From Condrieu, Gaul; see de Ridder 2764; cf. Cles-Reden Pl. 67; Richter, *Dumbarton Oaks* 37, Pl. 17. See the figure in the basilica near the Porta Maggiore.

23. The feather crown is different from the flower crown represented on figures of women (Fig. 62) and of fabulous animals such as the centaurs of this same Bernardini bronze (Curtis, *MAAR* 3 [1919] 83, nn. 1, 5). Luisa Banti ("Rapporti fra Etruria e Umbria avanti il V sec. a.C.," *Primo Convegno di Studi Umbri* [Gubbio 1963] 167-169) cites examples of plumed or petal-like crowns on human busts from Vetulonia and Marsiliana d'Albegna. Cf. Cristofani, *Nuove letture* 43, Pl. 15, 1 (infra n. 27).

24. On ivory-handled fans, see Curtis, *MAAR* 5 (1925) 24-26, Nos. 22-27, Pls. 9-11, and, for an example from Marsiliana d'Albegna, M. Cristofani and F.

Nicosia, *StEtr* 37 (1969) 352–353, Pl. 86. A representation of a female attendant using such a fan (*"flabello"*) is found on the seventh-century ossuary of Montescudaio, in Florence, Museo Archeologico, recently restored; see F. Nicosia, *StEtr* 37 (1969) 387–388, Pl. 98 b, c, and cf. Fig. 15, with bibliography. For importation of (undecorated) ostrich eggs into Etruria, see M. Torelli, "Un uovo di struzzo dipinto conservato nel Museo di Tarquinia," *StEtr* 33 (1965) 329–365. For the source of ostrich feathers, see the Nubians bearing tribute, including ostrich feathers (ca. 1460 B.C.), in Davies, *Tomb of Rekh-mi-Re* Pl. 2.

25. See the Sumerian *"personnage aux plumes"* from Tello in the Louvre, Early Dynastic period (Frankfort 20). Moortgat (33) believes that this headdress was not made of feathers or plumes but of leaves and suggests it might be the predecessor of the Sumerian god-crown, before it developed into the horned crown; these statements are hard to prove or disprove (see T. A. Carter's review in *AJA* [1970] 191). See also a contemporary stone vase from Bismaya. Frankfort (19, Pl. 11A) mentions the low "feather crowns" worn by all the musicians but not the plumes of some of them. A limestone stele found at Ras Shamra, dated 2000–1800 by the excavator, is shown in C. F. A. Schaeffer, *Syria* 12 (1931) Pl. 8, No. 2; cf. *Ugaritica* II (1949) Pl. 22, center pp. 90–93, 95–99. Cf. also the list in Richardson, *MAAR* 27 (1962) 188, n. 158, Figs. 72–73.

26. The literature on "feather crowns" is further complicated by the fact that the term is used to describe four completely different coiffures. Richardson (*MAAR* 27 [1962] 187) refers to the short "feather crown" on the figure of a foreign musician on a relief from the palace at Nineveh: see Moortgat Pl. 283; illustrated and discussed in R. D. Barnett, *Assyrian Palace Reliefs* (London 1958) Pl. 54, and Barnett, "Assyria and Iran: The Earliest Representations of Persians," in A. U. Pope, ed., *A Survey of Persian Art from Prehistoric Times to the Present* XIV (London and New York, 1967) 2997–3007, Fig. 1065; cf. Ashurbanipal's Elamite archers from Nineveh, in the Fogg Museum of Art, in *The Art of the Ancient Near East* (Museum of Fine Arts, Boston 1962) Fig. 27. D. Curtis (*MAAR* 3 [1919] 83, n. 2), F. Poulsen (*Jahrbuch* 29 [1911] 230f.) and G. M. A. Hanfmann (*Altetr. Plastik* 80) refer instead to the controversial, so-called Syrian or Philistine feather-crown of the Philistines on the Medinet Habu reliefs, for which see R. D. Barnett, "The Sea Peoples," *CAH* II 28, fasc. 68 (1969) 15–16. Made of reeds, leather strips, or horsehair, it was apparently a warrior's helmet; see E. Porada, "The Warrior with Plumed Helmet," *Berytus* 7 (1942) 57–63. It is also represented on Cyprus; see Barnett 19; G. A. Wainwright, *JEA* 47 (1961) 74–77. T. Dothan ("The Philistine Problems," *Antiquity and Survival* 2, 2/3 [1957] 157) points out the similarity between these headdresses and those of anthropoid coffin lids from Beth Shan; see the references in J. C. Waldbaum, *AJA* (1974) 94. This second type of headdress in turn must not be confused with a third type, that of the Phaistos disc (and perhaps, too, the Lycian feather hat mentioned in Hdt. 7.92; see Barnett 7), or a fourth, the real crowns of feathers in Mesopotamia and Iran (see, e.g., the baked clay plaque in H. Frankfort, S. Lloyd, and T. Jacobson, *The Gimilsin Temple* [Chicago 1940] Fig. 123; cf. Pritchard Fig. 524 and Frankfort Pls. 71, 174A).

27. E.g., a bronze handle from Città di Castello with a figure wearing a feather hat, surrounded by lions, in Banti, *Etruscan Cities* Pl. 64; cf. other similar figures from Vetulonia and Marsiliana d'Albegna mentioned supra n. 23, in Banti 256–257, and in Camporeale, *Commerci di Vetulonia* Pls. 19, 21.

28. Cf. the bronze vase from Bisenzio with figures performing a war dance around a chained animal (bear?), in the Villa Giulia Museum, Rome, early seventh century B.C., in *Mostra* No. 13, Pl. 3.

29. Taranto 8263, by the Karneia painter. See A. D. Trendall, *The Red-Figured Vases of Lucania, Campania and Sicily* (Oxford 1967) No. 280, Pl. 24.

30. Walter O. Moeller, "Juvenal 3 and Martial *De Spectacularis* 8," *CJ* 62 (1967) 369–370: "*pinnas sumere* seems to have been a way of saying 'to become a gladiator.'" Martial, in fact, refers to a beast-fighter or bear-tamer, which is even closer to our original animal tamers wearing feather crowns: cf. the Assyrian musician with lion on the Ashurbanipal palace relief (supra n. 26).

31. Luisa Banti (supra nn. 23, 27) does not believe in the "reality" of this hat decoration and points out that the closest comparisons for the Bernardini figures are handle decorations: this fact, she claims, contradicts an interpretation of them as dancing figures. The use of dancers or acrobats as decorative motifs can be documented from many periods, however: see Figs. 35, 38, 43, 81; Chapter 2, *passim*; Banti Pls. 54, 57; S. Haynes, *Etruscan Bronze Utensils* (London 1965) 22; and tumbler handles from Praeneste in G. Battaglia, *Corpus of Praenestine Cistae* (forthcoming).

32. For the Etruscan arrangement, see the head of the Egyptian divinity Bes, crowned with a palmette-shaped stylization of the ostrich plumes, in E. Porada, *Ancient Iran* (London 1965) 165, Fig. 83. M. Guido (*Sardinia* [London 1963] 174) sees a Punic ancestry for the feather crowns of Sardinian bronze statuettes, like those of the god Bes (see infra Chapter 7, n. 2). Many of these Bes figurines were imported into Etruria, beginning early in the seventh century. For bronzes, see Montelius, *Vor. Chron.* Pl. 51, Fig. 15; an example from Veii is in *NSc* 24 (1970) 267, Fig. 52, dated by M. Torelli 700–675 B.C.; see also Camporeale, *Commerci di Vetulonia* 99, Pl. 34. In fact, as Edith Porada suggests, in order to find comparisons closer to those in Etruria we must turn to Egyptian monuments, to the great "ostrich-plume" decoration of divinities, rulers, foreigners, and entertainers. See Smith, *Anc. Egypt*, on the panache of horses, Pls. 142–143, 144A, 160B; for Nofretari in her tomb, see Smith Pl. 159B; and see William Hayes, *Scepter of Egypt* pt. 2 (New York 1959), s.v. "feathers" and "plumes." In Etruria, the plumes became more "floral," perhaps influenced by the contemporary "flower-crown" ornament spreading out in many petals. Cf. an ivory caryatid from Nimrud in the British Museum, in Barnett S211, Pl. 75.

Perhaps the most intriguing example is the feather crown on the Master of Animals on the pendant from the Aegina Treasure, where the context, remarkably close to our Etruscan examples, may argue a date close to the seventh century. The crown seems to be of the eight-feather type, with four feathers in front and, presumably four in back; see Marshall, *B. M. Jewellery* No. 762; Higgins 64–65, 201, Pl. 3B, color pl. Bl. The controversy over the date of the piece and of the Aegina Treasure in general is summarized in R. A. Higgins, "The Aegina Treasure Reconsidered," *BSA* 52 (1957) 42–57 (with preceding bibliography); Higgins argues for a late Minoan (sixteenth-century B.C.) date on the basis of the technique and parallels with individual details. Most details of costume and decoration are also characteristic of the Orientalizing period, however, such as the "shorts" or "kilt" represented on Orientalizing ivories in Etruria (infra Chapter 2). In favor of a seventh-century date are Becatti, in *Oreficerie antiche* 38, No. 122, Pl. 25, "Arte Geometrico-Orientalizzante"; Demargne, in *Crète Dédalique* 126; and C. Hopkins, in *AJA* 66 (1962) 182–184. Hopkins (184) sees, correctly in my opinion, "the costume of the youthful male figure of the pectoral with his short kilt-like skirt and close-fitting, short-sleeved leather jacket" as borrowed from Asiatic fashions, with close parallels in Greek art of the seventh century: "It obviously marked the well-dressed superman and hero, or god." (For "jacket" read "chiton.") John

Boardman's remark on the Egyptian influence ("Egyptian scene of a prince wearing an Egyptian feather crown" [*Pre-Classical* 24, Fig. 8]) perhaps also fits this later chronological context better than a Minoan one.

A recent study on the motif of the crouching monkey, developed in Phoenician art and extremely popular throughout the Mediterranean world in the seventh century (D. Rebuffat Emmanuel, "Singes de Maurétanie Tingitane et d'Italie—Réflexions sur une analogie iconographique," *StEtr* 35 [1967] 633–644, esp. 642, Pl. 136a, and cf. J. Szilágyi, *RA* [1972] fasc. 1, 111–126), gives the proper context for another pendant of this group, with crouching monkeys on either side.

33. For the back braid, see Hanfmann, *Altetr. Plastik* 17f., and Banti, *StEtr* 28 (1960) 281; Richardson, *MAAR* 27 (1962) 190–191; and Bonfante Warren, *Brendel Essays*, Pls. 3–5. Pareti (272–273) is wrong in listing the back braid as typical of both male and female costume. The earliest example we have is a primitive bronze nude statuette from Vetulonia; see Richardson, *MAAR* 21 (1953) Pl. 6, 170, Figs. 20–21. Cf. the amber amulets from Vetulonia, Circolo dei Monili, in Hoernes 448–455, MacIver 107, Fig. 25, Falchi 101, Pl. 7. 4; and a bronze statuette from Arezzo, in Richardson Fig. 15C.

34. For hair fasteners (of a different form) found in Etruria and Cyprus, see bibliography in Hus 166, n. 2. Compare the rendering of the round fastener on a terracotta figure from Chiusi, infra Fig. 5, with the round clips represented on bases from Lemnos, infra Figs. 163–164. A. Stenico first recognized their similarity to Etruscan models in *Acme* 5 (1952) 599.

35. Some seventh-century figures are only apparent exceptions. The two female terracotta figures from Cerveteri (infra Appendix I), originally seated on thrones with high backs, were meant to be seen only from the front: the braid may have been indicated on the back of the original female body; it may have been attached separately, as on contemporary heads of "canopi" from Chiusi: see O.-W. von Vacano, *RömMitt* 75 (1968) 4–33, Pls. 4–5, and Gempeler 239–240. The hair, pulled sleekly back, produced the effect of this hair style; see Banti 303. One of the fragmentary stone female figures of the Pietrera tomb from Vetulonia (cf. Fig. 57) may also originally have had a back braid; see Banti, *StEtr* 28 (1960) 281, n. 23.

36. See especially Banti, *StEtr* 28 (1960) 277f.

37. Cf. the form of the back braid on early statue-busts from Chiusi, in Hus 59 (not illustrated).

38. Cf. Fig. 56, female heads on the gold earring from the Regolini-Galassi tomb, a fragmentary statue from the Pietrera tomb (Fig. 57), and the ivory caryatids in the Vatican (Fig. 63).

39. For the Hathor curl, see O. J. Brendel, *AJA* 47 (1943) 205, n. 31; Banti, *StEtr* 28 (1960) 281, n. 24; Hus 111, 139f.; Frankfort Pl. 167. The fashion found favor in Cyprus too; see a stone capital from Larnaka in the Louvre, in Bossert, *Altsyrien* Fig. 24, ca. 500 B.C.

40. The same fashion can also be seen in profile, worn together with the back braid, on a set of ivory relief plaques in Bologna (Fig. 17). Most interesting, in view of the early contacts of Sardinia with Etruria and the Near East, is a Sardinian bronze male statuette with two thick braids and a pointed hat, found in Vulci, now in Rome, Villa Giulia Museum; see R. Bartoccini, *Vulci* (Rome 1960) Pl. 17; Falconi Amorelli (supra Chapter 2, n. 20).

41. They are often erroneously labeled "*armille*," an improbable identification considering their average size, only 2 or 3 cm. in diameter. Examples can be seen in museums at Orvieto, etc. See *NSc* 21 (1967) 231, 248, Fig. 98 (from Veii); Higgins 93, 102: "uncertain purpose," "possible hair ornaments."

42. For the single- and double-curl fashions, which have parallels in Greece but are characteristically Etruscan, see Ducati 187; *StEtr* 2 (1928), 45–47;

Banti, *StEtr* 28 (1960) 282. Two curls on the relief of the Camucía are shown in Banti 117.

43. The gesture occurs in just this form, outside Etruria, on an ivory figurine from the sanctuary of Artemis Orthia of the seventh century, contemporary with our Etruscan figures; see Dawkins, *Artemis Orthia* Pl. 170, 5. A similar gesture is seen on a female figure grasping the cords of her tympanum, on an archaic Cretan terracotta; see E. H. Dohan, *MMStud* 3 (1930-31) 221, Fig. 27.

44. On many examples, braids and corkscrew curls are hard to distinguish. Braids appear on the stone busts from Chiusi (Hus 59f.).

45. On the Syrian motif, see the bibliography in Hus 264, n. 1. A variant gesture, on statues from Vetulonia with the hands flat on the chest or held thumbs up, can be compared to that of a figure on a contemporary gold plaque from Rhodes in the British Museum, in Coarelli, *Jewellery* Pl. 2. For an Etruscan misinterpretation of the typical gesture of the Near Eastern fertility goddess (infra Fig. 153; cf. Fig. 161), the nude goddess holding her breasts, imported into the West, see a gold earring with a bust of Isis from Sardinia, dated sixth or fifth century B.C., in D. Harden, *The Phoenicians* (New York 1962) 212, Fig. 79. This type, without the gesture of holding the breasts, was adopted reluctantly and briefly in Athens (see the nude ivory statuettes with polos, in R. Lullies, *Propyläen* I 3; Boardman, *Pre-Classical* Fig. 43) and in Etruria (see the ivory statuette from Marsiliana d'Albegna, infra Fig. 161; *Mostra* No. 22, Pl. 7, dated seventh century; and the naked goddess from Orvieto, in A. Andrén, "Marmora Etruriae," *Antike Plastik* 7 [1967] n. 1). Cf. also Moortgat Pl. 33 for the gesture, signifying a greeting, on an Early Dynastic *kudurru*. See G. Camporeale, *Gnomon* 35 (1963) 292; cf. 298, a review of Hus: if one admits the "reality" of these gestures in Etruria it is not so important to explain their development; cf. also Banti, text to Pl. 24; Boardman 44, with refs.; and Bonfante Warren, *Brendel Essays* nn. 17-22.

46. Cf. the Near Eastern type of goddess dressed in a chiton, but still holding the breasts, on archaic terracottas from Crete; Dohan, *MMStud* 3 (1930-31) 222, Figs. 30-32.

47. Munich, Antikensammlung, Inv. 6158.

48. Oriental models for this style are, for the most part, found on male figures; see one from Megiddo in Pritchard Fig. 496; H. G. May, *Material Remains of the Megiddo Cult, OIP* 26 (Chicago 1935) 33-34, Pl. 34, No. 357; Frankfort Pl. 152; an ivory with a banquet scene of men and women in Loud, *Megiddo Ivories* Pl. 32; a ninth-century relief from near Aleppo in Pritchard Fig. 499; W. F. Albright, *BASOR* 87 (1942) 23-29, 90 (1943) 30-34 (with G. Levi Della Vida).

49. See a winged deity in the Berlin Antiquarium, a bucchero figurine from Falerii (Civita Castellana) in Rome, Villa Giulia Museum, Inv. 488; Poulsen Fig. 99, Montelius, *Civ.* 309, 24. For the hat, cf. the sixth-century Cypriot statue (male) shown infra Fig. 116; Poulsen 112f.

50. See the bronze statuette of a centaur in Hanover, Kestner Museum, Inv. 3097, 11.5-cm. high, in Giglioli, *StEtr* 4 (1930) 360f., Pl. 27; von Vacano Pl. 64. The figure of Avile Tite seems somewhat earlier, however, than Luisa Banti's dating of it as a provincial survival in the early fifth century; see Banti Pl. 51. On the *etagenperücke*, see Poulsen 137-160; cf. Dawkins 247; Dohan, *MMStud* 3 (1930-31) 215 f., 220, Figs. 14-21; Hus 148. See also D. Mitten, *AJA* 74 (1970) 109: "may have been largely limited to such specific areas as the Peloponnesus and Crete."

51. For the Oriental polos, see the ivories from Megiddo in Frankfort Pl. 151A and B, Fig. 75; the ivories from Nimrud in Frankfort Pls. 166A, 167F; and Moortgat 46-47, 117, Pls. 104, 239. Frankfort says (191): "It is a remarkable

instance of the persistence of habits of dress in the East that the flat caps . . . are practically the same. . . . The caps are not shown on Assyrian monuments and confirm the Levantine origin of the ivories." See Müller, *Polos*.

52. In the Museo Etrusco Gregoriano, formerly thought to be from the Regolini-Galassi tomb: see Hanfmann, *Altetr. Plastik* 68, No. 2a. The hat is worn with the long braid and back mantle of the period. Cf. also several figures from Cerveteri, in the Albertinum, Dresden (Hanfmann No. 2B) and another in the Berlin Antiquarium (Hanfmann No. 2c, Figs. 3 and 4 *left*). There is a figure in the University Museum, Philadelphia (MS 1626), on which the stylized flower is quite different: it is a bud, without any petal "brim" (Hanfmann 67, No. 1, Figs. 6 and 7).

53. B.M. 126624-5, in Jacobsthal 47, Fig. 211. See also a similar flower on a bronze decoration from Cyprus, in L. Cesnola, *Cyprus: Its Ancient Cities, Tombs and Temples* (New York 1878) Pl. 30, from Kourion.

54. Jacobsthal (48f.) gives examples: "The Etruscans were very fond of such flowers and used them in manifold contexts of decorations." See Banti Pls. 10, 13, 14. For bucchero examples in the Vatican, see Pareti Pls. 56, 58, and cf. Pl. 60; see also Camporeale, *Commerci di Vetulonia* Pls. 2, 11, 12, 14, 18, 20, 22, 24.

55. Cf. Frankfort Pl. 166b; Barnett Pl. 79 (palm and lotus capitals).

56. Hanfmann, *Altetr. Plastik* 68; cf. 76. See infra Notes to the Illustrations.

57. De Ridder Nos. 820–835. Cf. Jacobsthal (46f.) for Greek flower ornaments.

58. Roncalli 90.

59. Pritchard Figs. 646, 647. Wings spring from the waist, e.g., on a figure on a relief from Tarquinia dating from around the middle of the sixth century but still containing Orientalizing motifs. See *Mostra*, No. 43, Pl. 10, detail in center panel; Camporeale, *Tomba del Duce* 104.

60. See a six-winged creature in Frankfort Pl. 59B; M. von Oppenheim, *Tel Halaf* 3 (1955) Pl. 95a and Pls. 89B, 91, 92, 156 (wings in front).

61. Etruscan mirrors and vases offer many examples of these four-winged persons: see the Pontic amphora in Paris with running figures illustrated in Hampe-Simon 33, Fig. 7 (for its authenticity, see infra Appendix I, n. 14); another vase, M. Lombardo, "Vaso etrusco a figure nere del gruppo di la Tolfa," *StEtr* 29 (1961) 311ff., Fig. 1, Pls. 39–40; a mirror showing a winged female figure running off with a naked youth in Gerhard 4, 363, 1 (the last two representations show wings on the feet as well); a mirror from Palestrina with a running Eros, also with four wings, in Gerhard 1, 120, 1. For the Etruscan representations of wings, see Camporeale, *Tomba del Duce* 103f., 108, n. 149.

62. See the bronze tripod basin from the Barberini tomb, Rome, Villa Giulia Museum, Inv. 13131. Curtis, *MAAR* 5 (1925) 43, Pl. 25, describes the sirens' limbs as "two broad, upraised portions which might be termed either arms or wings."

63. Camporeale, *Tomba del Duce* 150, Pl. 35b.

64. Bronze handle in Munich, Inv. 3833. For the gesture, see supra nn. 43–46.

65. Supra n. 47.

66. Supra Chapter 2, n. 34.

67. For the Pontic amphora, see infra n. 85. For the Caeretan hydriae, probably painted by a Greek artist in Etruria, see Cook, *Greek Painted Pottery* 160f., 348; Hemelrijk *passim*. According to Luisa Banti ("Tripodi Loeb"), the Loeb tripods and other metalwork of this type were made at Cerveteri; the similarity of style and costume agrees with this attribution to a single center. For the Ionian fashion, see Akurgal Figs. 162–164.

68. Cf. the long curls of his companion, the female Kourotrophos from Veii, and the figures from the Tomba delle Leonesse.

69. From the Stroganoff collection. For illustrations of the *speira*, see Daremberg-Saglio, s.v. *"speira"*; Sprenger 55, Pls. 25 (female), 37 (male).

70. Picard 274 (bibliography). After 480 B.C. all Greek men wore short hair: before that time, from about the middle of the sixth century, only athletes cut their hair short. Thucydides (I.6) says that almost up to his time Athenian aristocrats wore their hair pinned up in a knot (κρωβύλος) fastened with gold pins in the shape of grasshoppers. *Krobylos*, a foreign word, probably Semitic (not Indo-European; see Daremberg-Saglio) was borrowed in Asia Minor along with the fashion; it seems to have come into Greece along with the hair style, which Ionian cities adopted from their neighbors in the sixth century B.C. (see the Assyrian "club" hair style of monuments). For the krobylos worn by women in Greece, see Arias-Hirmer 99 and infra n. 71.

71. Sprenger 57, Pls. 29, 30 (male), 36 (female). An Etruscan bronze figure of a "togatus" with krobylos is shown in Kassel, *Antike Bronzen* No. 35, Pl. 12.

72. Banti, "Tripodi Loeb" 79; she includes Hercules, but except for the type of young god for which Alexander's features are eventually substituted, Hercules continues to be bearded in the Classical period.

73. Arias-Hirmer 173-175. Cf. the farcical story about the monkey-like Cercopides, illustrated on a metope from Selinus, who make fun of Heracles' black (hairy?) bottom (Roscher, s.v. *"kerkopen"*; F. Dürrbach, in Daremberg-Saglio, s.v. "Hercules").

74. For the bronze kouroi from Castello, see supra Chapter 2, n. 34. For the Loeb tripods, see Banti, "Tripodi Loeb" 79, showing Hercules and the Nemean lion, Pls. 2, 3 2: "Eracle è giovanile e sbarbato, come nei vasi a figure rosse a partire della fine del VI sec. a.C." Cf. supra n. 6. An exception is the giant Tityos (Banti, "Tripodi Loeb" 89).

75. If this chronological difference holds true, it invalidates the dating criterion cited in the note above.

76. See Richardson 159 on the archaic bearded Hercules. On the borrowing of the Hercules type from Cyprus, see Bayet, *Hercule romain* (110-111, followed by Richardson 68, 105, 133, Pl. 24a. For an opposing view see M. Pallottino's review of Richardson, *The Etruscans*, in StEtr 34 (1966) 427.

77. See Mark I. Davies, "The Suicide of Ajax: A Bronze Etruscan Statuette from the Käppeli Collection," *Antike Kunst* (1971) 148-157, on the luxuriant beard and handlebar mustache of a bronze figure of ca. 460 B.C. Richardson (144, Pl. 43) writes: "This Etruscan gentleman [on the Boston sarcophagus] is clean-shaven, which would suggest a date after the beginning of Alexander's reign were he Greek, but we are not quite sure about Etruscan fashions; in the Archaic period, mature men wore full beards, as in Greece, and they sometimes did so in the Classical period, but perhaps not so often as in Greece."

78. Livy 5.41 and Ogilvie, ad loc. I have suggested elsewhere (*JRS* 60 [1970] 49-66) that Livy might have used, as pictorial evidence for these scenes of early Rome, archaic Etruscan paintings like the painted terracotta plaques from Cerveteri. A good illustration of this scene would be the painting of two old men dressed in purple robes and holding staffs—close enough to the *vestes triumphales* the old Romans were said to have put on—sitting facing each other on ivory seats like the Roman *sellae curules* (Roncalli 90-91).

79. Bronze examples are found in S. Haynes, "Ludiones Etruriae," *Festschrift H. Keller* (Darmstadt 1963) 13-21, with references. For the Tomba del Pulcinella, see Romanelli, *Tarquinia* Fig. 33; Becatti-Magi; and Tomba delle Olimpiadi, in Bartoccini-Lerici-Moretti 55, Fig. 19 (erroneously called a

tutulus). Bartoccini-Lerici-Moretti suggest the following chronological sequence: 540–530, Tomba degli Auguri; 530–520, Tomba del Pulcinella; 525–520, Tomba delle Olimpiadi.

80. Fest. 484.32: "tutulum vocari aiunt flaminicarum capitis ornamentum, quod fiat vitta purpurea innexa crinibus et exstructum in altitudinem." For the most complete recent discussion, emphasizing the fact that the Etruscan tutulus was a hair style, and not a hat, see Rumpf, "Antonia Augusta" 30. The following account substantially reproduces Rumpf's argument.

81. See Ernout-Meillet: "fait partie d'un groupe de mots à redoublement, *populus, tutulus*, qui semblent être d'origine étrusque."

82. Varro *LL* 7.44: "id tutulus appellatus ab eo quod matres familias crines convolutos ad verticem capitis quos habent vitta velatos dicebantur tutuli." Cf. Fest. 484.32, quoted above. The word "tutulus" was extended, in Roman times, to the hat of the flamines (Varro 7.44; Körte, *Göttinger Bronzen* 25, 35). Modern scholars have erroneously called both the *mitra*, or Greek kerchief, and the conical Etruscan hat "tutulus." See A. Rumpf, *AJA* 60 (1956) 74f., a review of Pallottino, *Etr. Painting*.

83. According to some etymologies, "tutulus" indicates the swelling shape, connected with *tumeo* (see Walde-Hofman). Certainly Festus and Varro emphasize this feature in describing the tutulus; Varro (7.44) compares it to a *meta*, the conical column or goal in the Roman circus.

84. Paris, Louvre, Br. 236, ca. 500 B.C. For further examples, see Schilling, *Vénus*. He identifies bronze statuettes wearing this type of hair style as representing Turan, the Etruscan Aphrodite; cf. Körte, *Göttinger Bronzen* 35f., Pl. 9, Fig. 7; Bonfante Warren, *ANRW* I₄ 596, Pl. 43, Fig. 8.

85. On the Pontic amphora (cf. supra n. 67; Chapter 5, n. 20) the artist distinguished male and female figures by their dress. Female figures are identified by the high profile of the tutulus worn under a mantle and the shoes hung up beside them. In contrast, the fourth figure, a male, wears the hair in the straight, windblown fashion of monuments of this period in the Ionian style—see the charioteers on Caeretan hydriae, or carved bone plaques—and his shoes are nowhere in sight. The following representations on late sixth-century monuments, appearing to show men wearing the tutulus, can perhaps be differently explained: bone plaques with reliefs from Tarquinia in the Louvre, in M. Renard, *AntCl* 7 (1938) 247–259, Nos. 5, 6; cf. *Schimmel Coll.* 90 and *Mostra* No. 239, Pl. 34; an Etruscan-inspired Campanian black-figure amphora in Berlin, in E. Rohde, *WZUR*, Gesellschafts- und Sprachwissenschaftliche Reihe, 7/8 (1967) 502, Pl. 73, 2; an Etruscan black-figure hydria in Heidelberg, in R. Herbig, *StEtr* 7 (1933) 345, Pl. 15, 2, 4; and a painted terracotta plaque from Cerveteri, in Roncalli 93–94, No. 40, Pl. 22. The first two show pictures of banqueters, the third (and fourth?) running revelers. The hair style, really a Greek mitra rather than an Etruscan tutulus, is probably worn as an effeminate costume appropriate for Ionian banqueters. It is interesting to notice that Herbig expresses some doubt about the sex of at least one of these figures on the monument he illustrates on quite different, purely anatomical grounds. On the Campanian vase in Berlin the male figure is wearing a hat (not a tutulus), for which the closest comparison is that of a female figure on an Etruscan monument. Perhaps we have here a misunderstanding on the part of the Campanian artist, who does not know that in Etruria this hat was a fashion for women.

86. Richardson 103: "The popularity of the pointed caps in Etruria is, indeed, good evidence that the 'Ionian' period there was directly affected by the cities of Ionia and not merely, as in Greece, the result of the spread of Ionian

fashions through the Mediterranean." Real hats and real shoes, imported from Ionia, become "naturalized" in Etruria, while in Athens similar fashions made an appearance, in real life and in art, only as exotic styles: see supra Chapter 5, "Pointed Shoes."

87. For Cypriot hats, see Young and Young, *Figurines* 196ff.; supra n. 1. On the Villa Giulia sarcophagus, too, the woman wears a hat and high boots, while the husband is bareheaded and barefoot.

88. For the Phrygian hat, see Daremberg-Saglio, s.v. "tiara"; Young and Young, *Figurines* 202–203. For the hat of Perseus on Loeb tripods B and C, with front and back as well as side pieces, see Banti, "Tripodi Loeb" 80, Pls. 3, 9.

89. For the statuette in the Louvre, see infra Notes to Fig. 157. For another almost identical example in the Vatican, Museo Etrusco Gregoriano, see G. Q. Giglioli, "Tre enigmatici bronzetti etruschi," *StEtr* 4 (1930) 418–419, Pl. 34, and E. Galli, "Hereklu," *StEtr* 15 (1941) Pl. 6, Fig. 3. The third figure, which comes from Este, is bearded: Lamb 110, Pl. 40C; Galli, *StEtr* 15 (1941) Pl. 6, Fig. 2; T. Campanile, "Statuetta di Eracle in bronzo d'arte etrusca," *BdA* ser. 2, 3 (1924) 453–462, Pl. 3; and Fogolari, *Mus. Naz. Este* Pl. 70.

90. Villa Giulia Museum. Pallottino (*Mostra* No. 235) dates it ca. 540–520 B.C., "uno dei più antichi esempi di figurine votive fittili." It is a sizable piece of sculpture, 27 cm. high. The right arm is missing entirely; the left still holds a piece of lead wire, probably the remnant of a bow. The animal skin is here worn over a tunic.

91. Galli, de Ridder, and Giglioli (supra n. 89) all express doubts as to its identification as Hercules. Galli and Giglioli remark on the exotic, barbaric, even Scythian appearance that the Phrygian cap and the quiver give the figure.

92. Richardson 234.

93. Richardson 144.

94. Museo Gregoriano Etrusco, Vatican, Banti 344, Pl. 110, and *Etruscan Cities* Pl. 42; cf. Higgins 120–121, 150, 158, Pl. 41. For the Tomba degli Scudi (Tomb of the Shields), see Banti 339, Pl. 98, and *Etruscan Cities* Pl. 38.

95. "The bulla, originally a lentoid pendant hanging from a broad loop, was to become the typical Etruscan ornament, the *Etruscum aureum* of the Romans. . . . it does not seem to have been in general use before the fifth century. . . . The earliest recorded examples are in bronze and come from Faliscan tombs at Narce of the mid-seventh century" (Higgins 140–141, Pls. 42, 44). Gold bullae were found in some of the earliest graves; see Richardson 35; Higgins Pls. 42, 44. For bronze bullae, see R. Bloch, *Recherches archéologiques en territoire Volsinien . . . de la préhistoire à la civilisation étrusque*, Bibliothèque de l'École Française d'Athènes et de Rome 220 (Paris 1972) 138–141; Amorelli, *Coll. Massimo* No. 37 (ninth to seventh century B.C.). Bracelets with bullae were represented worn on the upper arm by male figures of the second half of the sixth century: see a painted terracotta fragment from Cerveteri in Berlin, Staatliche Museum, in Roncalli 26, No. 11, Pl. 10, 1; and Kassel, *Antike Bronzen* No. 35, Pl. 12, a "togatus" of 500–475 B.C. Most numerous, however, are the fourth-century examples: they are worn on a red-figure cup from Vulci, in the Vatican, Museo Gregoriano Etrusco, by a woman (abducted by a bearded god, probably Zeus; see Banti 337, Pl. 87, "first half of the fourth century"). They were often worn by gods or heroes; as on a terracotta fragment from Orvieto representing the torso of a youth, in Sprenger 60–61, Pl. 33; the Ficoroni cista, dated by Beazley before 336 B.C., in Helbig[4] 2976; a red-figure Etruscan crater of the fourth century, in Banti 336, Pl. 83 (see H. Jucker's review of Banti in *Gnomon* 37 [1965] 303 and cf. Beazley, *EVP* 34, on the Argonaut crater in the Louvre, "not much after the first decade of the fourth

century"); and a mirror from the vicinity of Perugia showing Perseus with the head of Medusa (Hermes wears a bulla bracelet) which Banti (335, Pl. 80) dates as fourth or third century, though Jucker, in his review (303), would not date it later than the fourth. See infra Fig. 122. A number of gold bullae of the fifth and fourth century have been found; see Helbig[4] 766-67; Banti 334, Pl. 78, and *Etruscan Cities* Pl. 41. For a gold bulla in the Walters Art Gallery, see G. M. A. Hanfmann and E. Fiesel, *AJA* 39 (1935) 189-199; cf. Richardson Pl. 40a, 152-153.

96. See the cinerary urn from Chianciano, in Banti 331, Pl. 73 ("diadema caratteristico di Chiusi e Orvieto"); Higgins Pl. 41. The dress of the female figure is a typical fourth-century outfit: see Jucker's review of Banti in *Gnomon* 37 (1965) 304. See also a red-figure cup from Vulci, in Banti 337, Pl. 87; a terracotta antefix, in Banti 332, Pl. 75 ("beginning of fourth century"); and another cinerary urn from Chianciano, the so-called Mater Matuta (Banti 332, Pl. 74; *Etruscan Cities* Pl. 77), whose tomb context dates it to 475-450, as shown by Cristofani in *Nuove letture* 89-93. On the fourth-century sarcophagus from Vulci in Boston it is worn by the woman lying on the lid and by the two female figures on the side; see Banti 340, Pls. 102-103; Richardson 143-146, Pls. 43-44. The crown-like diadem of a bronze statuette in the British Museum, with its incised circles, may be an attempt to represent this diadem in metal (Richardson 133, Pl. 39a), while the same ornament is represented in painting on the lady in the Tomba degli Scudi (Banti 339, Pl. 98).

97. Richardson (144) describes the hair style of the lady on the Boston sarcophagus: "the soft waves (are) parted in the center and bound with a braid, a fashion known also in fourth century Athens." For the krobylos, see above. There is a stylized but recognizable version on a red-figure crater from Volterra (in the Museo Guarnacci) in Banti 336, Pl. 86.

98. The torque is represented on the figure of a bronze sarcophagus lid in Leningrad: see A. Votschinina, *StEtr* 33 (1965) 317-328; Bianchi Bandinelli-Giuliano 338, "ca. 300 B.C." On this special necklace, the *torques* (στρεπτός, Hdt. 3.20; Xen. *Cyr.* 1.3.2; from *torqueo*, "twist"), see Isid. *Orig.* 19.31. 11: "dictae autem torques quod sunt tortae." They are spiral, twisted neck bands with open, decorated ends, widely worn in northern Europe and Asia, from Ireland to the territory of the Scyths, from the Bronze Age on. See C. F. A. Schaeffer, "Les porteurs de torques," *Ugaritica* II (1949) 49-120, for examples dated around 2000 B.C. in Ugarit and Byblos. Examples of gold, silver, and bronze torques were found in the British Isles, France, Russia, etc. Gallic warriors wore them into battle (Strab. 4.4.5: χρυσοφοροῦσι τε γάρ, περὶ μὲν τοῖς τραχήλοις στρεπτὰ ἔχοντες ; cf. Pliny *HN* 33.15; Polyb. 2.31.4). See the Pergamene statue of the dying Gaul in the Capitoline museum in Rome, and other monuments, in H. Hubert, *Les Celtes* (Paris 1932) 124-126. The Romans became acquainted with this ornament in war: Manlius Torquatus was so called after he tore a torque from an enemy corpse and put it on (Livy 7.10.11), and torques were given as prizes for valor. Among the Romans only men wore torques (Isid. *Orig.* 19.31, 11.2). The Etruscans borrowed this ornament from the Gauls and represented it often, on men and women, from ca. 400 B.C. on. The Greeks learned of it from the Medes and Persians (Hdt. 8.113.3, 7.80.4, etc.), whose nobles were distinguished by this torques (see the Alexander mosaic from Pompeii).

99. For the jewelry, see Higgins 149-153, Pls. 41-44, and M. F. Briguet, *La revue du Louvre* 24 (1974) 247-252. Earrings in the form of conventionalized grape clusters (Richardson 192; Higgins 151-52, Pl. 42D) are worn by figures of women with diadems: see a terracotta antefix, in Banti 78B, a red-figure cup from Vulci, in Banti Pl. 87, *Etruscan Cities* Pl. 49; the Tomba dell'Orco, Pl. 95,

Etruscan Cities Pl. 36; the Tomba degli Scudi, Pl. 98, *Etruscan Cities* Pl. 38; a skyphos in Boston, in Richardson 150–151, Pl. 42; and a mirror, infra Fig. 122. Actual gold earrings of this type, found in tombs, are in the British Museum (Banti, *Etruscan Cities* Pl. 42B; cf. Higgins 151, Pl. 42D), the Metropolitan Museum in New York (Richardson 152, Pl. 40c), and the Louvre (Briguet [supra] Fig. 4). Pendant earrings (Banti, *Etruscan Cities* 42C) which may be a later style than the clusters, are shown on a winged figure with krobylos on a red-figure crater from Volterra (Banti 336, Pl. 86) and on a mirror in Florence (infra Fig. 160) worn by Artemis and Athena (or Minerva), dressed in typical fourth-century fashion. For hair style, sakkos, and jewelry represented on women in the fourth and third century on Caeretan-Faliscan kylikes, see M. Del Chiaro, *MAAR* 27 (1962) 204–208.

100. See the bronze head of a youth from Cagli (Pesaro), Villa Giulia Museum, in *Mostra* No. 323, Pl. 67, dated around the middle of the fourth century. For the "tradizionale stilizzazione a ciocche fiammeggianti striate," see some terracotta heads from Orvieto (*Mostra* No. 317, Pl. 64, No. 319, Pl. 66) or the "testa Malavolta" from Veii (*Mostra* No. 324). See also *Roma Medio Repubblicana* Pls. 20, 30, 37, 39, 41, 44. For a straight-haired style see *Roma Medio Repubblicana* Pl. 38; Sprenger *passim*.

101. M. Bieber, *ProcPhilSoc* 93, 5 (1949) 373–426, and *Alexander the Great in Greek and Roman Art* (Chicago 1964) 53, 62; Richardson 144, 159, 161.

102. Examples are found in Banti Pls. 114–115, *Etruscan Cities*, Pls. 89–90; from Perugia, second century B.C., in *Mostra* Nos. 403, 409, 410, Pls. 99, 101, 100; and from Volterra, second or first century B.C., in *Mostra* Nos. 403, 409. An ash urn from Chiusi, mid-second century, is shown in Richardson 163–165, Pl. 45; cf. Bianchi Bandinelli-Giuliano 339.

103. Richardson 158–159; *EAA* s.v. "*Carsóli*," "*Italica, arte.*"

104. *Stephane*: see Higgins Pl. 45B. Richardson says (161): "The Gaulish torque began to be worn in Italy during the third century: the ogival *stephane* seems to be commoner in the second."

105. See the billowing hair on a bronze statuette of a priestess, Florence, Museo Archeologico, 554; M. Buffa, *StEtr* 7 (1935) 451–456, Pl. 25; Richardson (160–161, Pl. 47b) also points out that "the tendril of hair on the cheek is a Hellenistic detail but cannot be dated too closely." For women's hair styles on third- to second-century urns and sarcophagi, see N. Pacchioni, *StEtr* 13 (1939) 485–496, Pls. 39–42.

106. Terracotta sarcophagus of Seianti Thanunia Tlesnasa, from Chiusi, British Museum D 786, *NSc* 1877, 142; Banti Pl. 107, *Etruscan Cities* Pl. 82, ca. 150 B.C.; bullae, Bianchi Bandinelli-Giuliano 356, from Chiusi.

107. For the Praxitelean hair style, knotted at the crown, see the terracotta head in Banti Pl. 116, *Etruscan Cities*, Pl. 15. For the plain style, see the votive terracotta head from Cerveteri in Banti Pl. 117, *Etruscan Cities* Pl. 16 ("first century"). See the terracotta statuette of a girl combing her hair, a local provincial work from Sarteano, in *Mostra* No. 417, Pl. 104. Its genuineness has been doubted, but see Bianchi Bandinelli-Giuliano 376–377. See supra Chapter 3, n. 44.

108. The stylization of the hair found on a group of mirrors first identified by Beazley as "Group Z" was connected by Herbig with a group he called the "Kranzspiegelgruppe," and dated to ca. 150 B.C., in *StEtr* 24 (1955–66) 205. Figures on ivory reliefs from Palestrina, usually dated to the fourth century (*Mostra*, Nos. 328, 329, Pl. 68; *Roma Medio Repubblicana* Nos. 435, 436, Pls. 96, 97), show, with a linear stylization, coil-like locks of hair. For these I suggested a date around 100 B.C., along with a number of other cistae and mirrors related to Herbig's group, in *AJA* 68 (1964) 35f.; though this is

probably too late, the group does have a unified Praenestine style. On the rectangular bronze cista from Palestrina, the figures (O. J. Brendel, *AJA* 64 [1960] 45, Pl. 8.4; *Mostra* No. 362, Pl. 85) have their hair smoothly brushed back in a straight-haired Hellenistic style.

109. Of the bronze from the Bernardini tomb, Brown (24–25) says: "The workshop was still under powerful Eastern influence." The plumes are Egyptian but are modified on such monuments as North Syrian or Phoenician ivories.

110. Bonfante Warren, *Brendel Essays*.

111. Ivory head found at Nimrud in 1951, from the "Burnt Palace," C. K. Wilkinson, "Some New Contacts with Nimrud and Assyria," *BMMA* 10 (1951–52) 235, seventh century B.C.

112. See the "Assurattasch" from Olympia, in Matz Pl. 59. Other examples are in Ducati, *StEtr* 2 (1928) 45–47; Banti, *StEtr* 28 (1960) 282, n. 25. Double locks eventually replace the single lock in both Greece and Etruria.

113. Hanfmann (*Altetr. Plastik* 15f.) compares the Etruscan fashion with that of Greek Geometric heads; Riis (*Tyrrhenika* 73) compares it with later examples such as the Rampin head. Cf. Richardson, *MAAR* 27 (1962) 185.

114. Higgins 149: "Etruscan jewellery again becomes plentiful about 400 B.C. It now has a character entirely its own, in many ways entirely unlike Early Etruscan, and is remarkable in that, once developed, it remained without any significant changes for some one and a half centuries. . . . our evidence for the transitional period, 474–400 B.C., is slight, and is confined to the far North, which was probably apart from the main current."

7. FOREIGN INFLUENCES AND LOCAL STYLES

1. L. Bonfante Warren, "Etruscan Dress in North Italy," forthcoming.

2. Richardson, *MAAR* 27 (1962) 191: "Types whose costumes, and gestures are unmistakably derived from the Near East, as is their style"; H. Kantor, "A Bronze Plaque with Relief Decoration from Tell Tainat," *JNES* 21 (1962) 93–117: cf. infra Fig. 150, a bronze relief from the Bernardini tomb. O. W. Muscarella, in "Near Eastern Bronzes in the West: The Question of Origin," *Art and Technology* 109–128, has written a relevant passage on the question of Oriental imports in the West: "It is an academic question when one group of scholars claims that foreign immigrant-craftsmen came west and there made the early Oriental objects recovered, and another group suggests that the Oriental objects were imports; the same historical-archaeological implications result, namely that Western art and ideas were in contact with art and ideas from the East. . . . [The] Orientalizing objects are more important for documenting *influence*, whereas an import only informs us that *contact* and exposure occurred." Poulsen's epoch-making study of 1912, in which the author traces in detail Oriental influences in Orientalizing Greek art, has proved invaluable in writing this book. Of course, new finds and studies have added to our knowledge of artistic influence and cultural and commercial contact. Particularly in Etruscan studies the rhythm of discovery has accelerated within the past ten years, so that scholars can barely keep pace with the next turn of the spade, which is more than likely to turn up surprising new evidence about Etruria's foreign contacts. Etruscan-Phoenician relations are coming more into focus than was once thought possible by the find of the inscribed gold tablets at Pyrgi (the original report, by Pallottino and others, appeared in *ArchCl* 16 [1964] 49–117; the latest bibliography can be found in J. Ferron, *ANRW* I₁ 189–216) and by the exploration of Phoenician sites (I have

not seen J. MacIntosh, *Etruscan-Punic Relations* [Ph.D. dissertation, Bryn Mawr College, 1975]). Excavations at Graviscae illustrate the Greek presence in Etruria (M. Torelli, *NSc* [1971] 195-299 and *Parola del Passato* 26 [1971] 44-67); further reports are found in D. Ridgway, "Archaeology in Central Italy and Etruria, 1968-1973, Archaeological Reports for 1973-1974," (1974) 49-51, nn. 53-54; most important will be the publication of the material from Pithekoussai, documenting the arrival of the first Western Greeks in the first half of the eighth century B.C. (D. Ridgway, "Archaeological Reports for 1973-1974," [1974] 46, n. 27) and illuminating Greek, Etruscan, and Eastern contacts in that early period.

Meanwhile useful books and articles are bringing order to material already known but scattered or improperly understood. E. Akurgal's *Orient und Okzident, Die Geburt der Griechischen Kunst* (Baden Baden 1966) is "a systematic and modernized version" of Poulsen, and of T. J. Dunbabin's *The Greeks and Their Eastern Neighbors* (London 1957); see J. L. Benson's informative review in *AJA* 75 (1971) 338-339. For imports of bucchero vases, especially kantharoi, from Etruria to Greece, see J. MacIntosh, "Etruscan Bucchero Imports in Corinth," *Hesperia* 43 (1974) 34-45. For the chronology of Etruscan Orientalizing, J. G. Szilágyi's studies of Italo-Corinthian pottery are of capital importance (*StEtr* 26 [1958] 273ff.; *WissZUnivRostock* 16 [1967] 543ff.; *ArchCl* 20 [1968] 1ff.; *RA* [1972] 111-126). Cf. G. Colonna, *ArchCl* 13 (1961) 9-24. On Near Eastern imports to Etruria, see Strøm 109-137, with refs.; specifically on tridacna shells, see S. Stucchi, *BdA* 44 (1959) 158-166, and Amandry 73ff.; on ostrich eggs, see M. Torelli, *StEtr* 33 (1965) 329-365. On Egyptian faience objects found in Cerveteri, see F. W. von Bissing, SBMunich (1941), and *University of London, Institute of Classical Studies* 16 (1969) 4ff.; it is not clear whether these are imports from Egypt or from the Phoenician world. See supra Chapter 6, n. 32, for the many figurines of the god Bes found in Etruscan tombs. Like M. Guido (*Sardinia* [London 1963] 174), I see a Punic ancestry for seventh-century feather crowns, perhaps related to that of the dwarf-god Bes. On the Phoenician presence in the Western Mediterranean, see W. Culican, "Almuñecar, Assur, and Phoenician penetration of the Western Medieterranean," *Levant* 2 (1970) 28-36, and R. D. Barnett, "Nimrud Bowls in the British Museum," *Rivista di Studi Fenici* 2 (University of Rome 1974) 11-33, Pls. 1-18, with bibl.; M. Pallottino, "La Sicilia fra l'Africa e l'Etruria: problemi storici e culturali," *Kokalos* 18-19 (1973) 48-76.

For the reconstruction of a lost import, see M. Pallottino, "Orientalizing," in *EWA* X 794; G. Camporeale, *StEtr* 35 (1967) 31-40, 601; Bonfante Warren, *Studi Banti* 81-87; Canciani 123. Routes are discussed by A. Hus, *MélRome* 71 (1959) 38ff. Camporeale, *Commerci di Vetulonia*, charts imports and imitations in Vetulonia, not only from abroad but from other Etruscan cities. He does not believe that Vetulonia received foreign imports directly; for a contrary opinion, see F. W. von Hase, *RM* 79 (1972) 155ff.

3. See Vermeule 193, 212, on ceremonial Minoan costume vs. Mycenean clothes. Minoan dress was represented as archaic "divine" costume on mainland female figures, as on an ivory from Mycenae (Vermeule Pl. 39A), apparently in imitation of such figures as the ivory group of goddesses with a child (Vermeule 220, Pl. 38). For Mycenean dress, see Marinatos, *Kleidung*; E. French, *BSA* 66 (1971) 101-187; cf. 109 (Minoan).

4. For cultural contacts in the eastern Mediterranean in the second millennium, see T. B. L. Webster, *From Mycenae to Homer* (London, 1958). Charlotte Long is probably right (*AJA* 58 [1954] 147-148) in seeing a linen chiton (similar to the "proto-Ionic" chiton of Etruria) on Mycenean figurines of the LM III C period. This garment and the long (Mycenean) back braid

could have come into Mycenean fashion at the same time. (See supra Chapter 6, n. 33.)

5. For the vitality of Mycenean elements surviving into the early Greek period, see Della Seta, "Lemno" 131; Pallottino, "Fond. miceneo"; E. T. Vermeule, "Painted Mycenean Larnakes," *JHS* 85 (1965) 123–148, especially 147.

6. A. Blakeway, "Demaratus," *JHS* 25 (1935) 144. Cf. Richardson, *MAAR* 27 (1962) 164.

7. See J. Boardman, *The Greeks Overseas* (Penguin 1964) 84, on the "non-Oriental (though perhaps Cypriot) bloomers" of the central figure of the Cretan shield. The pants were perhaps more properly Cretan than Cypriot. Supra Chapter 2, n. 40.

8. E.g., an Orientalizing vase from Crete in Berlin, Staatliche Museum, ca. 670–650 B.C., in Doro Levi, *Hesperia* 14 (1945) Pl. 26; Greifenhagen, *Staatl. Mus.* 42, No. F 307, Pl. 35 ("ornaments . . . reminiscent of Minoan"); Bonfante Warren, *Brendel Essays*, Pl. 3f–g.

9. See J. Heurgon, "La Magna Grecia e i santuari del Lazio," *La Magna Grecia e Roma nell'età Arcaica, Atti dell'VIII Convegno di Studi Sulla Magna Grecia* (Taranto 1968) 12–13, on the greater importance of the sea than the land route for Greek contacts, especially the port of Caere: "L'importazione dalla Ionia si è fatta senza nessuno scalo conosciuto." Many elements came directly to southern Etruria from Asia Minor.

10. See also Corinthian comparisons for the dress of the Vix statuette in M. Gjødesen, *AJA* 67 (1963) 335, esp. 340; supra Chapter 4. For the legend that Demaratus brought Corinthian artists to Tarquinia with him, see Pliny *HN* 35.16, 152; Banti 55.

11. The plaid pattern and the short capelet of some Laconian figurines are common to other areas of the Orientalizing world. An interesting sequence of Greek influence in the Orientalizing period, however, is traced by G. Colonna, "Una nuova iscrizione etrusca . . . ," *MélRome* 82 (1970) 672, from epigraphical evidence. The Etruscan alphabet, received no earlier than 700 B.C. from the Greeks of Campania, was first modified under Corinthian influence, then, around 630 B.C., under East Greek influence. Dorian features of Greek borrowings in Etruscan in the early period underline the importance of Dorian-speaking East Greeks—Rhodians, Cnidians, Halicarnassans, and others—in close contact with the Etruscans at that time (M. Cristofani, "Sull'origine e la diffusione dell'alfabeto etrusco," *ANRW* I$_2$ 466–489, esp. 474).

12. E. A. Lane, *BSA* 34 (1933–34) 186: "The greatest proportion of exported Lakonian vases was found in Etruria, and they naturally contributed some ingredients to what may be called the 'Etruscan pie.'" For examples of decorative motifs which include the bud and pomegranate frieze, taken over in Etruscan art, see Lane 187. Laconian connections with Etruscan costume, e.g., the calcei repandi, are evident during this same period; and see a bronze statuette (supra Chapter 2, n. 14) for similarity of style as well as dress.

13. W. H. Gross considers the crater to be of Tarentine manufacture (private conversation). See infra Notes to Illustrations.

14. For the metope from Selinus see supra Chapter 4, n. 9. See also an architectural terracotta fragment from Paestum with pointed sandals, in B. Neutsch *AA* 71 (1956) 418–419, Fig. 138; P. Sestieri, *Nuova Antologia* No. 1853 (1955) 73. See Chapter 4, n. 35, for the poncho style.

15. See supra Chapter 4, nn. 45–46, for female statuettes from southern Etruria wearing the diagonal mantle; and infra, n. 19. For contacts between Magna Graecia and northern Italy, see D. Mustilli, "Magna Grecia e Italia Settentrionale," *Atti del I Congresso Internazionale di Archeologia Settentrionale* (Bologna 1963) 33–43.

98. The torque is represented on the figure of a bronze sarcophagus lid in Leningrad: see A. Votschinina, *StEtr* 33 (1965) 317-328; Bianchi Bandinelli-Giuliano 338, "ca. 300 B.C." On this special necklace, the torques($\sigma\tau\rho\epsilon\pi\tau\delta\varsigma$, Hdt. 3.20; Xen. *Cyr.* 1.3.2; from *torqueo*, "twist"), see Isid. *Orig.* 19.31. 11: "dictae autem torques quod sunt tortae." They are spiral, twisted neck bands with open, decorated ends, widely worn in northern Europe and Asia, from Ireland to the territory of the Scyths, from the Bronze Age on. See C. F. A. Schaeffer, "Les porteurs de torques," *Ugaritica* II (1949) 49-120, for examples dated around 2000 B.C. in Ugarit and Byblos. Examples of gold, silver, and bronze torques were found in the British Isles, France, Russia, etc. Gallic warriors wore them into battle (Strab. 4.4.5: $\chi\rho\upsilon\sigma\sigma\phi\rho\rho\tilde{\upsilon}\sigma\iota$ $\tau\epsilon$ $\gamma\dot{\alpha}\rho$, $\pi\epsilon\rho\dot{\iota}$ $\mu\dot{\epsilon}\nu$ $\tau\tilde{\sigma}\iota\varsigma$ $\tau\rho\alpha\chi\dot{\eta}\lambda\sigma\iota\varsigma$ $\sigma\tau\rho\epsilon\pi\tau\dot{\alpha}$ $\dot{\epsilon}\chi\sigma\nu\tau\epsilon\varsigma$; cf. Pliny *HN* 33.15; Polyb. 2.31.4). See the Pergamene statue of the dying Gaul in the Capitoline museum in Rome, and other monuments, in H. Hubert, *Les Celtes* (Paris 1932) 124-126. The Romans became acquainted with this ornament in war: Manlius Torquatus was so called after he tore a torque from an enemy corpse and put it on (Livy 7.10.11), and torques were given as prizes for valor. Among the Romans only men wore torques (Isid. *Orig.* 19.31, 11.2). The Etruscans borrowed this ornament from the Gauls and represented it often, on men and women, from ca. 400 B.C. on. The Greeks learned of it from the Medes and Persians (Hdt. 8.113.3, 7.80.4, etc.), whose nobles were distinguished by this torques (see the Alexander mosaic from Pompeii).

80

81

82

82. Bronze statuette, Baltimore, Walters Art Gallery, Inv. 54.99. Height 38.9 cm. Ca. 400 B.C. Reinach, *Rép. st.* III Pl. 197, 2; Hill No. 240, Pl. 46; Teitz No. 69, Pl. 170.
83. Venus, Adonis, Minerva, and a seated divinity (a Fate?). Bronze mirror. Ca. 400 B.C. Gerhard Pl. 112; *TLE* No. 752. On the shield of Minerva, an inscription reads: "Tite Cale: atial: turce: malstria: cver," or "Titus Calus gave this mirror to his mother as a gift."
84.-85. Deceased couple (Fig. 84) and couple with attendants (Fig. 85). Sarcophagus from Vulci. Boston, Museum of Fine Arts. Lent by the Boston Athenaeum. Acc. Ath. 1281. 84. Length 2.115 m. Ca. 300 B.C. Vermeule and Chase 202, 203, Figs. 185 a–c, 186; Banti Pl. 103; Herbig 13–14, No. 5, Pl. 40; Hanfmann, *JHS* 65 (1945) 47, Pl. 8; Richardson 143–146, Pls. 43, 44; Hus, *Vulci* Pl. 24a.
86. Hercules and Minerva at a goat sacrifice in the Garden of the Hesperides. Bronze mirror. Ca. 300 B.C. Gerhard 140 (the artist mistook Hercules' club as a caduceus); Bayet, *Herclé* 52, 128–130, 135–137, Pl. 3.

83

84

85

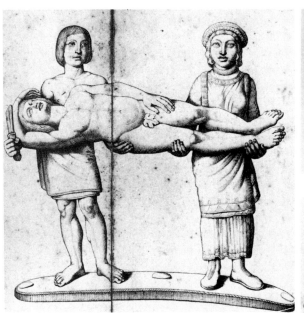

86

87

87.-88. Man and woman carrying a dead man. Bronze handle of Praenestine cista from Castel Clementino, in Picenum (evidently exported). Once in the Museo Kircheriano; now lost. Height 7.7 cm. Fourth century B.C. G. Marchi, *La cista atletica del Museo Kircheriano* (Rome 1848) Pl. 2; A. Sambon, *Collection Warnecke: Catalogue des objets d'art antique* (Paris 1905) No. 137, Pl. 9; G. Battaglia, *Corpus di ciste prenestine* (forthcoming).

88

89

90

89. The murder of Eriphyle. Funerary urn from Volterra. Volterra museum. Height 40 cm., length 54 cm. Third century B.C.(?) Laviosa, *Sc. Volterra* 68, No. 11, Pls. 33–37.

90. Death of Oenomaus. Funerary urn from Volterra. Florence, Museo Archeologico, Inv. 5703. Height 45 cm., length 80 cm. Third-second century B.C. Brunn-Körte 2, 111, Pl. 41,2; Laviosa, *Sc. Volterra* 104, No. 19, Pls. 61–64.

91. Meleager and Atalanta, flanked by the aged king Oeneus and the son of Thestios. Meleager wears hunting boots, Atalanta a torque and necklace. Bronze mirror, unknown provenance. Paris, Louvre Museum. Height 21.3 cm., diameter 13 cm. Hellenistic period, perhaps third century B.C. De Ridder 1749; Gerhard 175; Cles-Reden Pl. 59; Ciasca 49, No. 30, Pl. 24,2 (with bibl.).

92. Reclining figure of bejeweled female on the lid of a funerary urn with a relief showing a farewell scene of husband and wife. Palermo museum. Fourth century B.C.

93. Necklace of gold bullae. Vatican, Museo Etrusco Gregoriano. Fourth or third century B.C. Bonfante Warren, *Archaeology* 26 (1973) 242; cf. Helbig[4] 776, 767, 809; Banti Pl. 78; Banti[2] Pl. 41; Bianchi Bandinelli-Giuliano Pls. 349–350; Coarelli, *Jewellery* Pl. 54.

91

92

93

MANTLES

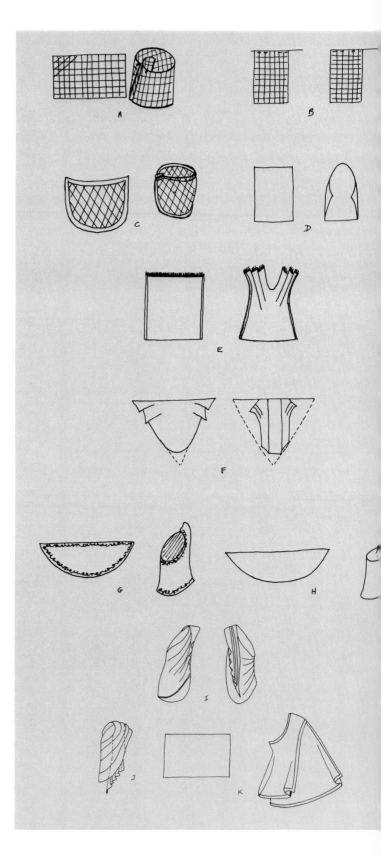

94. Forms and patterns of mantles in Etruria and an oval mantle from Gerömsberg, Sweden.

A–B, seventh-century cloaks, *A*, for men, and *B*, for women; *C*, mantle of statuettes from Cerveteri (Figs. 14–16), rectangular; *D–E*, rectangular mantles for women; *F*, mantle of statuette from Vulci (Fig. 99); *G–I*, tebenna draped diagonally; *J–K*, himation draped diagonally; *L–O*, mantles worn with ends in back: *L* and *M*, short rounded scarf, *N*, long rounded laena, *O*, long triangular mantle; *P–T*, mantles worn with ends in front: *P*, rectangular mantle; *Q–S*, rectangular mantles with sewn ends; *T*, long rounded mantle; *U*, later form of the tebenna (Arringatore, Fig. 109); *V*, early oval rounded mantle, from Gerömsberg, Sweden (cf. Fig. 1).

95. Woman wearing a "rain-cape" type of mantle with armholes, originally holding out an object in each hand (the lituus probably was not on the original). Bronze statuette. London, British Museum. Height 5.5 in. Ca. 600 B.C. C. Smith, *The Forman Collection* (London 1899) Pl. 2, No. 55; Körte, *Göttinger Bronzen* 20, 6; Riis, *Tyrrhenika* 59–60, Pl. 10, 1; Strong, *Early Etr.* 57.

96. Woman with mantle and pointed shoes, so-called "*xoanon.*" Bronze statuette. Florence, Museo Archeologico, 678. Height 24 cm. 540–530 B.C. *Mostra* 25, No. 79, Pl. 17. Cf. several figures of this type in Monaco, *StEtr* 16 (1942) Pl. 31, and Magi, *StEtr* 12 (1938) Pl. 48.

97. Female figure wearing mantle and pointed shoes. Greek bronze statuette from Vix. Châtillon-sur-Seine, Musée Archéologique. Height 19 cm. Ca. 540 B.C. Joffroy, *Vix.* Greifenhagen, *Propyläen* I 150 (text), dates it 530 B.C. and follows G. Vallet and F. Villard, *BCH* 79 (1955) 50f., who assign it to a South Italian workshop.

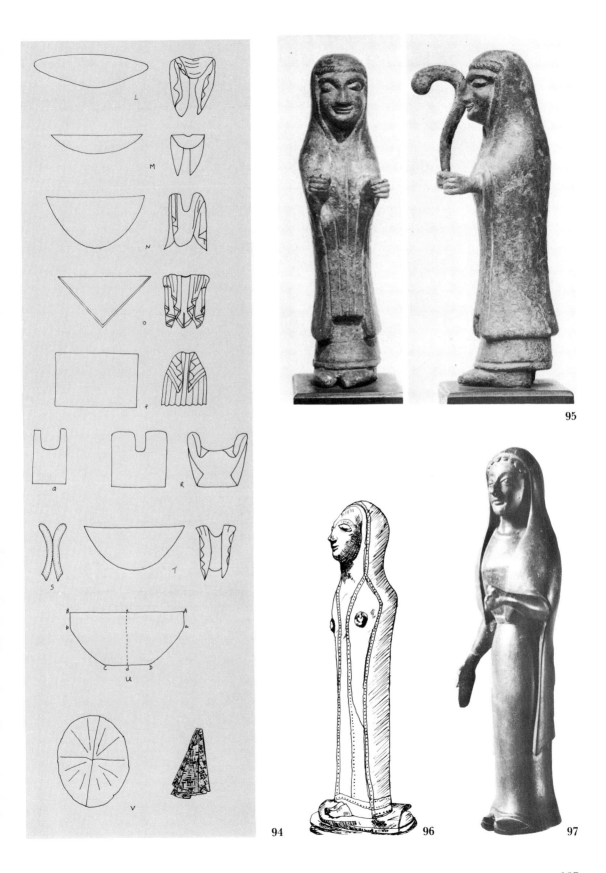

94

95

96

97

98

98. Choros leader, and women, dancing around a central figure, wearing Dedalic capelets. Relief on fragmentary circular stone cippus from Chiusi. Palermo museum, Collezione Casuccini, No. 205. Height 24 cm., width 2.50 cm. Ca. 550 B.C. Johnstone, *Dance in Etr.* 56–58, U3, Pl. 2, Fig. 5; *Mostra* 23, No. 72; Bonfante Warren, *Studi Banti* 81–87, Pl. 19a.

99. Statuette from Vulci, Tomb of Isis, Necropolis of Polledrara, of alabaster-like gypsum, wearing chiton, himation with gilt belt, and sandals. The hem of the chiton was decorated with a Corinthian-style lotus flower border; traces of the original paint are still visible. London, British Museum. Height 88 cm. Ca. 570 B.C. Banti, *StEtr* 28 (1960) 277ff., Pls. 52–54; Richter, *Korai* 41, No. 45, Figs. 159–162; S. Haynes, *Antike Plastik* 4 (1965) 13–26; Hus, *Vulci*, Pl. 2; Banti 302–303, Pl. 33; Banti² 309, No. 43a; V. Poulsen, *Etruskische Kunst* (Königstein am Taunus 1969) Pls. 44–45 (good side views).

100. Back of Fig. 99.

101. Funeral procession. Fragment from a circular funerary stone cippus from Chiusi. Palermo museum, Collezione Casuccini, No. 245. Height 101 cm. Ca. 540 B.C. Paribeni, *StEtr* 12 (1938) 67, Pl. 7,1; Banti, *StEtr* 28 (1960) 285, Pl. 53b.

101

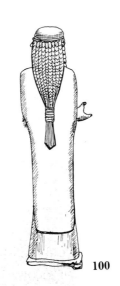

100

99   102   103

102. Bronze statuette of a youth. Paris, Bibliothèque Nationale, No. 938. Height 8 cm. Ca. 480 B.C. Babelon-Blanchet 413, No. 938; Heuzey 235; Bonfante Warren, *ANRW* I₄ Fig. 3. For the style, cf. B. M. bronze No. 500 in S. Haynes, *Art and Technology* 184, Figs. 11, 12.

103. Back of Fig. 102.

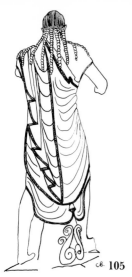

104.–105. Apollo. Terracotta statue from Veii. Rome, Villa Giulia Museum. Height 1.75 m. 500–490 B.C. Banti, Pls. 44–45; *Propyläen* I 411; Helbig⁴ 2556.

106. Female figure wearing diagonally draped himation and pointed shoes. Bronze statuette. Paris, Bibliothèque Nationale, Cabinet des Médailles, No. 1040. Height 25.8 cm. Ca. 500 B.C. *Mostra* 64, No. 255, Pl. 43; Bonfante Warren, *Archaeology* 26 (1973) 246. Cf. two similar statuettes in the Vatican, Museo Etrusco Gregoriano, Invs. 12043, 12047: T. Dohrn, in Helbig⁴ 701, dates them ca. 520 B.C.

107. So-called Vertumnus. Bronze statuette from Isola di Fano (Picenum). Florence, Museo Archeologico, Inv. 72725. Height 27.5 cm. Ca. 500 B.C. Richardson *Art Quarterly* 19 (1956) Fig. 8, and *MAAR* 27 (1962) Fig. 36; Riis, *Tyrrhenika* 59.

108. Detail from the shoulder of Fig. 107.

109. Aulus Metellius, the *Arringatore*. Bronze statue. Florence, Museo Archeologico. He is dressed as a Roman citizen, with a short toga, *exigua* and *praetexta*, on the border of which is inscribed an honorary inscription in Etruscan; the tunic with *angustus clavus*; the gold ring of the knight; and *calcei*. Height 1.79 m. 100–80 B.C. Dohrn, *Arringatore* (with previous bibl.); D. K. Hill, *AJA* 74 (1970) 116–117; H. Lauter, *Gnomon* 43 (1971) 423–425; L. Richardson, Jr., and E. H. Richardson, *YCS* 19 (1966) 261–263, Fig. 13; E. Birbari, "Stitchery in Classical and Renaissance Art," *JWarb* 34 (1971) 318–320. K. Fittschen, *RM* 77 (1970) 177–184, examines the dress; A. Neppi Modona, in Solari Pl. 24, Fig. 42, the shoes; M. Pallottino, *BdA* 49 (1964) 115–116, the inscription (*TLE* 651). For the toga, see Wilson 25. His name is Etruscan: Aule Meteli.

104

106

107

108

109

110

112

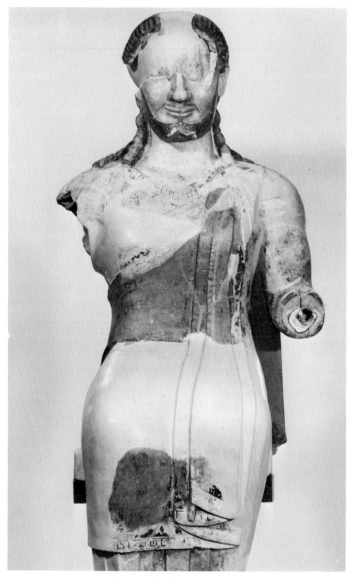

111

110. Seated group of gods receiving homage. Relief terracotta plaque from Velletri. Naples, Museo Nazionale. Height 38 cm., 1.49 cm. End of sixth century B.C. Van Buren 69–70; Andrén 412, Pl. 128; Mazzarino 58–75; A. Alföldi, *AJA* 63 (1959) 3. See bibliography in Pallottino 208.

111.–112. Seated Zeus, with diagonally draped red himation over light yellow long-sleeved chiton. Painted straps on the legs probably indicate laced sandals (the feet are missing). Greek terracotta cult statue. Paestum museum. Height 90.5 cm. Ca. 510 B.C. P. C. Sestieri, *BdA* 40 (1955) 193–212 and *RivIstArch* 5–6 (1956–57) 65ff.; Langlotz, *Westgriechen*, Pls. 3, 4.

113.–114. Dancers (Fig. 113) and banquet (Fig. 114), Tomba dei Leopardi, Tarquinia. Height 84 cm. Ca. 470 B.C. Pallottino, *Etr. Painting* Pl. 67f. and plates on 67–71; Banti[2] Pl. 34.

113

114

115. Heracles carrying off Apollo's tripod. Attic red-figure cup from Cerveteri. Vatican, Museo Etruseo Gregoriano, Inv. 16579. Diameter 24 cm. Ca. 500 B.C. Helbig⁴ 658.

116. Man with mantle. Terracotta statuette from Aja Irini, Cyprus. Height 102 cm. 510–500 B.C. Gjerstad, *Swed. Cyprus Exp.* II 706, Nos. 1044 and 2495, Pls. 205, 2, 206, 2, 3; Törnkvist 25: "understood as an oblong, rectangular piece of cloth." Cf. *Medelhavsmuseet* 3 (1963) No. 1071, Fig. 20.

117. Hermes. Bronze statuette from Vulci. Paris, Bibliothèque Nationale. Height 11.6 cm. Ca. 480 B.C. De Ridder No. 269, Pl. 24; Hus, *Vulci*, Pl. 7b.

118

116

117

118. Youth with rounded mantle. Bronze statuette. Minneapolis Institute of Arts, Acc. 47. 39. Height 17.7 cm. Ca. 470–460 B.C. Arndt-Amelung II 3509–3510; Langlotz, *Fr. Bild.* 179, n. 15; *Master Bronzes* No. 167.

119. Hermes. Bronze statuette. Paris, Louvre Museum, Br. 269. Height 10.2 cm. Usually identified as Athena; E. Richardson identifies it as Hermes. Height 10 cm. 500–480 B.C. J. Charbonneaux, *BMF* (1946) 16. Cf. another example in Munich, Antikensammlung, Inv. 4313; R. Lullies, *AA* 72 (1957) 402–404, Figs. 22, 23.

120. Back of Fig. 119.

119

120

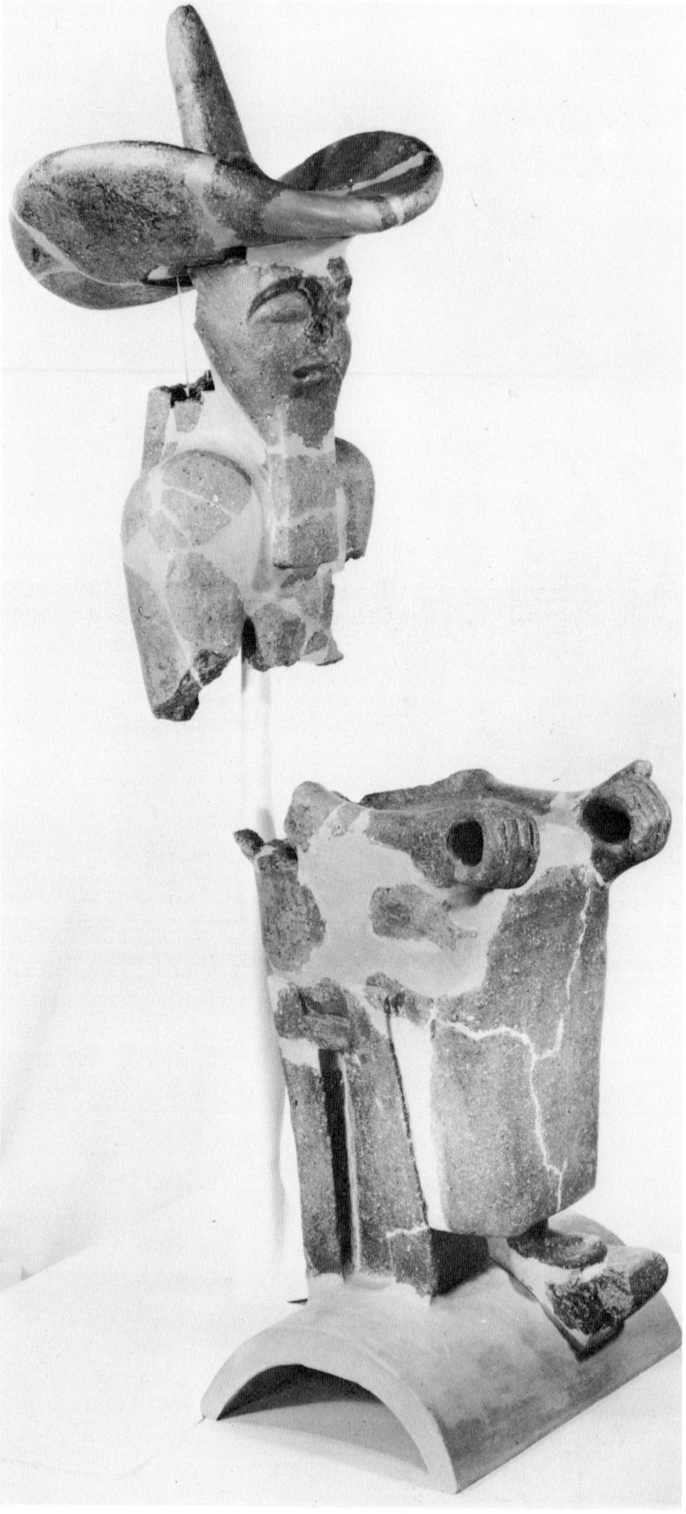

121. Seated male figure, bearded, wearing wide-brimmed hat, long robe, and laced, pointed shoes. Terracotta akroterion from Poggio Civitate (Murlo). Siena, Palazzo Pubblico. Height of original statue, 1.49 m. (life size). 570–550 B.C. I. Gantz, *Dial-Arch* 6 (1972) 167–235, Figs. 1–6, 16–20, and cf. 21–34 and color plate; R. Bianchi Bandinelli, *DialArch* 6 (1972) 236–247, Figs. 1, 2, 4; Bianchi Bandinelli-Giuliano 374, Fig. 446.

122. Bronze mirror with the Judgment of Paris. In the center Athena and Hera, wearing typically Etruscan earrings and bracelets with bullae, face the seated Aphrodite. All the figures are labeled with inscriptions giving their Etruscan names: "Menrva" (Minerva), "Uni" (Juno), "Turan" (Aphrodite), and, flanking the three goddesses, "Elcsntre" (Paris Alexander) and "Althaia." In the Judgment of Paris the goddesses are usually shown standing. Here the iconography is rather that of the dressing of Helen, a frequent and appropriate subject for mirrors, in which Helen, or her Etruscan counterpart, Malavesh, admires herself in her mirror as her attendants adorn her. Cf. for example Gerhard 215 or 384, and see E. Gerhard, "Die Schmückung der Helena," *Viertes Programm zum Berliner Winckelmanns-fest* (Berlin 1844). "Althaia," the name of the figure on the right, may be a misunderstanding for "Aithra," the name of Helen's attendant in such a scene (Rebuffat-Emmanuel 547, 606, No. 1297). Aithra, wife of Aegeus and mother of Theseus,

121

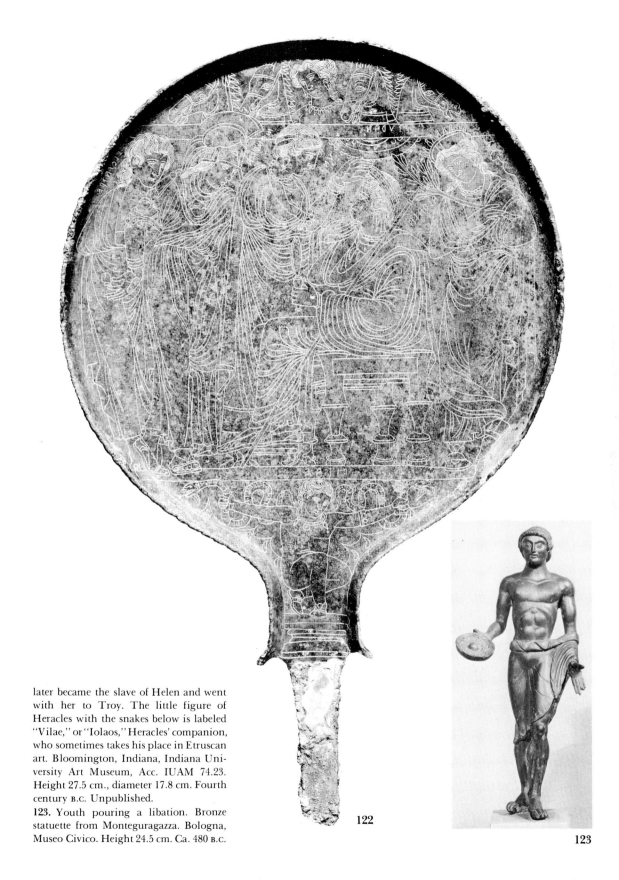

later became the slave of Helen and went with her to Troy. The little figure of Heracles with the snakes below is labeled "Vilae," or "Iolaos," Heracles' companion, who sometimes takes his place in Etruscan art. Bloomington, Indiana, Indiana University Art Museum, Acc. IUAM 74.23. Height 27.5 cm., diameter 17.8 cm. Fourth century B.C. Unpublished.

123. Youth pouring a libation. Bronze statuette from Monteguragazza. Bologna, Museo Civico. Height 24.5 cm. Ca. 480 B.C.

122

123

124

124. Preparations for a wedding (or a
funeral?). Relief panel, originally painted,
of a funerary cippus from Chiusi. Palermo
museum, Casuccini collection. Height 51
cm., width 67 cm. Ca. 480 B.C. (see Fig.
127). Gábrici, *StEtr* 2 (1928) Pl. 8.
125. Bronze statuette. Paris, Bibliothèque
Nationale, 213. Height 11.6 cm. Ca. 480
B.C. Babelon-Blanchet No. 213; Homann
Wedeking, *RM* 58 (1943) 87f., Pl. 6.
126. Back of Fig. 125.
127. Preparations for a wedding (or a
funeral?). Relief panel, originally painted,
of a funerary cippus from Chiusi. Rome,
Museo Barracco. Height 48.5 cm. Ca. 475
B.C. (see Fig. 124). Poulsen, *Etr. Paintings*
55, Fig. 42; Helbig[4] 1849. Cf. a similar
relief in the Ny Carlsberg Glyptotek, Cat.
No. H205.

125

126

127

128. Female figure dressed in chiton with long overfold and *sakkos* or pointed bonnet on the head. Bronze statuette from Rapino (province of Chieti). Chieti, Museo Nazionale. Height 11.6 cm. Fifth century B.C. E. Galli, *StEtr* 13 (1939) 231–248, Pls. 14, 15; Colonna, *Bronzi umbro-sabellici* 137, No. 417; Bianchi Bandinelli-Giuliano 101, Fig. 113 ("third century B.C."); Cianfarani Fig. 105.

129. Female figure wearing a chiton with a long overfold and laced, slightly pointed shoes. Greek bronze mirror support. Dublin, National Museum of Ireland, 1885:1. Height 9.5 in. Early fifth century B.C. Boardman, *Greek Art* Fig. 155; Congdon.

128

129

130   131

132   133

130.–131. Female figure wearing a tutu-lus and a fitted and sewn mantle made up of separate parts. Bronze statuette. Florence, Museo Archeologico, Inv. 261. Height 16 cm. Ca. 510 B.C. E. Baggio, *Italy's Life* 24 (1957) 63; M. Carrà, *Italian Sculpture* (London, 1970) Pl. 49.

132.–133. "Morgan statuette" of a female figure from Etruria. Bronze. New York, Metropolitan Museum of Art, Acc. 17.190.2066, gift of J. Pierpont Morgan. Height 29.4 cm. Ca. 500 B.C. Richter, *AJA* 16 (1912) 343–349, Pls. 3–4, and *Greek, Etr. and Rom. Br.* No. 56; Teitz 44, No. 30, Pls. 146–47; Bonfante Warren, *AJA* 75 (1971) 278, Figs. 1, 7.

134. Horseman wearing a short, rounded tebenna. Bronze statuette. Courtesy of The Detroit Institute of Arts, No. 46.260. Height 26.7 cm. Ca. 430 B.C. Richardson, *MAAR* 21 (1953) 115–116, Fig. 33; *Master Bronzes* No. 179; *Propyläen* I 405.

135. Portrait of Vel Sathies, wearing black sandals and triumphal *vestis picta*, dark wine-red in color, decorated with figures of naked soldiers armed with sword and shield, dancing the Pyrrhic dance. Beside him, in red-bordered tunic, is his dwarf, Arnza. Wall painting from the François tomb, Vulci. Rome, Villa Albani (property of the Torlonia family). Height 81 cm. Fourth century B.C. See another painted picture of a *triumphator* on a door *in situ* in the François tomb in Vulci, in Moretti-Maetzke Pl. 105; P. Goidanich, *StEtr* 9 (1935) 107–118; *Mostra* 128–129, No. 420, Pl. 107; Helbig⁴ 3239; F. Zevi, *Omaggio a R. Bianchi Bandinelli* (Rome 1970) 65–73; Bianchi Bandinelli-Giuliano 258, Fig. 297.

134

135

136

137

136. Greek shepherd. Bronze votive statuette from Andritzena, Arcadia. New York, Metropolitan Museum of Art, Acc. 08.258.7. The inscription says it was dedicated to Pan by Phaulos. Height 10 cm. Ca. 525 B.C. Richter, *Greek, Etr. and Rom. Br.* No. 58; Albright Gallery *Master Bronzes* (Buffalo, N.Y. 1937) No. 68.

137. Haruspex. Bronze statuette. Vatican, Museo Etrusco Gregoriano, Inv. 12040. The inscription says that Vel Sveitus dedicated it ("In turce Vel Sveitus," *TLE* 736). Fourth century B.C. Pallottino, *RendLinc* (1930), 51f., Pl. 2, and *Etruscologia* 265, 338, Pl. 30; Helbig[4] 708; Guzzo 157–160, Pl. 28, 1.

138. Haruspex. Bronze statuette. Rome, Villa Giulia Museum, one of two, Inv. 24 478/79. Height 33 cm. Hellenistic period. *Mostra* Nos. 345, 346, Pl. 80; Helbig[4] 2667.

138

SHOES

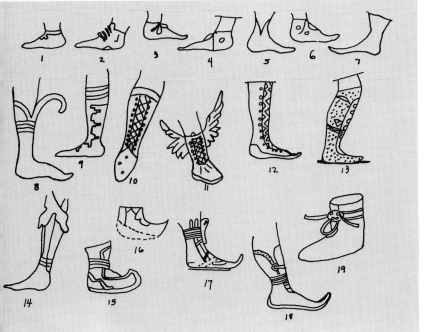

139

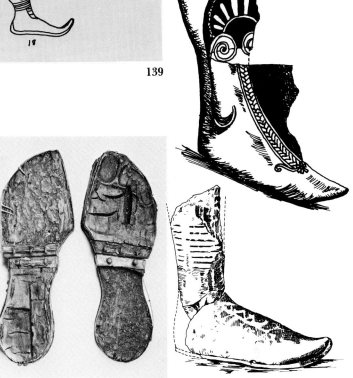

139. Forms of Greek, Etruscan, and Roman shoes and sandals: *1-7*, soft shoes; *8-19*, boots. Nos. *1-18* are adapted from Erbacher; *1-2* are Persian; *3-11, 13-14*, and *16* are Greek; *12* is Assyrian; *17-18* are Etruscan; *19*, a Roman boot with leather *luna*, comes from F. Cumont, *Fouilles de Dura Europos (1922-1923)* (Paris 1926) Pl. 94, 1.

140. Etruscan wood and bronze sandals from Bisenzio, tomb 80. Rome, Villa Giulia Museum, Inv. 57156 A, B. Maximum length 25 cm. End of sixth century B.C. Helbig⁴ 2552; cf. 697, and *Arte e civ. degli Etruschi* Nos. 71-72. Note marks of toes on right sandal.

141. Shoes from Sicily. Ca. 540 B.C. *A*, terracotta boot, fragmentary, with pointed toes, black crosswise laces, and horizontal laces above the ankle, from the excavations of the Athenaion. Syracuse. Syracuse, Museo Nazionale. Height 18.7 cm.: P. Orsi, *MonAnt* 25 (1919) 628 f., Fig. 218. *B*, terracotta foot from the archaic temple of Gela; *Dedalo* 6 (1925-1926) 362; cf. P. Orlandini, "Nuovi acroteri fittili a forma di cavallo e cavaliere dall'acropoli di Gela," *Scritti in onore di* G. *Libertini* (Florence 1958) 117-128, with bibl.

140

141

142

143

142. "Juno Sospita." Bronze base from Perugia. Munich, Antikensammlung. Height 28 cm. 530–520 B.C. Petersen, *RM* 9 (1894) 296f., No. 19, Fig. 5; *Mostra* 49–50, No. 176.

143. A ritual scene, Hera's adoption of Heracles. Olympian gods stand by as witnesses. Engraved bronze mirror from Volterra. The tablet bears the inscription, "Eca sren twa ixnac Hercle Unial clan thrasce," "This shows how (?) Hercules, son of Uni (Juno, Hera), drank milk (?)." Florence, Museo Archeologico. Diameter 29.5 cm. Ca. 300 B.C. Gerhard 5, 60; *Mostra* 106–107, No. 359. *TLE* No. 399; E. Fiesel, *AJP* 57 (1936) 130–136; M. Renard, in *Hommages à J. Bayet*, Collection Latomus 70 (Paris 1964) 611–618, Fig. 3.

144. Reclining couple. Terracotta sarcophagus from Cerveteri. Rome, Villa Giulia Museum, Inv. 6646. Height 1.41 m., length 1.91 m. Ca. 520 B.C. Helbig[4] 2582; *Propyläen* I 407; F. Magi, *RendPontAcc* 43 (1970–71) 27–45.

145. Detail of Fig. 144: note how the man's mantle covers the woman.

146. The Judgment of Paris. Pontic amphora by the Paris Painter, from Vulci. Munich, Antikensammlung, No. 837 WAF. Height 33 cm. Ca. 540 B.C. Furtwängler-Reichhold Pl. 21; *Mostra* 27, No. 82; Arias Pl. 38; Hampe-Simon Pl. 17; *Propyläen* I 413.

146

144

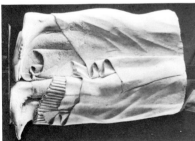

145

147. Four figures reclining: Achilles among the women at Skyros(?). Pontic amphora by the Paris Painter. New York, Metropolitan Museum of Art, Acc. 55.7, Gift of N. Koutoulakis, 1955. Height 35 cm. 540–530 B.C. D. von Bothmer, *BMMA* 14 (1955–56) 127–132; Cook, *Greek Painted Pottery* Pl. 34 (back); *Propyläen* I 413; Banti, *EAA* 6, 374, Fig. 414; Hampe-Simon Pl. 15.

147

148

148. Perseus, with Minerva seated on his right, prepares to behead the sleeping Medusa ("Metus"). Bronze mirror from Chiusi. Third century B.C. Helbig, *BullInst* (1885) 201; Gerhard 5, 67.

149. Helen, Paris Alexander, Hermione, and Turan (Aphrodite). Bronze mirror from Praeneste. Rome, Villa Giulia Museum, Inv. 16691. Height 22 cm., diameter 16 cm. Ca. 450 B.C. Gerhard 379; *Mostra* 73, No. 281, Pl. 50; Hampe-Simon 43, Fig. 9; Helbig[4] 2963; Rebuffat-Emmanuel 541–543, Pl. 91.

149

HATS, HAIR STYLES, AND BEARDS

A   B   C   150

151

152

150. Flower-hat, feather hat, and Bes figurine. 650–625 B.C. *A*, centaur wearing a flower-hat in the hunting scene on the bronze fitting from the Bernardini tomb, Praeneste, Rome, Villa Giulia Museum, 640–620 B.C., height 8 cm.: Curtis, *MAAR* 3 (1919) 82–84, Nos. 90–91, Pls. 65–66; Jacobsthal 49; Brown 24–25, Pl. 12 a–b; Richardson, *MAAR* 27 (1962) 186 and cf. 188; Steinberg, *Bronzes* 129–140, Figs. 111–113 and cf. 344; Bianchi Bandinelli-Giuliano 157. *B*, running male figure from same group, wearing a feather hat, height 8.3 cm.; cf. a bronze handle with flower decoration and figure with feather hat in V. Poulsen, *Etruskische Kunst*, back cover. *C*, the Egyptian divinity Bes, wearing a feather hat, fayence pendant from Veii, Tomb Ya. Height 5.3 cm. 700–675 B.C.: E. Fabricotti, M. A. Meagher, and M. Torelli, *NSc* 24 (1970) 266–267, Fig. 52, No. 97; cf. Montelius, *Vor. Chron.* Pl. 51, Fig. 15, bronze figure of Bes.

151. Bucchero statuette from the Tomb of Isis, Vulci, wearing diadem, originally of gold foil (polos?). Munich, Antikensammlung, Inv. 2365. Height 9 cm. Seventh century B.C. Ducati Pl. 60, Fig. 187.

152. Sirens. *A*, Greek winged siren on archaic shield band from Olympia, Olympia museum, 575–550 B.C.: E. Kunze, *Olympia Forschungen* II 242, Pl. 28, IX a. *B*, Etruscan bronze decorative support or handle in the form of a winged siren, Munich, Antikensammlung, Inv. 3833, ca. 600 B.C.

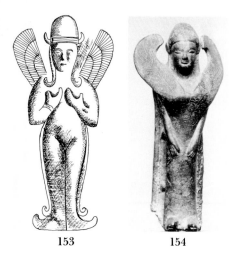

153   154

153. Winged goddess holding her breasts, with a veil hanging down behind her and framing her naked body. Stone orthostat relief from Carchemish, from the long wall of sculpture. Seventh century B.C. Riemschneider Pl. 42; R. D. Barnett, in L. Woolley, *Carchemish* III (London 1952) 157, Pl. B40.

154. Winged goddess. Bronze statuette from Perugia. Berlin, Staatliche Museum, Inv. Fr. 2153. Height 14 cm. Ca. 550 B.C. Herbig, *Götter und Dämonen* Pl. 16, 1; Mühlestein Fig. 187; Greifenhagen 80–81.

155. Bronze relief plate with winged "Mistress of Animals" in South Etruscan style. Copenhagen, Ny Carlsberg Glyptotek, No. H81a. Height 16 cm. 620–600 B.C. Johansen, *Reliefs* 11–15, 61–70, Pls. 2–7, 29, and *Guide to the Collection* (1972) 62–63; J. G. Szilágyi, *Gnomon* 45 (1973) 834–836.

156. "Master of Animals" and frontal female figure with wings or "tails." Bronze handle with relief decorations from the Bernardini tomb, Praeneste. Height 12.3 cm. 675–650 B.C. Rome, Villa Giulia Museum. Curtis, *MAAR* 3 (1919) Pl. 27, 2; Steinberg, *Bronzes* B8, 103–104, Fig. 80; Strøm Figs. 103, 150–154.

157. Silvanus (Selvans) or Heracles. Bronze statuette. Paris, Louvre Museum. Height 10.8 cm. Early fifth century. De Ridder No. 223; T. Campanile, "Statuetta di Eracle in bronzo d'arte etrusca," *BdA* ser. 2, 3 (1924) 458–459, Figs. 5–8. Cf. a similar bearded statuette from Este in Giglioli 124, 3; Campanile Figs. 1–4; Bianchi Bandinelli-Giuliano Fig. 56.

155

156

157

158. Silvanus (Selvans) or a hunter. Terracotta statuette from Veii, località Campetti. Traces of red paint. Rome, Villa Giulia Museum. Height 27 cm. Early fifth century. Pallottino, *Le Arti* 2 (1939–1940) 23f., Pl. 9; L. Banti, *StEtr* 17 (1943) 188, No. 3; *Mostra* 57, No. 235 ("540–520; Ionian influence").

158

159

159. Deceased man with Vanth, female demon of death. Stone sarcophagus from Chianciano. Florence, Museo Archeologico, Inv. 94352. Height 80 cm., length 1.20 cm. Ca. 400 B.C. Banti Pl. 73; Sprenger 72-74, No. 7, Pl. 36 (heads, "400-380 B.C.").

160. Minerva, Hercules, Apollo, and Artemis ("Menrva," "Hercle," "Artumes," "Aplu"). Bronze mirror from Bomarzo. Florence, Museo Archeologico, Inv. 84806. Acquired 1911. Diameter 18 cm. Third century B.C. Milani, *Mus. Arch. Firenze* 143, Pl. 48; Ducati 447-448, Fig. 522; Giglioli 301, 3. On the upper border an inscription reads, *Mi Titasi cver menaxe,* "I was given as a gift to Tita" (*TLE* 282).

161   162

161.–162. Naked female figure with long back braid. Ivory statuette from Circolo della Fibula, Marsiliana d'Albegna. Florence, Museo Archeologico. Height 9.5 cm. 675-650 B.C. Huls 40, No. 13, Pl. 9; *Mostra* No. 22, Pl. 7; Richardson, *MAAR* 27 (1962) 176, Figs. 35-37. See F. Nicosia, *StEtr* 37 (1969) 352, Pl. 84, *Restauri arch.* 17, Pl. 2, and *Propyläen* I 395b,c, for new photograph, without the gold leaf, which had been erroneously restored; M. Benzi, *RendLinc* 21 (1966) 271f.; Bonfante Warren, *Brendel Essays* Pl. 5f-g.

163. Goddess with armed god, perhaps Venus and Mars. Vase from Lemnos. Athens, National Museum. Height of panel 21 cm. Seventh century B.C. A. Della Seta, *ArchEph* 1937B, 649-651, No. 7, Fig. 5; Bonfante Warren, *Brendel Essays* n. 13, Pl. 4e, with bibl. Ch. Picard (*RA* 20 [1943] 97-124) believes the scene illustrates the Homeric story (*Od.* 8.256ff.) about Ares' and Aphrodite's love affair, and suggests a date in the second half of the seventh century, or even the sixth. K. Friis Johansen (*The Iliad in Early Greek Art* [Copenhagen 1967] 38-39, n. 59) believes instead that the vase, a piece of local craftsmanship, refers to a local legend unknown to us, and accepts a sixth-century date, following Schefold 143, who dates the vase around 550 B.C.

164. Goddess wearing polos, enthroned, receiving homage from cithara player and boy. Vase from Lemnos. Athens, National Museum. Height of panel 17 cm. Seventh century B.C. Della Seta, *ArchEph* 1937B, 643-646, No. 5, Fig. 4; Bonfante Warren, *Brendel Essays* n. 13, Pl. 4d, with bibl.

160

163

164

BIBLIOGRAPHY AND ABBREVIATIONS

Abbreviations used are listed in AJA 74 (1970) 1ff., with exceptions listed below.

Abruzzo	V. Cianfarani, ed. *Antiche civiltà d'Abruzzo.* Rome 1969.
Ākerstrom	Å. Åkerstrom. "Untersuchungen über die figurlichen Terracottafriese aus Etrurien und Latium." *Opuscula Romana* 1 (1954).
Akurgal	E. Akurgal. *Die Kunst Anatoliens von Homer bis Alexander.* Berlin 1961.
Akurgal, *Orient und Okzident*	E. Akurgal. *Orient und Okzident, Die Geburt der griechische Kunst.* Baden-Baden 1966.
Akurgal, *Reliefs*	E. Akurgal. *Griechische Reliefs des VI Jahrhunderts aus Lykien.* Berlin 1942.
Alföldi	A. Alföldi. *Der frührömische Reiteradel und seine Ehrenabzeichen.* Baden-Baden 1952.
Alföldi, *Early Rome*	A. Alföldi. *Early Rome and the Latins.* Ann Arbor, 1963 [1965].
Alföldi, "Insignien"	A. Alföldi. "Insignien und Tracht der römischen Kaiser." *RM* 50 (1935) 3–158; *Die monarchische Repräsentation in römischen Kaiserreiche.* Darmstadt 1970. Pp. 121–276.
Alföldi, *Die Trojanischen Urahnen*	A. Alföldi. *Die trojanischen Urahnen der Römer.* Basel 1957.
Amandry	P. Amandry. "Objets orientaux en Grèce et en Italie aux VIII et VII siècles avant J. C." *Syria* 35 (1958) 73ff.
Amelung	W. Amelung. *Die Gewandung der alten Griechen und Römer,* text to Plates 16–20 of S. Cybulski. *Tabulae quibus antiquitates Graecae et Romanae illustrantur.* Leipzig 1903.
Amorelli, *Coll. Massimo*	M. T. Falconi Amorelli. *La Collezione Massimo.* Quaderni di Villa Giulia 3. Milan 1968.
Andrae, "Gravierte Tridacna-Muscheln"	W. Andrae, "Gravierte Tridacna-Muscheln aus Assur." *Zeitschrift für Assyriologie* 45 (1939) 98f.
Andrén	A. Andrén. "Architectural Terracottas from Etrusco-Italic Temples." *Acta Instituti Romani Regni Sueciae.* Lund-Leipzig 1940.
ANRW	H. Temporini, ed. *Aufstieg und Niedergang der römischen Welt.* Berlin-New York 1972-.
Antiken, Bonn	*Antiken aus dem Akademische Kunstmuseum Bonn.* Kunst und Altertum am Rhein No. 19. Düsseldorf 1969.
Antike Plastik	W. Amelung, *Antike Plastik.* Berlin 1928.

Arias	P. E. Arias. *Archeologia e storia dell'arte greca. Enciclopedia Classica* XI, Bk. V.
Arias-Hirmer	P. E. Arias and M. Hirmer. *1000 Years of Greek Vase Painting.* New York 1962.
Arndt-Amelung	P. Arndt, W. Amelung, and G. Lippold. *Photographische Einzelaufnahmen antiker Skulpturen.* Munich 1893–1940.
Art and Technology	S. Doeringer, D. G. Mitten, and A. Steinberg, eds. *Art and Technology: A Symposium on Classical Bronzes.* Cambridge, Mass. 1970.
Arte e civ.	A. Maiuri. *Arte e civiltà dell'Italia antica.* Milan 1960.
Arte e civ. degli Etruschi	*Arte e civiltà degli Etruschi.* Turin 1967.
Artemis Orthia	R. M. Dawkins. *The Sanctuary of Artemis Orthia at Sparta.* London 1939.
Aubet	E. Aubet. *Los marfiles orientalizantes de Praeneste.* Barcelona 1971.
Babelon-Blanchet	E. Babelon and J. A. Blanchet. *Catalogue des bronzes antiques de la Bibliothèque Nationale.* Paris 1895.
Banti	L. Banti. *Il mondo degli Etruschi.* Rome 1960.
Banti²	L. Banti. *Il mondo degli Etruschi.* 2d ed. Rome 1969.
Banti, "Div. fem. a Creta"	L. Banti. "Divinità femminili a Creta nel Tardo Minoico III." *Studi e Materiali di Storia delle Religioni* 17 (1941) 1f.
Banti, *Etruscan Cities*	L. Banti. *The Etruscan Cities and Their Culture.* Translated by Erika Bizzarri. Berkeley and Los Angeles 1973.
Banti, *StEtr* 28 (1960)	L. Banti. "Scultura etrusca arcaica: la statua della Polledrara." *StEtr* 28 (1960) 277ff.
Banti, "Tomba dei Tori"	L. Banti. "Problemi della pittura arcaica etrusca: la Tomba dei Tori a Tarquinia." *StEtr* 24 (1955–56) 143–181.
Banti, "Tripodi Loeb"	L. Banti. "Bronzi arcaici etruschi: i tripodi Loeb." *Tyrrhenica* (1957) 77f.
Barnett	R. D. Barnett. *Catalogue of the Nimrud Ivories.* London 1957.
Bartoccini-Lerici-Moretti	R. Bartoccini, C. M. Lerici, and M. Moretti. *Tarquinia, La Tomba delle Olimpiadi.* Milan 1959.
Baur, *Centaurs*	P. Baur. *Centaurs in Ancient Art.* Berlin 1912.
Bayet, *Herclé*	J. Bayet. *Herclé; étude critique des principaux monuments relatifs à l'Hercule étrusque.* Bibliothèque des Écoles Françaises d'Athènes et de Rome 132. Paris 1926.
Bayet, *Hercule romain*	J. Bayet. *Les Origines de l'Hercule romain.* Bibliothèque des Écoles Françaises d'Athènes et de Rome 132. Paris 1926.

Beazley, *ABV*	J. D. Beazley. *Attic Black-Figure Vase-Painters.* Oxford 1942.
Beazley, *Dev.*	J. D. Beazley. *The Development of Attic Black-Figure.* Berkeley and Los Angeles 1951.
Beazley, *EVP*	J. D. Beazley. *Etruscan Vase-Painting.* Oxford 1947.
Becatti, *Oreficerie antiche*	G. Becatti. *Oreficerie antiche dalle minoiche alle barbariche.* Rome 1955.
Becatti-Magi	G. Becatti and F. Magi. *Tarquinii III–IV: Le Pitture delle Tombe degli Auguri e del Pulcinella.* Monumenti della Pittura Antica Scoperti in Italia 1. Rome 1955.
Bellinger	Louisa Bellinger. "The Bible as a Source Book for the Study of Textiles." *Workshop Notes 18.* Washington, D.C. 1958.
Bernoulli, *Aphrodite*	J. J. Bernoulli. *Aphrodite.* Leipzig 1873.
Bianchi Bandinelli, "Clusium"	R. Bianchi Bandinelli. "Clusium." *MonAntLinc* 30 (1925).
Bianchi Bandinelli, *Storicità dell'arte classica*	R. Bianchi Bandinelli. *Storicità dell'arte classica.* Florence 1950.
Bianchi Bandinelli-Giuliano	R. Bianchi Bandinelli and A. Giuliano. *Les Étrusques et l'Italie avant Rome.* Paris 1973.
Bickerman	E. J. Bickerman. "Some Reflections on Early Roman History." *RivFilClass* 97 (1969) 394–396.
Bieber	M. Beiber. *Griechische Kleidung.* Berlin and Leipzig 1928.
Bieber, *AA* (1973)	M. Beiber. "Charakter und Unterscheide der griechischen und römischen Kleidung." *AA* (1973) 425–447.
Bieber, *Cassel Mus.*	M. Bieber. *Die antiken Skulpturen und Bronzen des k. Mus. Fr. in Cassel.* Marburg 1915.
Bieber, "Costume"	M. Bieber. "Costume, Historical Development. The Ancient World: The Near East, The Aegean and Greece, Italy and Rome." *Encyclopedia of World Art* IV (1961) 19–26.
Bieber, *Entwicklungsgeschichte*	M. Bieber. *Entwicklungsgeschichte der griechischen Tracht.* 2d ed. Berlin 1967.
Bieber, *Greek and Roman Theater*	M. Bieber. *History of the Greek and Roman Theater.* 2d ed. Princeton 1961.
Bieber, *Hellenistic Sculpture*	M. Bieber. *The Sculpture of the Hellenistic Age.* 2d ed. New York 1961.
Bieber, "*Romani Palliati*"	M. Bieber. "Roman Men in Greek Himation (*Romani Palliati*)." *ProcPhilSoc* 103 (1959) 377ff.
Blinkenberg	C. S. Blinkenberg. *Fibules grecques et orientales.* Copenhagen 1926.
Boardman	J. Boardman. "Two Archaic Korai in Chios." *Antike Plastik* 1 (1962) 43–45.

Boardman, *Anatolia*
6 (1961–62)

J. Boardman. "Ionian Bronze Belts." *Anatolia* 6 (1961–62) 179–189.

Boardman, *Cretan Collection*

J. Boardman. *The Cretan Collection in Oxford*. Oxford 1961.

Boardman, *Greek Art*

J. Boardman. *Greek Art*. New York 1964.

Boardman, *Pre-Classical*

J. Boardman. *Pre-Classical*. Baltimore 1967.

Boisacq

E. Boisacq. *Dictionnaire étymologique de la langue grecque*. Paris 1923.

Bonfante Warren, *AJA*
75 (1971) 277–284

L. Bonfante Warren. "Etruscan Dress as Historical Source: Some Problems and Examples." *AJA* 75 (1971) 277–284.

Bonfante Warren,
ANRW I₄

L. Bonfante Warren. "Roman Costumes: A Glossary, and Some Etruscan Derivations." *Aufstieg und Niedergang der römischen Welt* I₄. Berlin and New York 1973. Pp. 584–614.

Bonfante Warren,
Archaeology 26 (1973)
242–249

L. Bonfante Warren. "Etruscan Women: A Question of Interpretation." *Archaeology* 26 (1973) 242–249.

Bonfante Warren,
Arethusa 6 (1973)
91–101

L. Bonfante Warren. "The Women of Etruria," *Arethusa* 6 (1973) 91–101.

Bonfante Warren,
Brendel Essays

L. Bonfante Warren. "The Orientalizing Context of the Etruscan Back Braid." *In Memoriam Otto J. Brendel. Essays in Archaeology and the Humanities*. Mainz 1975.

Bonfante Warren, *JRS*
60 (1970) 49–66

L. Bonfante Warren. "Roman Triumphs and Etruscan Kings: The Changing Face of the Triumph." *JRS* 60 (1970) 49–66.

Bonfante Warren,
Kerns Studies

L. Bonfante Warren. "Roman Triumphs and Etruscan Kings: The Latin Word *Triumphus*." *Studies in Honor of J. Alexander Kerns*. Edited by R. Lugton and M. Saltzer. Ianua Linguarum Ser. Maior 44. The Hague 1970. Pp. 108–120.

Bonfante Warren,
Studi Banti

L. Bonfante Warren. "Riflessi di arte cretese in Etruria." *Studi in onore di Luisa Banti*. Rome 1965. Pp. 81–87.

Bossert, *Altanatolien*

H. Bossert. *Altanatolien*. Berlin 1942.

Bossert, *Altkreta*

H. Bossert. *Altkreta*. Berlin 1923.

Bossert, *Altsyrien*

H. Bossert. *Altsyrien*. Tübingen 1951.

von Bothmer, *Amazons*

D. von Bothmer. *Amazons in Greek Art*. Oxford 1957.

von Bothmer, *Anc. Art*

D. von Bothmer. *Ancient Art from New York Private Collections*. New York 1961.

Breitenstein

N. Breitenstein. *Catalogue of Terracottas, Danish Nat. Mus*. Copenhagen 1941.

Brendel, *AJA* 62 (1958)
240–242

O. J. Brendel. Review of Becatti-Magi. *AJA* 62 (1958) 240–242.

Brendel, *Erotic Art*

O. J. Brendel. "The Scope and Temperament of Erotic Art in the Greco-Roman World." *Studies in Erotic Art*. Edited by T. Bowie and C. V. Christenson. Studies

	in Sex and Society, Institute for Sex Research, Indiana University. New York and London 1970. Pp. 3-107.
Brendel, *Etruscan Art*	O. J. Brendel. *Etruscan Art.* Forthcoming.
Broholm-Hald, *Bronze Age Fashion*	H. Broholm and M. Hald. *Bronze Age Fashion.* Copenhagen 1948.
Broholm-Hald, *Costumes*	H. Broholm and M. Hald. *Costumes of the Bronze Age in Denmark.* Copenhagen and London 1940.
Brommer, *Vasenlisten*	F. Brommer. *Vasenlisten zur griechischen Heldensage.* 3d ed. Marburg 1973.
Brunn	W. L. Brown. *The Etruscan Lion.* Oxford 1960.
Brown-Bruckmann	H. Brunn and F. Bruckmann. *Denkmäler griechischer und römischer Sculptur* III. Munich 1888-1916.
Brunn-Körte	H. Brunn and G. Körte. *I rilievi delle urne etrusche.* 3 vols. Rome and Berlin 1870-1916.
Bryant, "Greek Shoes"	A. Bryant. "Greek Shoes in the Classical Period." *HSCP* 10 (1899) 57.
Buschor	E. Buschor. *Griechische Vasen.* Munich 1940.
Camporeale, *Commerci di Vetulonia*	G. Camporeale. *I Commerci di Vetulonia.* Florence 1969.
Camporeale, *Tomba del Duce*	G. Camporeale. *La Tomba del Duce a Vetulonia.* Florence 1967.
Canciani	F. Canciani. *Bronzi orientali e orientalizzanti a Creta nell'VIII e VII sec. a.C.* Rome 1970.
Carcopino	J. Carcopino. *La Vie quotidienne à Rome.* Paris 1939.
Cesnola	L. Cesnola. *Collection of Cypriote Antiquities in the Metropolitan Museum of Art* I. Boston 1885.
Chantraine	P. Chantraine. *Dictionnaire étymologique de la langue grecque, A-K.* Paris 1968-70.
Charbonneaux, *Br. grecs*	J. Charbonneaux. *Les Bronzes grecs.* Paris 1958.
Cianfarani	V. Cianfarani. *Culture adriatiche d'Italia.* Rome 1970.
Ciasca	A. Ciasca. *Il capitello eolico in Etruria.* Florence 1962.
Civiltà del Ferro	*La Civiltà del Ferro, studi pubblicati nella ricorrenza centenaria della scoperta di Villanova. Documenti e studi a cura della Deputazione di Storia Patria per la Provincia di Romagna* VI. Bologna 1959.
Cles-Reden	S. Cles-Reden. *Les Étrusques.* Paris 1955.
Coarelli, *Jewellery*	F. Coarelli. *Greek and Roman Jewellery.* London 1970.

Colonna, *Bronzi umbro-sabellici*

G. Colonna. *Bronzi votivi umbro-sabellici a figura umana. I: Periodo "arcaico."* Florence 1970.

Comstock-Vermeule

E. Comstock and C. Vermeule. *Greek, Etruscan and Roman Bronzes in the Museum of Fine Arts, Boston.* Boston 1971.

Congdon

L. O. Keene Congdon. *Caryatid Mirrors of Ancient Greece.* Forthcoming.

Conway, Whatmough

R. Conway and J. Whatmough. *The Prae-Italic Dialects of Italy.* London 1933.

Cook, *Greek Painted Pottery*

R. M. Cook. *Greek Painted Pottery.* London 1960.

Cristofani, *Nuove letture*

M. Cristofani. *Nuove letture di monumenti etruschi dopo il restauro.* Florence 1971.

Cristofani, *Statue-cinerario*

M. Cristofani. *Statue-cinerario chiusine di età classica.* Rome 1975.

Cristofani, *T. Monte Michele*

M. Cristofani. *Le Tombe di Monte Michele nel Museo Archeologico di Firenze. Veii* I. Florence 1969.

Curtis, *MAAR* 3

C. Densmore Curtis. "The Bernardini Tomb." *MAAR* 3 (1919).

Curtis, *MAAR* 5

C. Densmore Curtis. "The Barberini Tomb." *MAAR* 5 (1925).

Daremberg-Saglio

Daremberg-Saglio. *Dictionnaire des antiquités grecques et romaines.* Paris 1873–1917.

Davenport, *Costume*

M. Davenport. *The Book of Costume.* New York 1948.

Davies, *Rekh-mi-Re*

N. de G. Davies. *Paintings from the Tomb of Rekh-mi-Re at Thebes.* New York 1935.

Davies, *Tomb of Rekh-mi-Re*

N. de G. Davies. *The Tomb of Rekh-mi-Re at Thebes.* The Metropolitan Museum of Art Egyptian Expedition 21. New York 1943.

Dawkins, *Artemis Orthia*

R. M. Dawkins. *The Sanctuary of Artemis Orthia at Sparta.* London 1939.

Delbrueck

R. Delbrueck. *Spätantike Kaiserporträts.* Berlin and Leipzig 1933.

Delbrueck, *Consulardiptychen*

R. Delbrueck. *Die Consulardiptychen.* Berlin 1929.

Della Seta, "Lemno"

A. Della Seta. "Arte Tirrenica di Lemno." *ArchEph* 1937B, 629–654.

Demargne

P. Demargne. *The Birth of Greek Art.* New York 1964.

Demargne, *Crète Dédalique*

P. Demargne. *La Crète Dédalique.* Paris 1947.

De Marinis

S. De Marinis. *Tipologia del banchetto in Etruria.* Rome 1961.

Dennis

J. Dennis. *Cities and Cemeteries of Etruria.* London 1873.

de Simone

C. de Simone. *Die Griechischen Entlehnungen im Etruskischen* II. Wiesbaden 1970.

DialArch

Dialoghi di Archeologia.

Dickins, *Acr. Mus.*	G. Dickins. *Catalogue of the Acropolis Museum.* Cambridge 1912.
Dohan	E. H. Dohan. "A Ziro Burial from Chiusi." *AJA* 41 (1935) 203f.
Dohrn, *Arringatore*	T. Dohrn. *Der Arringatore.* Monumenta Artis Romanae 8. Berlin 1968.
Dohrn, *Grundzüge*	T. Dohrn. *Grundzüge etruskischer Kunst.* Baden-Baden 1968.
Ducati	P. Ducati. *Storia dell'arte etrusca.* Florence 1927.
Ducati, *Historia* 1929	P. Ducati. "Osservazioni sui primordi dell' arte figurata a Felsina e ad Este." *Historia* 1929, 29–60.
Ducati, "Laminette eburnee"	P. Ducati. "Laminette eburnee del Museo Civico di Bologna." *StEtr* 2 (1928) 39–47.
Ducati, *Mus. Civ. Bologna*	P. Ducati. *Guida del Museo Civico di Bologna.* Bologna 1923.
Ducati, *Pittura Etr. Italo-Greca e Rom.*	P. Ducati. *Pittura Etrusca, Italo-Greca e Romana.* Novara 1942.
Ducati, *Pontische Vasen*	P. Ducati. *Pontische Vasen.* Berlin 1932.
Ducati, "Sit. Certosa"	P. Ducati. "La Situla della Certosa." *Mem. R. Acc. delle Scienze dell'Ist. di Bologna.* Classe di Scienze Morali ser. 2, V–VI (1920–23) 23–95.
Ducati, *Tombe delle Leonesse e dei Vasi Dipinti*	P. Ducati. *Tarquinii, Le Pitture delle Tombe delle Leonesse e dei Vasi Dipinti.* Monumenti della Pittura Antica Scoperti in Italia. Rome 1937.
Duell	P. Duell. "The Tomba del Triclinio at Tarquinia." *MAAR* 6 (1927) 23.
Dumézil	G. Dumézil. *La Religion romaine archaïque.* Paris 1966.
Dumézil, *ARR*	G. Dumézil. *Archaic Roman Religion.* Chicago 1970.
EAA	*Enciclopedia dell'arte antica: classica e orientale.* Rome 1958–.
Erbacher	K. Erbacher. *Griechisches Schuhwerk.* Würzburg 1914.
Ernout-Meillet	A. Ernout and A. Meillet. *Dictionnaire étymologique de la langue latine.* 4th ed. Paris 1959–60.
Etruria interna	*Aspetti e problemi dell'Etruria interna. Atti dell'VIII Convegno Nazionale di Studi Etruschi ed Italici, Orvieto 1972.* Florence 1974.
Etruscan Culture	A. Boethius, ed. *Etruscan Culture, Land and People.* New York and Malmö 1962.
Études Étrusco-Italiques	*Études Étrusco-Italiques.* Louvain 1963.
Evans, *PM*	A. J. Evans. *The Palace of Minos at Knossos.* London 1921–35.

EWA   *Encyclopedia of World Art.* New York 1959–68.

Falchi   I. Falchi. *Vetulonia e la sua necropoli antichissima.* Florence 1891.

Ferri, "Tentativo di ricostruz."   S. Ferri. "Tentativo di ricostruzione di una figura femminile dai frammenti della Pietrera (Vetulonia)." *Atti del I Congresso Internazionale di Preistoria e Protostoria Mediterranea.* Florence, Naples, and Rome 1950.

Fogolari, *Mus. Naz. Este*   G. Fogolari. *Il Museo Nazionale Atestino in Este.* Rome 1957.

Fogolari, *Paleoveneti*   G. Fogolari. *Paleoveneti di Vicenza.* Mostra a Palazzo Chiericati 2 Maggio–2 Giugno. Vicenza 1963.

Forbes   R. B. Forbes. *Studies in Ancient Technology.* Leyden 1964.

Fraccaro   P. Fraccaro. *La Storia romana arcaica.* Milan 1952.

Frankfort   H. Frankfort. *The Art and Architecture of the Ancient Orient.* London 1954.

Frankfort, *Cylinder Seals*   H. Frankfort. *Cyclinder Seals.* London 1939.

Frisk   H. Frisk. *Griechisches etymologisches Wörterbuch.* Heidelberg 1960–70.

Frova   A. Frova. *L'Arte etrusca.* Milan 1957.

Furtwängler, *Berlin Antiquarium*   A. Furtwängler. *Beschreibung der Vasensammlung im Antiquarium.* Berlin 1885.

Furtwängler, *Olympia*   A. Furtwängler. *Olympia, Ergebnisse.* IV: *Die Bronzen.* Berlin 1890.

Furtwängler-Reichhold   A. Furtwängler and K. Reichhold. *Griechische Vasenmalerei.* Munich 1904–22.

Gábrici, *StEtr* 2 (1928)   E. Gábrici. "La Collezione Casuccini del Mus. Naz. di Palermo." *StEtr* 2 (1928) 55–81.

Gagé, *Matronalia*   J. Gagé. *Matronalia.* Paris 1963.

I. Gantz, *DialArch* 6 (1972)   I. Edlund Gantz. "The Seated Statue Akroteria from Poggio Civitate (Murlo)." *DialArch* 6 (1972) 167–235.

T. Gantz, *RM* 81 (1974)   T. Gantz. "The Procession Frieze from the Etruscan Sanctuary at Poggio Civitate." *RM* 81 (1974) 1–14.

T. Gantz, *StEtr* 39 (1971)   T. Gantz. "Divine Triads on an Archaic Etruscan Frieze Plaque from Poggio Civitate (Murlo)." *StEtr* 39 (1971) 3–24.

Gempeler   R. D. Gempeler. *Die etruskischen Kanopen.* Einsiedeln, n.d. [1974?].

Gentili   G. V. Gentili. *La Villa Imperiale di Piazza Armerina.* Rome 1954.

Gerhard   E. Gerhard. *Etruskische Spiegel.* Completed by A. Klugman and G. Körte. Berlin 1840–97.

Gerhard, *AV*   E. Gerhard, *Auserlesene griechische Vasenbilder.* Berlin 1840–58.

Ghirardini   G. Ghirardini. "Antichità Baratela di Este." *NSc* 1888, 3ff.

Giglioli   G. Q. Giglioli. *L'Arte etrusca.* Milan 1935.

Gjerstad, *Early Rome*   E. Gjerstad. *Early Rome.* 5 vols. Lund 1953–73.

Gjerstad, *Swed. Cyprus Exp.*   E. Gjerstad. *The Swedish Cyprus Expedition. 1927–1931.* Stockholm 1934–48.

Goldscheider   L. Goldscheider. *Etruscan Sculpture.* New York 1941.

Greifenhagen, *Staatl. Mus.*   U. Gehrig, A. Greifenhagen, and N. Kunisch. *Führer durch die Antikenabteilung, Staatliche Museum.* Berlin 1968.

Grenier   A. Grenier. *Bologne villanovienne et étrusque.* Paris 1912.

Gullberg-Åström   E. Gullberg and P. Åström. *The Thread of Ariadne, a Study on Ancient Greek Dress.* Studies in Mediterranean Archaeology 21. Göteborg 1970.

Guzzo   P. G. Guzzo, *Le Fibule in Etruria dal VI al I secolo.* Florence 1972.

Hampe   R. Hampe. *Frühe griechische Sagenbilder in Böotien.* Athens 1936.

Hampe-Simon   R. Hampe and E. Simon. *Griechische Sagen in der frühen etruskischen Kunst.* Mainz 1964.

Hanfmann, *Altetr. Plastik*   G. M. A. Hanfmann. *Altetruskische Plastik* I. Würzburg 1936.

Hanfmann, *Crit. d'Arte*   G. M. A. Hanfmann. "Origin of Etruscan Sculpture." *Critica d'arte* 2 (1937) 156–166.

Hanfmann, *Etr. Plastik*   G. M. A. Hanfmann. *Etruskische Plastik.* Stuttgart 1956.

Harris   W. V. Harris. *Rome in Etruria and Umbria.* Oxford 1971.

Hase, von   *See* von Hase.

Haynes   S. Haynes, "Zwei archaisch-etruskische Bildwerke aus Vulci." *Antike Plastik* 4. Edited by W. Schuchhardt (Berlin 1965). Pp. 13–26, Pls. 6–11; review by R. Bianchi Bandinelli in *DialArch* 1 (1967) 122–125.

Haynes, *Etruscan Sculpture*   S. Haynes. *Etruscan Sculpture.* London 1971.

Helbig[4]   W. Helbig. *Führer durch die öffentlichen Sammlungen klassischer Altertümer in Rom.* 4th ed. Edited by H. Speier; Etruscan entries by T. Dohrn. 4 vols. Tübingen 1963–72.

Hemelrijk   J. M. Hemelrijk. *De Caeretaanse Hydriae.* Rotterdam 1956.

Hencken, *Tarquinia*   H. Hencken. *Tarquinia, Villanovans and Early Etruscans.* American School of Prehistoric Research, Peabody Museum, Harvard University, Bulletin 23. Cambridge, Mass. 1968.

Herbig R. Herbig. *Die jüngeretruskischen Stein-sarcophage.* Berlin 1952.

Herbig, *Götter und Dämonen* R. Herbig. *Götter und Dämonen der Etrusker.* 2d ed. Mainz 1965.

Heurgon J. Heurgon. *La Vie quotidienne chez les étrusques.* Paris 1961.

Heurgon, *Daily Life* J. Heurgon, *The Daily Life of the Etruscans.* New York 1964. (An unreliable translation.)

Higgins R. A. Higgins. *Greek and Roman Jewellery.* London 1961.

Higgins, *Terracottas* R. A. Higgins. *Greek Terracottas.* London 1967.

Hill D. K. Hill. *Catalogue of Classical Bronze Sculpture in the Walters Art Gallery.* Baltimore 1949.

Hinks, *B. M. Paintings* R. P. Hinks. *Catalogue of the Greek, Etruscan and Roman Paintings in the British Museum.* London 1933.

Hoernes M. Hoernes. *Urgeschichte der bildenden Kunst in Europa.* Vienna 1898.

Hoffman-Raubitschek H. Hoffman and A. Raubitschek. *Early Cretan Armorers.* Mainz 1972.

Houston, *Anc. Greek, Rom. Byz. Cost.* Mary G. Houston. *Ancient Greek, Roman and Byzantine Costume.* 2d ed. London 1954.

Huls Yvonne Huls. *Ivories d'Étrurie.* Brussels-Rome 1957.

Hus A. Hus. *Recherches sur la statuaire en pierre étrusque archaïque.* Paris 1961.

Hus, *Vulci* A. Hus. *Vulci étrusque et étrusco-romain.* Paris 1971.

Jacobsthal P. Jacobsthal. *Greek Pins.* Oxford 1956.

Joffroy, *Vix* R. Joffroy. *Le Trésor de Vix.* Paris 1954.

Johansen K. F. Johansen. *Les Vases sicyoniens.* Paris and Copenhagen 1923.

Johansen, *Reliefs* F. Johansen. *Reliefs en bronze d'Étrurie.* Copenhagen 1971.

Johnstone, *Dance in Etr.* M. Johnstone. *The Dance in Etruria.* Florence 1956.

Kähler, *Metopenbild* H. Kähler. *Das Griechische Metopenbild.* Munich 1947.

Karo G. Karo. *Le oreficerie di Vetulonia,* in *Studi e materiali di archeologia e numismatica.* Florence 1899–1901.

Kassel, *Antike Bronzen* *Antike Bronzen. Kataloge der Staatlichen Kunstsammlungen Kassel.* 1972.

Kastelic, *Situlenkunst* J. Kastelic. *Situlenkunst.* Vienna and Munich 1964.

Körte, *Göttinger Bronzen* G. Körte. *Göttinger Bronzen.* Berlin 1917.

Kossack G. Kossack. "Über italische Cinturoni." *Praehistorische Zeitschrift.* Deutsche Gesellschaft für Anthropologie 34/35. Berlin 1949–50. Pp. 132–147.

Krauskopf	I. Krauskopf. *Der thebanische Sagenkreis und andere griechische Sagen in der etruskischen Kunst.* Schriften zur Antiken Mythologie 2. Mainz 1974.
Kunze	E. Kunze. *Kretische Bronzereliefs.* Berlin 1931.
Lamb	W. Lamb. *Greek and Roman Bronzes.* London 1929; reprinted Chicago 1969.
Langlotz, *Fr. Bild.*	E. Langlotz. *Frühgriechische Bildhauerschulen.* Nüremberg 1927.
Langlotz, *Westgriechen*	E. Langlotz. *Kunst der Westgriechen in Sizilien und Unteritalien.* Munich 1963.
Langlotz, *Zeitbestimmung*	E. Langlotz. *Zur Zeitbestimmung des strengrotfigurigen Vasenmalerei und der gleichzeitigen Plastik.* Leipzig 1920.
Laviosa, *Sc. Volterra*	C. Laviosa. *Scultura tardo-etrusca di Volterra.* Florence 1964.
Leisinger	H. Leisinger. *Les peintures étrusques de Tarquinia.* Lausanne 1953.
Levi, "Arkades"	D. Levi. "Arkades. Una città cretese all'alba della civiltà ellenica." *ASAtene* 10-12 (1927-29).
Levi, *Mus. Chiusi*	D. Levi. *Il Museo Civico di Chiusi.* Rome 1935.
Lewis and Short	C. Lewis and C. Short. *A Latin Dictionary.* Oxford 1962.
Lorimer	H. L. Lorimer. *Homer and the Monuments.* London 1950.
Loud, *Megiddo Ivories*	G. Loud. *The Megiddo Ivories.* Oriental Institute Publication 52, Chicago 1939.
Lucke-Frey	W. Lucke. *Die Situla in Providence, R.I.* Edited by O. H. Frey. Röm. Germ. Forschungen 26. Berlin 1962.
MacIntosh, *RM* 81 (1974) 15-40.	J. MacIntosh. "Representations of Furniture on the Frieze Plaques from Poggio Civitate (Murlo)." *RM* 81 (1974) 15-40.
MacIver	D. Randall McIver. *Villanovans and Early Etruscans.* Oxford 1924.
Marinatos	S. Marinatos and M. Hirmer. *Crete and Mycenae.* London 1960.
Marinatos, *Kleidung*	S. Marinatos. *Kleidung, Haar und Barttracht. Archaeologia Homerica* I A, B. Göttingen 1967.
Marshall, *B. M. Jewellery*	F. Marshall. *Catalogue of Jewellery in the British Museum.* London 1911.
Martha	J. Martha. *L'Art étrusque.* Paris 1889.
Masson	E. Masson. *Les plus anciens emprunts sémitiques en grec.* Paris 1967.
Master Bronzes	D. Mitten and S. Doeringer. *Master Bronzes from the Classical World.* Cambridge, Mass. etc. 1967.
Matz	F. Matz. *Geschichte des griechischen Kunst. I: Die geometrische und die früharchaische Kunst.* Frankfurt 1950.

Matz, *CMMS*	F. Matz. *Corpus der minoischen und myken-ischen Siegel.* Berlin 1964-.
Matz, *Kreta, Mykene, Troja*	F. Matz. *Kreta, Mykene, Troja.* Stuttgart 1957.
Matz, Duhn	F. Matz and F. von Duhn. *Antike Bildwerke in Rom* I. Leipzig 1881-82.
Mazzarino	S. Mazzarino. *Dalla monarchia allo stato repubblicano.* Catania 1945.
Medelhavsmuseet	Medelhavsmuseet. *Bulletin, Museum of Mediterranean and Near Eastern Antiquities.*
Micali	G. Micali. *Monumenti per servire alla storia degli antichi popoli italiani.* Florence 1832.
Milani, *Mus. Arch. Firenze*	L. A. Milani. *Il R. Museo Archeologico di Firenze.* Florence 1923.
Milani, *Mus. it.*	L. A. Milani. *Museo italiano di antichità classica.* Florence 1885.
de Miré, *Sicile Grecque*	G. de Miré and V. de Miré. *La Sicile grecque.* Paris 1955.
Momigliano	A. Momigliano. "An Interim Report on the Origins of Rome." *JRS* 53 (1963) 97ff.
Mommsen	T. Mommsen. *Le Droit public romain. Manuel des antiquités romaines.* 3 vols. Paris 1893. Also J. Marquardt, *La vie privée des Romains. Manuel* 15. Pp. 105-253.
Montelius, *Civ.*	O. Montelius. *La Civilisation primitive en Italie depuis l'introduction des métaux.* Stockholm 1895-1910.
Montelius, *Vor. Chron.*	O. Montelius. *Die Vorklassische Chronologie Italiens.* Stockholm 1912.
Moortgat	A. Moortgat. *Die Kunst des Alten Mesopotamien.* Cologne 1967.
Moretti, *Il guerriero*	G. Moretti. *Il guerriero italico di Capestrano.* Rome 1936.
Moretti	M. Moretti. *New Monuments of Etruscan Painting.* Translated by D. Kiang. University Park, Pa. 1970.
	M. Moretti. *Nuovi monumenti della pittura etrusca.* Milan 1966.
Moretti, *Mus. V. G.*	M. Moretti. *Museo di Villa Giulia.* Rome 1962.
Moretti-Maetzke	M. Moretti and G. Maetzke. *The Art of the Etruscans.* London 1970.
Mostra	*Mostra dell'Arte e della Civiltà Etrusca.* Milan 1955.
Mostra dell'Etr. Padana	*Mostra dell'Arte dell'Etruria Padana e della Città di Spina.* Bologna 1960.
Mostra delle situle	*Mostra dell'arte delle situle dal Po al Danubio.* Padua 1961.
Mostra dello sport	*Mostra dello sport nella storia e nell'arte.* Catalog of the Sports Exhibit at the XVII Olympic Games. Rome 1960.

Mueller-Deecke	K. O. Mueller and W. Deecke. *Die Etrusker.* Stuttgart 1877. Rev. A. J. Pfiffig, 1963.
Mühlestein	H. Mühlestein. *Die Kunst der Etrusker: Die Ursprünge.* Berlin 1929.
Müller, *Fr. Plastik*	V. Müller. *Frühe Plastik in Griechenland und Vorderasian.* Munich 1929.
Müller, *Polos*	V. Müller. *Der Polos, die griechische Götterkröne.* Berlin 1915.
Myres, *Cesnola Collection*	J. L. Myres. *Handbook of the Cesnola Collection of Antiquities from Cyprus.* New York, 1914.
Neppi Modona	A. Neppi Modona. *A Guide to Etruscan Antiquities.* Florence 1954.
Neppi Modona, *Emporium*	A. Neppi Modona. "Pitture etrusche arcaiche. Le lastre fittili policrome ceretane." *Emporium* 67 (1928) 27ff.
Neugebauer, *Gladiatorentypus*	K. A. Neugebauer. "Der älteste Gladiatorentypus." *Berliner Mus. Berichte aus d. Preuss. Kunstsamml.* Beiblatt z. Jahrbuch d. Preuss. Kunstsamml. 61 (1940). Pp. 7ff.
Ogilvie	R. M. Ogilvie. *Commentary on Livy* Books *1-5.* Oxford 1965.
Ohly, *Antikensamml.*	D. Ohly. *Die Antikensammlungen am Königsplatz in München.* Waldsassen/ Bayern, n.d.
Pallottino, *The Etruscans*	M. Pallottino. *The Etruscans.* Edited by D. Ridgway. Bloomington, Indiana, 1974.
Pallottino, *Etr. Painting*	M. Pallottino. *Etruscan Painting.* Geneva 1951.
Pallottino, *Etruscologia*	M. Pallottino. *Etruscologia.* 6th ed. Milan 1968.
Pallottino, "Fond. micenei"	M. Pallottino. "Fondamenti micenei dell'arcaismo greco." *Crit. d'Arte* 7 (1942). Pp. 1-17.
Pallottino, "Tarquinia"	M. Pallottino. "Tarquinia." *MonAntLinc* 36 (1937).
Pallottino, *TLE*	See *TLE.*
Palmer	L. R. Palmer. *The Latin Language.* London 1954.
Paoli	U. E. Paoli. *Vita romana.* Florence 1948.
Pareti	L. Pareti. *La Tomba Regolini-Galassi.* Rome 1947.
Paribeni, *StEtr* 12 (1938)	E. Paribeni. "I rilievi chiusini arcaici." *StEtr* 12 (1938) 57-139.
Paribeni, *StEtr* 13 (1939)	E. Paribeni. "I rilievi chiusini arcaici. II." *StEtr* 13 (1939) 179-202.
B. Payne, *Costume*	B. Payne. *History of Costume.* New York 1965.
Payne, *NC*	H. G. Payne. *Necrocorinthia.* Oxford 1931.
Payne, *Perachora*	H. G. Payne. *Perachora.* Oxford 1946.
Payne-Young	H. G. Payne and G. M. Young. *Archaic Marble Sculpture from the Acropolis.* London 1936.

Peroni

R. Peroni. *L'Età del bronzo nella penisola italica I. L'Antica età del bronzo.* Florence 1971.

Peruzzi, *Origini* I, II

E. Peruzzi. *Origini di Roma.* 2 vols. Bologna 1970, 1973.

Peruzzi, *Mic. in Lat.*

E. Peruzzi. "Prestiti micenei in Latino." *Studi Urbinati* 47 (1973) Suppl. Ling. 1.

Pfiffig, *Einführung*

A. J. Pfiffig. *Einführung in die Etruskologie. Probleme, Methoden, Ergebnisse.* Darmstadt 1972.

Pfiffig, *Etruskische Sprache*

A. J. Pfiffig. *Die Etruskische Sprache.* Graz 1969.

Pfiffig, *Religio etrusca*

A. J. Pfiffig. *Religio etrusca.* Graz 1975.

Pfuhl

E. Pfuhl. *Malerei und Zeichnung der Griechen.* Munich 1923.

Phillips, *Poggio Civitate*

K. M. Phillips. *Poggio Civitate (Murlo, Siena). The Archaic Sanctuary.* Florence 1970.

Picard

Ch. Picard. *Manuel d'archéologie grecque.* I–IV: *La Sculpture.* Paris 1935–54.

Pinza

G. Pinza. *Materiale per la etnologia antica toscano-laziale.* Milan 1915.

Platon

N. Platon. *A Guide to the Archaeological Museum of Heraclion.* 3d ed. Heraklion 1959.

Poggio Civitate

Poggio Civitate (Murlo, Siena). The Archaic Sanctuary. Florence 1970.

Porada, *Corpus*

E. Porada. *Corpus of Ancient Near Eastern Seals in North American Collections. The Collection of the Pierpont Morgan Library.* New York 1948.

Poulsen

F. Poulsen. *Der Orient und die frühgriechishe Kunst.* Berlin 1912.

Poulsen, *Etr. Paintings*

F. Poulsen. *Etruscan Tomb Paintings.* Oxford 1922.

V. Poulsen, *Etruskische Kunst*

V. Poulsen. *Etruskische Kunst.* Königstein im Taunus 1969.

Pritchard

J. Pritchard. *The Ancient Near East in Pictures.* Princeton 1954.

Propyläen I

K. Schefold. *Die Griechen und Ihre Nachbarn.* Propyläen Kunstgeschichte I. Berlin 1967. H. Jucker. "Vorrömische Kunst in Sardinien. Mittel- und Norditalien," Nos. 378–425.

Pryce, *B. M. Sc.*

F. N. Pryce. *Catalogue of Sculpture in the British Museum.* London 1928–35.

Ranke, *Anc. Egypt*

H. Ranke. *The Art of Ancient Egypt.* Vienna 1936.

RE

A. F. von Pauly-G. Wissowa. *Real-Encyclopädie der klassischen Altertums-Wissenschaft.* Stuttgart 1894–.

Rebuffat-Emmanuel

D. Rebuffat-Emmanuel. *Le miroir étrusque d'après la collection du Cabinet des Médailles.* Collection de l'École Française de Rome 20. Paris 1973.

Reinach, *Rép. st.*   S. Reinach. *Répertoire de la statuaire grecque et romaine.* Paris 1920–30.

Restauri arch.   *Restauri archeologici. Mostra dei restauri sulle opere d'arte del Mus. Arch. di Firenze danneggiate dall'alluvione del 4 Nov. 1966.* Florence 1969.

Richardson   E. H. Richardson. *The Etruscans.* Chicago 1964.

Richardson, *Dress*   E. H. Richardson. *Civilian Dress of the Classical World.* Slide collection of the Archaeological Institute of America. 1967.

Richardson, "Libation-Bearer"   E. H. Richardson. "An Archaic Etruscan Libation-Bearer." *Art Quarterly* 19 (1956) 125–137.

Richardson, *MAAR* 21 (1953)   E. H. Richardson. "Etruscan Origin of Early Roman Sculpture." *MAAR* 21 (1953) 77–124.

Richardson, *MAAR* 27 (1962)   E. H. Richardson. "The Recurrent Geometric in the Sculpture of Central Italy and Its Bearing on the Origin of the Etruscans." *MAAR* 27 (1962) 161f.

Richter, *Anc. Furn.*   G. M. A. Richter. *Ancient Furniture.* London 1966.

Richter, *Anc. Italy*   G. M. A. Richter. *Ancient Italy.* Ann Arbor 1955.

Richter, *Archaic Greek Art*   G. M. A. Richter. *Archaic Greek Art.* New York 1949.

Richter, *Dumbarton Oaks*   G. M. A. Richter. *Greek and Roman Antiquities in the Dumbarton Oaks Collection.* Cambridge, Mass. 1956.

Richter, *Greek Collection*   G. M. A. Richter. *Handbook of the Greek Collection.* Cambridge, Mass. 1953.

Richter, *Greek, Etr. and Rom. Br.*   G. M. A. Richter. *Greek, Etruscan and Roman Bronzes.* New York 1915.

Richter, *Handbook*   G. M. A. Richter. *Handbook of the Etruscan Collection.* New York 1940.

Richter, *Korai*   G. M. A. Richter. *Korai.* London 1968.

Richter, *Kouroi*   G. M. A. Richter. *Kouroi.* New York 1942. 2d ed. London 1960.

Richter, *Red-Fig. Vases*   G. M. A. Richter. *Attic Red-Figure Vases.* New Haven 1958.

Richter, *Sculpture*   G. M. A. Richter. *Sculpture and Sculptors of the Greeks.* 2d ed. rev. New Haven 1962.

de Ridder   A. de Ridder. *Les Bronzes antiques du Louvre.* Paris 1913.

Riemschneider   M. Riemschneider. *Die Welt der Hethiter.* Stuttgart 1955.

Riis, "Art in Etr. and Lat."   P. J. Riis. "Art in Etruria and Latium." *Les origines de la république romaine.* Entretiens sur l'Antiquité Classique 13. Geneva 1967. Pp. 90–91.

Riis, *Etr. Art.*   P. J. Riis. *Etruscan Art.* Copenhagen 1953.

Riis, *Tyrrhenika*   P. J. Riis. *Tyrrhenika.* Copenhagen 1941.

RM   *Mitteilungen des deutschen archäologischen Instituts, Römische Abteilung.*

Roma Medio Repubblicana	F. Coarelli and others. *Roma Medio Repubblicana. Catalogo della Mostra.* Rome 1973.
Romanelli	P. Romanelli. *Tarquinia.* Rome 1951.
Romanelli, *Tarquinia*	P. Romanelli. *Tarquinia.* Itinerari dei Musei e Monumenti d'Italia. Rome 1957.
Roncalli	F. Roncalli. *Le lastre dipinte di Cerveteri.* Florence 1966.
Ruesch	A. Ruesch and others. *Guida illustrata del Museo Nazionale di Napoli.* Naples 1908.
Rumpf, "Antonia Augusta"	A. Rumpf. "Antonia Augusta." *Abh. Preuss. Akad. d. Wissenschaften.* Berlin Phil.-Hist. Klasse 5. 1941.
Rumpf, *Chalk. Vas.*	A. Rumpf. *Chalkidische Vasen.* Berlin 1927.
Rumpf, *Wandmal.*	A. Rumpf. *Die Wandmalereien in Veii.* Leipzig 1915.
Ryberg	Inez Scott Ryberg. *Rites of the State Religion in Roman Art. MAAR* 22 (1955).
Schaefer, Andrae	H. Schaefer and W. Andrae. *Die Kunst des alten Orients.* Berlin 1925.
Schaeffer, *Ugaritica* I, II	C. F. A. Schaeffer. *Ugaritica, Mission de Ras Shamra.* 2 vols. Paris 1959-49.
Schefold	K. Schefold. *Orient, Hellas und Rom.* Berne 1959.
Schilling, *Vénus*	R. Schilling. *La Religion romaine de Vénus.* Bibliothèque des Ecoles Françaises d'Athènes et de Rome 178. Paris 1954.
Schimmel Coll.	*Ancient Art. The Norbert Schimmel Collection.* Edited by O. W. Muscarella. Mainz 1974.
Schmökel, *Ur. Assur, Babylon*	H. Schmökel. *Ur, Assur und Babylon.* Stuttgart 1955.
Singer	C. Singer. *History of Technology* I. Oxford 1954.
Small, *StEtr* 39 (1971) 25-61.	J. P. Small. "The Banquet Frieze from Poggio Civitate." *StEtr* 39 (1971) 25-61.
Smith, *Anc. Egypt*	W. S. Smith. *The Art and Architecture of Ancient Egypt.* Baltimore 1958.
Solari	A. Solari. *Vita pubblica e privata degli Etruschi.* Florence 1931.
Sprenger	M. Sprenger. *Die etruskische Plastik des V jahrhunderts v. Chr. und ihr Verhältnis zur griechischen Kunst.* Rome 1972.
Steinberg, *Bronzes*	E. A. Steinberg. *Bronzes of the Bernardini Tomb.* Ph.D. dissertation, University of Pennsylvania, 1966.
Strøm	I. Strøm. *Problems Concerning the Origin and Early Development of the Etruscan Orientalizing Style.* Odense University Classical Studies 2. Odense 1971; review, L. Bonfante Warren, *AJA* 77 (1973) 100-102.
Strong, *Early Etr.*	D. E. Strong. *The Early Etruscans.* New York 1968.

Strong, *Rom. Imp. Sc.*	D. E. Strong. *Roman Imperial Sculpture.* London 1961.
Studi Banti	*Studi in onore di Luisa Banti.* Rome 1965.
Studniczka	F. Studniczka. "Beiträge zur Geschichte der altgriechischen Tracht." *Abh. Arch.-Epigr. Seminar Univ. Wien* 6, 1 (1886).
Teitz	R. S. Teitz. *Masterpieces of Etruscan Art.* Worcester, Mass. 1967.
TEL	*Encyclopédie photographique de l'art.* Louvre. 3 vols. Paris 1936–38.
Tilke	M. Tilke. *Entwicklungsgeschichte des orientalischen Kostums.* Berlin 1923.
TLE	M. Pallottino. *Testimonia Linguae Etruscae.* Florence 1954.
Tod, Wace, *Sparta Mus.*	M. N. Tod and A. J. Wace. *Catalogue of the Sparta Museum.* Oxford 1906.
Törnkvist	S. Törnkvist. *Arms, Armour and Dress on the Terracotta Figures from Ajia Irini, Cyprus.* Ph.D. dissertation, University of Lund, Sweden, 1970.
Van Buren	E. D. Van Buren. *Figured Terracotta Revetments in Etruria and Latium.* London 1921.
van Ufford, *Terres-cuites siciliennes*	L. Quarles van Ufford. *Les Terres-cuites siciliennes.* Assen 1941.
von Hase	F.-W. von Hase. "Gürtelschliessen des 7. und 6. Jahrhunderts v. Chr. in Mittelitalien." *JdI* 86 (1971) 1–59, Figs. 1–44.
von Vacano	O.-W. von Vacano. *Die Etrusker.* Stuttgart 1955.
Vercoutter	J. Vercoutter. *L'Égypte et le monde égéen préhellénique.* Cairo 1956.
Vermeule	E. Vermeule. *Greece in the Bronze Age.* Chicago 1964.
Vermeule, Chase	C. C. Vermeule and G. N. Chase. *Greek, Etruscan and Roman Art. The Classical Collection of the Museum of Fine Arts.* Boston 1963.
Vieyra	M. Vieyra. *Hittite Art 2300–750 B.C.* London 1955.
Vighi, *Mus. V. G.*	R. Vighi. *Catalogo del Museo di Villa Giulia.* Rome 1955.
Walde-Hofmann	A. Walde and J. B. Hofmann. *Lateinisches etymologisches Wörterbuch.* 3d ed. Heidelberg 1930–56.
Walters, *B. M. Bronzes*	H. B. Walters. *Catalogue of the Bronzes, Greek, Roman and Etruscan, in the Department of Greek and Roman Antiquities, British Museum.* London 1899.
Walters, *B. M. Terracottas*	H. B. Walters. *Catalogue of Terracottas in the Department of Greek and Roman Antiquities, British Museum.* London 1903.
Weege	F. Weege. *Etruskische Malerei.* Halle 1921.

Wild, *Textile Manufacture* J. P. Wild. *Textile Manufacture in the Roman Provinces.* Cambridge 1970.

Wilson L. Wilson. *The Clothing of the Ancient Romans.* Baltimore 1938.

Wilson, *Toga* L. Wilson. *The Roman Toga.* Baltimore 1924.

Wunderlich E. Wunderlich. *Die Bedeutung der roten Farbe im Kultus der Griechen und Römer.* Breslau and Tübingen 1925.

SOURCES FOR ILLUSTRATIONS

1. Adapted from Forbes 188, Fig. 25; Singer I, 443, Fig. 279; and Peroni 100, Fig. 31.

2. Mus. Civ. Arch., Bologna, Nos. 8164/L250, 8165/L251.

3. Drawing by Kathleen Mills Liotta, from Archivio Fot. Coll. Mus. Vatican, No. XXVIII-23-402.

4. Univ. Mus., Philadelphia, No. 5073.

5. Univ. Mus., Philadelphia.

6.-8. Staatl. Antikenabteilung, Berlin, photo I. Luckert.

9. Drawing by Lisa Kayne from Sopr. Ant. Etr., Florence, No. 1032.

10. Photo Felbermeyer.

11. Drawing adapted from G. Q. Giglioli, *StEtr* 3 (1929) Pl. 26.

12. Drawing by LB and Lisa Kayne.

13. From Ducati Pl. 59, Fig. 181.

14.-15. Brit. Mus. photo.

16. Musei Capitolini photo.

17. Bologna, Mus. Civ. Arch.

18. Drawings by Lisa Kayne from R. Demangel, *BCH* 45 (1921) Figs. 2, 4.

19. From Dawkins Fig. 121c.

20. Brit. Mus. photo.

21. From A. Furtwängler, *Olympia* Pl. 59.

22. From Andrae Pl. II, Fig. 1.

23. Drawings by LB and Lisa Kayne.

24. Met. Mus., No. 16142.

25. From Amorelli, *Coll. Massimo* 29.

26. Walters Art Gallery, No. 5587

27. Mus. Naz. photo.

28. From Hus Pl. 2, No. 13.

29.-30. Louvre Mus. photo.

31.-33. Sopr. Ant. Etr., Florence, Nos. 3405, 3408, 19741/7.

34. Met. Mus., No. 87704.

35. Drawing by S. Walzer and Lisa Kayne.

36.-38. Drawings by Kathleen Mills Liotta.

39. Drawing by Catherine Barré.

40. Met. Mus., No. 112873.

41. Drawing by Lisa Kayne.

42. From Hus Pl. 15, 1.

43. Alinari, No. 20220.

44. Barnett Pl. 43; Brit. Mus. photo.

45. Sopr. Ant. Etr., Florence, No. 10156.

46. Alinari, No. 26104.

47. Palermo, No. 1259.

48. Furtwängler-Reichhold 51.

49. Drawing by Lisa Kayne.

50. Met. Mus., No. 88069.

51. Staatl. Antikensamml., Munich, No. W1326.

52. Sopr. Ant. Campania, Naples Mus., No. MN B2835.

53. From Bieber Figs. 17, 19; Bellinger Fig. 1.

54. Adapted from Met. Mus., No. 78307.

55. Staatl. Antikensamml., Munich, photo G. Wehrheim.

56. Deutsch. Arch. Inst., Nos. 35.2088, 35.2089.

57. Sopr. Ant. Etr., Florence, No. 6874.

58.-59. Brit. Mus., Nos. XX D (27), XX D (24).

60. Drawing by Catherine Barré.

61. From Richter, *Greek, Etr. and Rom. Br.* 23-24.

62. Alinari, No. 35622; Mus. Civ. Arch., Bologna, No. 3288/F 190.

63. Villa Giulia Mus., Rome.

64. Staatl. Mus., Berlin, photo J. Tietz-Glagow.

65. Drawings by Lisa Kayne.

66. Met. Mus., No. 154681.

67. From Akurgal, *Reliefs*, Fig. 11.

68. Drawing by Lisa Kayne.

69. From Giglioli Pl. 68, Fig. 205.

70. Sopr. Ant. Etr., Florence, Nos. 7145, 6542.

71. From Ducati, *Pittura Etr. Italo-Greca e Rom.* Pl. 4.

72. Reconstruction drawings by M. Butterworth, S. Ferranti, and H. Linden, courtesy of K. M. Phillips.

73.-75. Brit. Mus., Nos. C3752, C3753, C3754.

76.-80. Staatl. Antikensamml., Munich, Nos. SL67, SL66, SL66, SL68, SL68.

81.-82. Drawings by Kathleen Mills Liotta.

83. From Gerhard 112.

84.-85. Courtesy Museum of Fine Arts, Boston, Nos. C6626, C6627.

86. From Gerhard 140.

87.-88. From G. Marchi, *La cista athletica del Museo Kircheriano* (Rome 1848) Pl. 2.

89.-90. Sopr. Ant. Etr., Florence, Nos. 22902, 22874.

91. Louvre, photo Franceschi.

92. Sopr. Ant., Palermo, No. 5869.

93. Alinari, No. 35556.

94. Drawings by LB and Lisa Kayne.

95. Brit. Mus., No. B. 249, XCVICI.

96. Drawing by Kathleen Mills Liotta.

97. Archives Photographiques, Paris, Nos. S4-P2030, 18619.

98. Palermo Mus. No. 930.

99. Brit. Mus., No. III D C267.

100. From Hus Pl. 4.2.

101. Palermo Mus., No. 947.

102.-3. Bibliothèque Nationale, Paris, No. 938.

104. From Bianchi Bandinelli-Giuliano 161, Fig. 185.

105. Drawing by Catherine Barré.

106. Archives Photographiques, Paris, No. ES 5-3930-013-AE-1, 18619.

107. Alinari, No. 43851.

108. Sopr. Ant. Etr., Florence, Nos. 27187, 27186.

109. Alinari, P.e I.a, No. 2544.

110. From G. Pellegrini, *Studi e Mat. Arch.* I, Fig. 12.

111. Hirmer Photoarchiv, No. 601.3430.

112. Sopr. Ant., Salerno.

113. Alinari, No. 26090.

114. Alinari, No. 26089.

115. Vatican, Mus. Etr. Greg.

116. Medelhavsmuseet, Nos. MM 2861, 2862, MM A.1. 10 4-2495, from Gjerstad, *Swed. Cyprus Exp.* II Pls. 205:2, 206:3.

117. Bibliothèque Nationale, Paris, Service de Doc. Phot., No. 64-F-413.

118. Minneapolis Institute of Arts, No. 9657.

119.-20. Photo M. Chuzeville.

121. Sopr. Ant. Etr., Florence, No. 25787.

122. Indiana University Art Museum photo.

123. Mus. Civ. Arch., Bologna, No. 7544/0.271.

124. Sopr. Ant., Palermo, No. 14616.

125. Deutsch. Arch. Inst., No. 3856.

126. Drawing by S. Walzer.

127. Alinari, No. 34842.

128. Mus. Chieti photo.

129. National Museum of Ireland photo.

130.-31. Drawing by S. Walzer.

132.-33. Met. Mus., Nos. 40180, 45242.

134. Detroit Institute of Arts, No. 7013.

135. Deutsch. Arch. Inst., No. 63.790.

136. Met. Mus., No. 109126.

137. Arch. Fot. Coll. Mus. Vatican, No. III-39-22.

138. Alinari, No. 283448.

139. Drawings by LB and Lisa Kayne, after Erbacher.

140. Villa Giulia Mus. photo.

141. From P. Orsi, *MonAnt* 35 (1919) Fig. 218, and *Dedalo* 6 (1925–26) 362.

142. Staatl. Antikensamml., Munich, photo.

143. From Gerhard 5, 60.

144. Deutsch. Arch. Inst., No. 11299F.

145. Deutsch, Arch. Inst., No. 61.728.

146. Staatl. Antikensamml., Munich, No. W493.

147. Met. Mus., No. 158697.

148. From Gerhard 5, 67.

149. From Gerhard 4, 379.

150. *A*, Milani 25; *B*, Milani 24; *C*, *NSc* 24 (1970) No. 97, Fig. 52.

151. Staatl. Antikensamml., Munich, No. Kb 3/15.

152. *A*, from E. Kunze, *Olympia Forschungen* II, 242, Pl. 28, IXa; *B*, drawing by Kathleen Mills Liotta.

153. Drawing by LB and Lisa Kayne.

154. Staatl. Mus., Berlin, photo Abteilung, No. Ant. 3453.

155. Ny Carlsberg Glyptotek.

156. Deutsch. Arch. Inst. No. 63.514.

157. Louvre photo.

158. Sopr. Ant. Etr., Rome, No. 1264.

159.-62. Sopr. Ant. Etr., Florence, Nos. 14319, 3131, 6543, 1929.

163.-64. Drawings by Kathleen Mills Liotta (adapted by Lisa Kayne).

INDEX

Vienna, Kunsthistorisches Museum, Fig. 48
Villanovan belt. *See* belts
Villanovan fashions, 132, 134
Villa of the Mysteries, 41, 121
vittae (ribbons), 76, 142
Vix crater, statuette, 47, 48, 56, 86, 123, 148, Fig. 97
vocabulary, 101-4, 153-54. *See also* Etruscan language
Volterra, 34, 43, 54, 61, 63, 72, 113, 121, 122, 129, 134, 144, 145, Figs. 68, 69, 89, 90, 143
Volterra, Museo Guarnacci, 144, Figs. 68, 89
Vulci, 14, 47, 53, 59, 60, 79, 83, 111, 118, 121, 124, 127, 129, 130, 131, 138, 143, 144, Figs. 25, 58-59, 84-85, 99-100, 117, 135, 146, 151. *See also* François tomb; Polledrara tomb; tridacna shells; tripod bases

wake, 131. *See also* funerary rites
war dance (pyrrhic, sword dance), 21, 69, 110, 136, Figs. 52, 135
warm clothing. *See* climate
warriors, 26, 34, 62, 67, 68, 69, 116, 120, 131, 136, 144, Figs. 12, 27, 36, 39. *See also* armor; Capestrano warrior

Warrior vase, 9, 33, 68, 98, 117
weaving. *See* wool working
weddings, 132. *See also* marriage ceremony
wife, 89, 118. *See also* gestures; social status
wings, 71, 72-73, 97, 139, 140, 145, 152
women athletes, 21, 26, 29, 110, Figs. 24, 52. *See also* acrobats; dancers
women's graves, 23, 106, 122
wool, 11-17, 91, 93. *See also* chiton, Dedalic
wool working, 11, 106, 108, Figs. 1, 2. *See also* loom; plaid patterns
Worcester Art Museum, 121
workmen, 28, 68
wreaths, 9, 77, 78
wrestlers, 52, 109, 111, 112

Xenophon, 144

Zeus (Tinia, Jupiter), 36, 50, 74, 86, 117, 125, 126, 127, 143, Figs. 21, 111-12. *See also* Loeb tripods
Zinjirli, 116
"ziro" burial urns, 33, 45, 71, 98-99, 116, Figs. 4-9

Larissa Bonfante, an associate professor of classics at New York University,
is the author of *Bibliography of the Works of Margarete Bieber* (with Rolf
Winkes) and the translator of *Ancient Chronology*, by E. J. Bickerman.

THE JOHNS HOPKINS UNIVERSITY PRESS

This book was composed in Baskerville text and display type by Jones Compo-
sition Company from a design by Susan Bishop. It was printed by Universal
Lithographers, Inc., on 60-lb Glatco Smooth paper and bound in Joanna
Arrestox cloth by Murphy-Parker, Inc.

Library of Congress Cataloging in Publication Data

Bonfante, Larissa.
   Etruscan dress.

   Bibliography: pp. 213–30.
   Includes index.
   1. Costume—Etruria.   I. Title.
GT560.B66   391'.00937'5   75-11344

ISBN 0-8018-1640-8